# Preferred Lies

# Preferred Lies

A Book of Golf Anecdotes and Trivia

Myles Dungan

POOLBEG

Published 1996
by Poolbeg Press Ltd
123 Baldoyle Industrial Estate
Dublin 13, Ireland

A catalogue record for this book is available from the British Library.

ISBN 1 85371 670 7

Cover photography by The Slide File
Cover design by Poolbeg Group Services Ltd
Set by Poolbeg Group Services Ltd in Garamond 9.5/13.5
Printed by ColourBooks Ltd, Baldoyle Industrial Estate, Baldoyle, Dublin 13

## *About the Author*

Myles Dungan is a presenter for RTE Television and Radio. He also fronts major golf events such as the Murphy's Irish open, the British Open and the US Masters. His previous book *A Good Walk Spoiled* was published in 1994 by Poolbeg.

*This book is dedicated to*

Aidan Butler
Ronan Collins
Julian Davis
Mary Davis
Noel Gavin
Dave Halloran
Jerry Kelly
Anne Lyster
John Walshe

*All of whom can be relied upon to favour a quick, early morning round of golf and with whom I have shared the usual quota of satisfaction and exasperation.*

# CONTENTS

# INTRODUCTION

Following on the egregious theft of the witticisms, solecisms and cataclysms of generations of golfers which was contained in that modest volume *A Good Walk Spoiled* it was decided to slide a follow-up on to the market. The decision was made by my publishers and my accountant/loan shark. The latter prefers to be called my Financial Excavator (he will always give me a dig out for 10% a week) and is a man with the unlikely name of Pat. (Unlikely because he normally employs a much heavier hand. He should probably have been named Thump instead.) He is something of a bibliophile, cherishing "big" books in particular; he once broke a man's arm with a hardbacked, large-print copy of *War and Peace* which weighed twelve pounds and measured two feet across from cover to cover. He is also an enthusiastic balletomane and is prone to humming the works of Russian composers as he executes a *pas de deux* with his less cultured friend Sam on one's private parts. But I digress.

When my accountant/loan shark pointed to my four skeletal children boiling nettles on a fire created by the flames licking around remaindered copies of my recent book of poetry *Ghastly Images from my Frontal Lobes,* I willingly agreed to bowdlerise, plagiarise and sodomise the anecdotes of those same generations of golfers. Of course, the moment he replaced the safety-catch on his elephant gun and started generously distributing stalks of fetid pampas grass amongst my starving infants, I was out the door. But the extradition laws between Ireland and Libya have been tightened up considerably since my last escape, hence the appearance of this volume of untruths and half truths, cleverly and ambiguously entitled *Preferred Lies*.

1

The book has been laid out in its present format for the sake of convenience (mine) and consists of everything from the apocryphal to the merely apocalyptic. It is designed to thrill, enthral and reduce you to tears. (A special derivative of CS gas has been added to the wood pulp expressly for the latter purpose.)

In case you come to this book unburdened with any information about the game of golf you might wish to know that it is defined as . . . "An outdoor game in which a small rubber-cored ball is hit with a wooden or iron-faced club. The club faces having angles and are styled for different types of shot . . ." and so on in quite tedious fashion. And now that we've got that out of the way, let's get on with it, Sarn't Major!

*Myles Dungan*

# CHAPTER ONE

## Statistics

*Some Utterly Trivial and Inessential Facts about Golf*

### Scoring

Bill Burke went around the back nine of the 6389 Normandie course in St Louis, Missouri in a total of 25 strokes on 20 May, 1970. (His card read 433–233–142.) He had played the front nine in 32!

The only golfer to make eleven birdies in a single round of an LPGA tournament is Vicki Fergon. She incinerated the Almaden Golf and Country Club course in San José in 1984 during the San José Classic in a round of 62.

Gene Sarazen established the reputation of the US Masters with his famous "shot that rang around the world" albatross at the 15th at Augusta in 1935. Jeff Maggert emulated that achievement in 1994 at the 13th in a far less significant round and, more recently, Per Ulrik Johanson scored an albatross at the Riviera Club in Los Angeles during the 1995 USPGA Championship. But the only golfer to have made an albatross (three under par on a single hole) in the history of the US Open Championship is Taiwan's Tze-Chung Chen. He accomplished that feat at Oakland Hills.

On the other side of the scoreboard, Willie Chisholm is the only player to have shot an 18 on a par-3 hole at the US Open. It happened in 1919 at the Brae Burn Country Club in West Newton, Massachusetts. His tee shot at the 185-yard 8th lodged against a boulder short of the

3

green. Chisholm swung at the ball 13 times before he could pry it loose and took 18 to complete the hole.

The lowest nine-hole score in a professional tournament is 27 strokes, shared by Mike Souchak, Andy North, Jose Maria Canizares (at Crans-sur-Sierre) and Robert Lee (Mount Agel during the Monte Carlo Open).

Souchak's 27 had an almost predestined quality about it. Souchak, a former American football player, born in 1927, was 27 years old at the time he set the record. His 72-hole aggregate for the tournament (257) was 27 under par and contained 27 birdies. In addition, the temperature on the last day of the tournament was 27 degrees Celsius.

RH Corbett's score of 27 in the 1916 Tangye Cup in Mullim in England was, however, a model of consistency compared to Souchak's. Corbett scored three on all nine holes for an eight-under-par total of 27. He had two eagles, four birdies and three pars.

In June 1994 an American club professional, Wayne Meyers, shot a 15-under-par 57 at Southern Oaks, South Carolina on a course measuring 6,449 yards. He had three eagles, nine birdies and no bogies. Coming to the 18th (a par 5) he needed a par to break sixty. Instead he chipped in with a 9-iron for an eagle.

Don't ever bet on yourself in a game against Monte Carlo Money (that's his real name). Aside from having a name which reeks of success at the gaming table, he's also a handy golfer who, on 11 March 1981 went round the Las Vegas Municipal Golf Club (where else?) in an eighteen-hole medal total of 58 shots. The par-72 course measures more than 6600 yards.

The Karen Country Club in Kenya has a par-five hole, the 15th, which measures 566 yards and which provided the occasion for a unique scoring achievement some years back. Playing in a four-ball, one of the club members shot a par five on the hole, another a birdie four, a third an eagle three and, incredible though it might sound, the fourth player carded an albatross.

In February 1993 the members of a four-ball playing at Reading Golf Club played the 140-yard 11th hole in an aggregate score of SEVEN. Two players holed out in one, one had a birdie two and the party pooper of the four-ball had a modest par. (Can you imagine the pressure on him to make his par putt?)

The magic target of breaking 60 in a professional tournament has been achieved twice in the USA. First by Al Geiberger in the Danny Thomas Classic at the Colonial course in Memphis Tennessee on 10 June, 1977 and then by Chip Beck in the third round of the Las Vegas Invitational at the Sunrise GC on 12 October, 1991.

The official card which Geiberger and playing partner Dave Stockton signed for that round ended up in the PGA World Golf Hall of Fame, in Pinehurst, North Carolina. Then, in 1995, an ad appeared in the Northern California edition of *Golf World* offering for sale an "Official scorecard recording Al Geiberger's historical '59'. Signed by Al Geiberger and Dave Stockton." The Hall of Fame wasn't pleased at this devaluation of their exhibit and some questions were asked. It appears that Geiberger, after the round, got hold of about 20 cards, filled in his score and got Stockton to countersign them. He then distributed them to a number of friends. The cards are interesting mementos, but not official scorecards.

The lowest 72-hole total in a professional tournament was scored by Peter Tupling in the Nigerian Open at Ikoyi GC in Lagos in February 1981. He shot 63, 66, 62, 64 for a 255 (29 under par).

Laura Davies is used to setting records but the four-round total she shot in the 1995 Guardian Irish Holidays Open at St Margaret's in Dublin will probably last for a while. After complaints following the 1994 staging of the event where she was the only player to finish under par, the grip of the course was relaxed by the Tournament Director for 1995. Once again, however, it was La Davies who benefited, she finished *twenty-five* under par (and they only played four rounds, just as in all the other WPGET tournaments).

Two Welshmen, David Llewellyn and Ian Woosnam, share the

distinction of having shot the lowest 72 total in a European PGA Tour event. Both have gone as low as 258, Llewellyn in the Biarritz Open in 1988 and Woosnam in the Monte Carlo Open in 1990. Woosnam shot a 60 in his final round.

USPGA Tour statistics show that 18% of first round leaders or co-leaders go on to win the tournament. 31% of second round leaders or co-leaders win while just under half, or 49%, of third round leaders or co-leaders come out ahead at the end.

Did you even know that the World One Club Championship existed? Well, it does, and in 1987 an American, Thad Daber, using a 6-iron, went around the 6037-yards Lochmore Golf Club in Cary, North Carolina in 70 shots to win the championship and claim the record for lowest score with a single club.

Jerry Pate must hold some sort of record for the biggest victory margin in a professional competition. In 1982, the year he won the TPC, he romped home in the Colombian Open by 21 shots.

Phillippe Porquier took almost that many shots on just one hole. During the 1978 French Open at La Baule, Porquier came to the par-5 13th. He left the hole having shot a 15-over-par 20. It stands as a record for the worst single hole score in European Tour history.

The lowest recorded score by a professional player on an 18-hole golf course, outside of competition, was the 55 shot by Alfred Smith at the par-70 Woolacombe GC in England on 1 January, 1936.

Mary Beth Zimmerman shot a record eight consecutive birdies in 1984 at the Illinois Rail Charity Classic. She shot a back nine of 28 in compiling a round of 64.

The lowest recorded score by a woman golfer over a regulation 18-hole course is believed to have been shot on July 11, 1929 by a teenager, Wanda Morgan, who took 60 shots to negotiate the Westgate and Birchington Golf course in Kent. Her nines scores were 31 and 29.

William Ingle got off to the sort of start statisticians dream about at Torphin Golf Course near Edinburgh on September 2, 1920. He aced the first, had a two on the second, a three on the third, a four on the fourth and a five on the fifth! (If he had continued his arithmetic progress through the entire 18 he would have shot a round of 171.)

## Putting

In the 1982 Ladies Michelob Open at the Brookfield West Golf and Country Club in Georgia, Joan Joyce required only 17 putts in the course of her round, establishing an LPGA record.

The longest recorded successful putt in a major tournament was slotted by the American pro Cary Middlecoff on the 13th green at Augusta in the 1955 US Masters. The putt was measured at 86 feet. (Middlecoff had a wonderfully sanguine attitude to the game of golf. He once said, "I think, what is the worst that can happen on this shot? I can whiff it, shank it or hit it out of bounds. But even if one of these bad things happens, I've got a little money in the bank, my wife still loves me and my dog won't bite me when I come home.")

(It should be noted that there are claims that Nick Faldo's putt on the 2nd green during his final round in 1989 measured at least 100 feet.)

George Archer holds the USPGA record for the least number of putts required in a 72 hole tournament. In 1980 at the Sea Pines Heritage classic at Harbour Town Golf Course in Hilton Head Island, Archer took only 94 putts, to beat the previous record by 5. This means he averaged 1.3 putts per hole (an interesting concept) and 23.5 putts per round.

Bobby Jones is reputed to have sunk a putt of over 100 feet on the massive fifth green at St Andrew's during the 1927 Open Championship.

Shades of Costantino Rocca! On 1 October 1976, Bob Cook of the USA sank a 140-foot putt on the 18th at St Andrew's in an international four-ball tournament.

In 1947 Colin Collen-Smith played 18 holes at Betchworth Park GC in Dorking in England, taking only 14 putts. He chipped in four times and single-putted fourteen greens. Andy North, twice US Open champion, took 18 putts in one round during the Anheuser Busch Golf Classic at Kingsmill GC.

## Winning

Chick Evans is the only golfer to have played in 50 consecutive US Amateur Championships. He first won the US Amateur in 1907. In 1916 he won the US Open and US Amateur, a feat achieved otherwise only by Bobby Jones.

In 1971, Laura Baugh became the youngest winner of the US Women's Amateur Championship at the age of 16.

Sandy Herd is probably the oldest winner of a non-Seniors event. In 1926, at the age of 58, he won the *News of the World* Match Play Championship playing against many golfers less than half his age.

The most one-sided US Amateur Championship final was the very first one in 1895. It was won by Charles McDonald. He defeated Charles Sands at the Newport Country Club, Rhode Island by 12 and 11.

On 11 March 1945, Byron Nelson began an amazing streak of victories which will probably never be equalled. Spurred by the desire to win enough money to buy a ranch and get out of golf, he won the first of eleven consecutive tournaments. His run of success began with a victory in the Miami Four-ball and finished on 4 August when he won the Canadian Open. He earned $30,250, more than enough for his ranch. Were he to have waited 50 years, he would have won anything between $2 and $3 million.

Hardly on a par with Byron Nelson's prolonged streak but almost as significant in its own right was the three-in-a-row streak of Lee Trevino in 1971 – except that they weren't victories in the Greater God Knows Where Pro-Am. In successive weeks he won the US, Canadian and British Open championships.

Not all Skins Games are necessarily as they seem, but in February 1995 Raymond Floyd sank an eight-foot putt on the 17th hole of the Senior Skins Game to win a total of $290,000, the largest single hole pay-out ever in a Skins game.

One of the most crushing defeats in first class golf was that experienced by Miss Mollie McBride in the 1921 Canadian Ladies Championship at the Rivermead Club in Ottawa. Playing over 36 holes, Miss McBride must have felt her back was to the wall after going 14 down by the turn. Three holes into the afternoon session she succumbed by 17 and 15 to her opponent Miss Cecil Leitch. She had won only one hole (the 9th) and halved two others.

Dorothy Campbell was probably one of the most successful amateur golfers ever. Born in Scotland she won the British and US Amateur Championships and a total of more than 750 other tournaments.

Charlotte Dod is the only player to have won a Women's Singles Title at Wimbledon and the Women's British Open. She won her first All England tennis title at the age of fifteen in 1887 and then won five more up to 1893. She turned her attention to golf and won the British Open in 1904.

The famous Babe Didrikson Zaharias dominated the US Open in 1954, winning it by 12 shots. The previous year it had seemed that she'd played her last round of golf when she had to undergo an operation for cancer. She was possibly the greatest all-round athlete ever. She won gold medals for the high jump, javelin and 80-metres hurdles at the 1932 Olympic games. She turned to golf in the 1940s and once won 14 consecutive tournaments, beating Byron Nelson's streak into a golf hat.

Kathy Whitworth is what the Americans like to call the "winningest" golfer in LPGA history. Between 1962 and 1985 she won 88 tour events. Her record is actually four more than that for the USPGA, held by the great Sam Snead.

Mickey Wright almost emulated in women's golf tournaments the great streak of Byron Nelson in 1945. In 1963 she won 13 tournaments on the LPGA tour. (Between 1958 and 1964 she also won four US Opens and four US PGAs. When she retired in 1978 she was just six victories short of Kathy Whitworth's record.)

## Driving

The longest drive in the history of the game might, technically at least, be one hit by a member of the John O'Gaunt Club near Biggleswade in England. His ball finished 42 miles away from the tee when it finally came to rest! After he teed off, his ball landed in a passing vegetable lorry and ended up in Covent Garden.

Rick Adams and Mark Glynn reckon they easily outclass John Daly when it comes to long driving. So much so that they make a profession out of it. They go on the road every summer with what they call the "Power Show". In July 1995 they engaged in a showdown with a rival celebrity claimant to driving distance, Karl Woodward, a German. Adams won the contest with a carry of 346 yards, Glynn was second with 341 and Woodward at least a club back at 319. Woodward, a sore loser it seems, made his excuses before he left. After the competition he loudly called for a painkiller and complained of a slipped disc.

On a cold icy day a Frenchman, Samuel Messieux, who taught his native language at the University of St Andrew's, with a slight wind behind him, drove his ball 361 yards at the fourteenth hole on the Old Course. If you watched John Daly win the 1995 Open at the same venue you might wonder what makes M Messieux's drive so special. It's timing and nature, that's what. The chilly day was in 1836 and the ball he was using was a "featherie". It's the longest recorded drive using this historical relic. He drove the ball from the Hole O'Cross green into the Hell bunker, a hazard he must have thought well out of range.

## Stuff That Wouldn't Fit Anywhere Else

In the US alone, more than 12,400 golf courses serve over 20 million people who play golf at least once a year.

Between 1910 and 1953, American Ralph Kennedy established some sort of record by playing on 3,615 different golf courses. He played on at least one course in every state in the USA and on courses in 13 other countries. His odyssey began at the Van Cortlandt Park public golf course in Manhattan and ended when he gave up the game at the age of 72 at the Hamilton Inn Golf Course in Lake Pleasant, New York. Like a binge golfer, he would often take on courses in groups. In 1933 he played eight Bermuda courses in two days. In one seven-day period in Chicago he played 21 different spreads. Fittingly, the 3,000th course he played was the Old Course at St Andrew's.

Catherine Duggan and Lynn Adams played the fastest round ever in LPGA history during the Sarasota Classic in Florida in 1984. Playing at the Bent Tree Golf Club, they completed their 18 holes in one hour and thirty-five minutes! For the record Duggan shot 72 and Adams 78. (A few years later John Daly and Mark Calcavecchia were actually *fined* for playing a round in less than two and a half hours!)

The only golfer to have played more than 10,000 holes of golf in one year is Ollie Bowersof of Gafney, South Carolina who squeezed in 10,075 holes (560 rounds) in one year. (That's an average of 1.53 rounds a day!) And yes, he must have had either a lot of time on his hands or a very tolerant wife/employer/family.

The record for throwing a golf club is not held by Tommy Bolt (that's for distance, not frequency, of course) but by the less well-known Randolph Timmerman. He threw a club 61 yards in the 1936 Throwing Tournament at Druid Hills Country Club in Atlanta. It certainly doesn't sound like a huge throw. Anyone care to try to beat it?

# CHAPTER TWO

## *Eccentrics*

*Golf's left-field heroes and heroines*

### Andrew McKellar

Towards the end of the 1700s it is recorded that one Andrew McKellar gave up his job as a butler, bought a tavern in Edinburgh and, leaving it to his wife to run, retired to play golf for the rest of his life. He spent every available hour on the golf course (Bruntsfield Links) without ever improving his game. He was not deterred by darkness, often playing by lamplight. Snow did not faze him, he simply painted his balls red and played over it. After a while, his good wife realised that she was being handed the soiled end of the stick on a daily basis and decided to embarrass her husband. So, one day, she brought his dinner out on to the course while he was playing. Mr McKellar, clearly a literalist, missed the point of the exercise entirely and advised his wife in unparliamentary language that he would eat his victuals when he had finished his round.

### Duke of Connaught

People with titles have a reputation, deserved or otherwise, for eccentricity. There's supposed to be a direct relationship between the lustre of the title and the degree of pottiness. The more exalted the title the more batty or scatty the title-holder, all the way up to the British Royal Family who are totally daft. It's just a theory. I don't necessarily share it. I merely mention it in the context of the Duke of Connaught who held the title at the turn of the century. He was playing a match with Lionel Hewson (one of the designers of Ballybunion) at the Curragh GC in 1904. Both men reached the first in regulation but Hewson was much closer to the hole, six inches as opposed to the thirty feet of the Duke. Imagine his surprise and chagrin when the Duke marched on to the green, pocketed his ball and explained to his opponent, "I always count two on the greens and avoid having to putt."

## Lord Castlerosse

Weighing in at up to twenty stone, Lord Castlerosse was truly a larger-than-life character. He was the first patron of Killarney Golf Club and an enthusiastic if unskilled amateur. He was, by profession (insofar as he had one), a newspaper columnist with the *Sunday Express* and his sybaritic lifestyle was largely subvented by his friend and employer Lord Beaverbrook. He was constantly in debt but, as one is taught to expect of true aristocrats, had absolute contempt for creditors. At the outbreak of war in 1939, he wrote in his column "I see my moneylender has gone off to war. I only hope he charges the enemy with the same enthusiasm that he charges me." He once ordered three dozen silk monogrammed shirts with money he didn't have and when he died left the whole lot to the the Presentation Convent in Killarney. (The Mother Superior laid claim to his slippers: for such a big man he had tiny feet.) His contribution to golf is, undoubtedly, the development of the beautiful Killarney club. His own game was devoid of expertise. Playing once with Henry Longhurst at Walton Heath he topped shot after shot until he pointed at the ball and instructed his caddie in the peremptory manner he adopted with flunkies, "Pick that up, have the clubs destroyed and leave the course".

## Walter Danecki

The qualifying rounds of the Open championship have seen enterprising and unskilled amateurs shade the truth somewhat in an effort to achieve their apotheosis by osmosis. Walter Danecki of Milwaukee was just such a soldier. To describe him as an averagely talented amateur golfer would be a calculated insult to averagely talented amateur golfers. He was a truly abysmal golfer. But he craved recognition, success and the opportunity to prove himself *in extremis.*

"I wanted that crock of gold", he said. That's why he chose to lie on his entry form for the 1965 Open and claim to be a professional. He carded a 108 for his first round over the par-70 Hillside course in Southport. By now struggling to make the cut for the Open proper (he would have had to shoot a 43 for his second round to have qualified), Walter succumbed to the pressure and took 113 strokes to get round Southport and Ainsdale the following day. He finished 81 over par and missed qualifying by 70 shots. Asked about his round afterwards, he appeared quite pleased with his performance but admitted to a stroke of good fortune. "I guess your small British ball helped me some," he commented. "If I'd had to play the big ball, I'd have been all over the place." Heaven forfend!

## Maurice Flitcroft

Most of us lead dull, stolid lives but Maurice Flitcroft, a seemingly ordinary North of England crane drivers has managed to launch himself into that mythic pantheon of the truly great just by being formidably dire. He is golf's answer to ski-jumper, Eddie the Eagle, and a candidate for canonisation.

Maurice first invaded the realm of the overpaid and pampered in the qualifying competition for the Open Championship in 1976. Playing over a windswept Formby links, his score plummeted to an undistinguished 121. His 60 for the back nine included an 11 at the 10th hole. He had only been playing the game for just over a year and had never actually completed a full eighteen holes. Quizzed by a curious press corps after his round Maurice commented, "I've made a lot of progress in the last few months and I'm sorry I did not do better. I was trying too hard at the beginning but began to put things together at the end of the round."

Disgusted at being hoodwinked, the Royal and Ancient returned the £30 entry fees paid by the two golfers who had partnered Maurice in his mould-breaking round.

Maurice Flitcroft never appeared at an Open Qualifier again. But Gene Pacecki did. In 1978, this American pro tried to make it into the Open at St Andrew's. In his qualifying round he took 70 strokes for the first nine and a half holes. He pulled out before reaching the tenth green and legged it to sanctuary as R & A officials recognised Mr Pacecki as their old adversary Maurice Flitcroft.

Two years later a Swiss pro (a Swiss golf professional – sounds rather like an oxymoron!) with the glorious name of Gerald Hoppy showed up at prequalifying for Muirfield. Mr Hoppy got as far as the ninth before his ball was appropriated by two gentlemen in blazers and he was removed from the course to the great relief and consternation of his partners who were unacquainted with the legend of the Flitcroft Pimpernel. He had taken a highly creditable 63 shots for the front nine.

There followed a long silence, akin to that of the inactivity of Carlos the Jackal before his final arrest. Then in 1990, having lulled the R & A into complacency Maurice struck again in the guise of another American, James Beau Jolley. Alas, security had improved (perhaps, on the verge of retirement, he had simply meant to test it out) and he only made it as far as the 3rd hole at Ormskirk before his round ended peremptorily.

Lacking a sense of humour, the R & A, in the form of its secretary Michael Bonnallack, views Maurice as "nothing more than an irritation and a nuisance." Well yes, of course, he is, no one would dispute that, but then so was Robin Hood.

### Simon Hobday

South African Simon Hobday, before he transferred to the Senior Tour, had a reputation for being sartorially challenged; he was, in a word, scruffy. He delighted in colours which clashed and in maintaining a generally high standard of inelegance. Such was his reputation that he never managed to secure a clothing contract with even the most outrageous golf-wear companies. He was so perturbed by this that he adopted an interesting device for extorting a contract from somebody, anybody: he wrote to one company threatening *to start* wearing their clothes if they didn't send him money on a weekly basis. Roddy Carr, golf agent and broadcaster, once roomed with Hobday when the two were on the European Tour. He recalls that when even Hobday grew disgusted with the state of his clothes he would pile them into a bath, pour in large dollops of detergent, fill the bath with water and stir the contents with a putter until he was satisfied that the most offensive stains had been removed. The wet clothes were then draped across the balcony to dry.

After going through a miserable period on the greens in the US Seniors Tour, Hobday decided that his Creator was to blame for all his troubles. In order to hoodwink this malevolent Deity into overlooking the fact that he was playing, Hobday decided, one day, to raise his sartorial standards to a level which was almost on a par with that of his fellows. The ploy didn't work, he three-putted the first green. In response Hobday railed at the heavens. "You Bastard," he howled, "I came out here with all new, clean clothes. You weren't supposed to recognise me with a crease in my trousers."

Gary Player once tried to get Hobday to change his ways, hoping to make a better player of him. As well as not being the last word in neatness, "Scruffy" was a party animal to whom an early morning tee-off without the benefit of sleep was not unknown. Player approached his fellow countryman one day and advised him to start getting to bed earlier. To which Hobday replied, "If I'm not in bed by nine . . . I go home."

Hobday oncé had a tremendous stroke of luck. He mishit a shot into a water hazard but its trajectory was so low that it actually skipped over the surface like a flat stone fired underarm. Hobday and the crowd enjoyed this turn for the better in his fortunes. Ever the showman, he then walked fully-clothed into the lake, exclaiming loudly, "If that ball can walk on water, so can I."

Never a patient sort, Hobday once found himself playing with Tony Johnstone of Zimbabwe, an excellent but "thorough" player. ("Thorough" is to speed what "thrifty" is to spending.) In one green Johnstone was taking what Hobday judged to be an unconscionably long time to line up his putt. Finally, as the Zimbabwean stooped to conquer, he asked Hobday to kindly move his body as his shadow was straddling the line of the putt. "Well, it wasn't there when you started," was the terse riposte.

Hobday, in the 1970s, was a member of a group of soul-mate pros nicknamed "The Wild Bunch". They included Hedley Muscroft, Jack Newton and John O'Leary. Some members of this group were once fined at the Dutch Open because the noise of their persistent sing-song in the clubhouse bar was bothering the late finishers on the 18th green.

At a PGA European Tour cocktail reception in Switzerland in the

1970s, Hobday was unable to gain admission because of a "ties only" rule, as clearly indicated by a sign outside the reception. He disappeared briefly and when he returned he was, by his own lights, properly dressed. The fact that he was, quite literally, wearing only a tie didn't appear to concern him.

### Craig Stadler

The otherwise amiable American pro Craig Stadler is the terror of aquatic life in golf venues all over the USA. This is because he tends to vent his frustration not on his fellow human beings but on his putters. Usually he tosses them into adjacent lakes. Once when a reporter noticed that Stadler was using a new putter, he asked the "Walrus" what had happened to the old one. "It didn't float!" came the reply. At the Las Vegas Invitational one year he missed a short putt and, conscious of his reputation as a hurler, someone in the crowd shouted, "Go on, throw it!" So he did.

In the 1985 Ryder Cup at the Belfry he missed a putt on the 18th, playing in a four-ball match. After the crowd around the green had scattered Stadler was still to be seen standing at the water's edge with his putter. Then, like a Knight of the Round Table disposing of Excalibur after the death of King Arthur, he tossed the offending club into the vasty deep.

Stadler is not the most sartorially elegant player on the US Tour and he once wore a pair of golf shoes which were well past their sell-by date. They had seen many wet and clinging roughs and were beginning to crack. When he was slagged off by Fuzzy Zoeller about them during a round, the Walrus merely took them off and shied them at Zoeller before continuing to play in his bare feet. Zoeller picked one of the shoes up, made a facial gesture and tossed the offending piece of footwear over his shoulder and into the grandstand.

### Clayton Heafner

Clayton Heafner is another of those great originals who refuse to conform to "normal" behavioural stereotypes. They just will not be squeezed into straitjackets (though, perhaps, in a literal sense they should). Heafner was once about to tee off for the 1941 Oakland Open when the public address announcer happened to mispronounce his name. Totally disgusted, Heafner stalked off the tee in high dudgeon and pulled out of the event.

In another tournament he revealed his acid sense of humour when he took a twelve at one hole. Asked by an enterprising hack why he had taken twelve strokes he replied, "Because I had a long putt for an eleven."

Heafner was renowned for his bad temper, which was not confined to the golf course. The great Jimmy Demaret once described Heafner as being the most even-tempered man he knew; on being challenged, he explained, "He was mad all the time."

He had a habit of abandoning rounds if he didn't like the smell of them. Once, after a bad opening drive in a tournament he sent his caddie after the ball and pulled out. On another occasion, in the middle of a mediocre round he hit a really bad shot and told his caddie to go and pick up the ball, he was going to withdraw. He was approached by an irate woman spectator who informed him that he could not pick up his ball because she had drawn him in a gambling pool. He studied the woman for a moment and nodded at his caddie. "OK, leave the ball," he conceded, and *then* he walked off the course.

### Carl Lohren

Carl Lohren was a contemporary of Heafner's who had a disconcerting habit of using every available minute on the road to practise, and I mean that quite literally. When he was driving, or being driven, between events, if the car he was in was stopped at traffic lights or in a jam of some kind he would hop out with a club and take a few swings. One day the inevitable happened. He was being driven across country by a fellow player to the Jacksonville Open. The car was stopped at a level-crossing and Lohren, sitting in the back seat, did as he always did, grabbed a club and leaped out of the car. But he neglected to tell anyone what he was about to do and the driver never noticed his absence. As soon as the train had passed and the crossing gates were raised he took off, leaving Lohren standing by the side of the road choking on the dust of the car in which he should have been a passenger.

## Tommy "Thunder" Bolt

American pro Tommy Bolt was quite a player. He won the US Open championship in 1958. But he was better known, and feared, for his vile temper. Fortunately, this was mainly directed against the contents of his golf bag. Nicknamed "Thunder" Bolt, he was an All American Club Thrower, one of the great chuckers. Fellow pro Jimmy Demaret once said of him, "His putter has spent more time in the air than Lindbergh." He would and did claim that his reputation was unfairly earned and that, in fact, he was a far more accomplished breaker of clubs than he was a thrower. He was especially given to breaking putters over his much-abused knees. "I probably became the world's foremost authority on how to putt without a putter." He once said.

On one occasion, Bolt had been having an especially bad round and the contents of his bag had suffered accordingly. He was faced with a long second shot to a par five and, studying the situation, he asked his caddie abstractedly to nominate a club. "A two- or a three-iron," ventured the caddie. Bolt looked at him, as if seeing him for the first time. "That's nearly 300 yards out there," he reminded the caddie. "Hell, Ole Tom cain't reach that green with a 2-, much less a 3-iron." "Mr Bolt," replied the caddie laconically, "all you got left in your bag are those two clubs, unless you want to use your putter, and that's missing its handle; you snapped it off on the first nine."

On another occasion he tossed a club straight into a lake after messing up a shot. His playing partner, inviting a string of oaths, observed, "You'd better throw a provisional, that one's likely to be lost."

Bolt did have certain rules. For example, "A cardinal rule for the club-breaker is never to break your putter and driver in the same match or you are dead." Or a practical hint for the amateur "chucker": "If you're going to throw a club in a temper, it's important to throw it ahead of you in the direction of the green. That way, you don't waste energy going back to pick it up."

He almost came to cherish his status as the orneriest cuss on the course and resented younger pretenders. He was unimpressed with the displays of temper of the young Arnold Palmer. "I have to say," he commented, "he was the very worst golf-club thrower I have ever seen. He had to learn to play well, he'd never have made it as a thrower."

In his entire career Tommy Bolt was never penalised for exceeding the legal limit of fourteen clubs per bag. That was probably the only thing he didn't break.

During the 1960 US Open at Cherry Hills in Denver (the one where Palmer drove the green on the par-4 first to ignite a tournament-winning round), Bolt had a bad day at the office even by his own uneven standards. At the 12th he dumped a shot into the lake and then had a row with a USGA official as to where he should drop his ball. Upset by what he saw as shabby treatment, he three-putted the next hole, bogied the fourteenth and then hooked two balls into the water on the 18th. In front of the huge gallery on the closing hole he marched off the tee to the edge of the water and ostentatiously tossed his driver into the blue lagoon at his feet. To his amazement, like a member of the cast of Baywatch, a young boy dived in, swam to the centre of the ripples, ducked underneath the water, re-emerged with the driver and swam for the shore to the cheers of the crowd. Even Bolt saw the funny side and, thus mollified, decided to forgive the driver. But the kid had other ideas. As he neared the shore he spotted Bolt heading to intercept him. When he landed he executed a shimmy and, to the chagrin of "Ole Tom", he took off for the perimeter wall of the course like greased lightning, clutching his prize. The crowd, unimpressed with Bolt's antics, were very much on the kid's side. They roared with approval and, as Bolt watched helplessly, someone in the gallery gave the kid a leg over the wall. "Ole Tom" never saw the driver again.

In the 1950s, some of the scorekeepers on the Tour complained about Bolt's flatulence. At one tournament he was actually warned that he would be fined if he didn't stop farting. He contiued to break wind whenever he saw fit and there was a further complaint. A fine of $100 was levied on him. Bolt objected that he was only doing what came naturally. The response of the tournmanent official who fined him was that the complainant hadn't been upset so much by the fart: "It was the fact that you kept lifting your leg and clutching your thigh in celebration."

During the US Open, which he won at Southern Hills in 1958, Bolt got annoyed at a Tulsa paper which gave his age as 49 in its coverage of the event. At a press conference after 36 holes, Bolt upbraided the reporter from the paper, who apologised profusely, insisting that it had been a typographical error. "Typographical error, hell," responded Bolt. "It was a perfect four and a perfect nine."

Bolt wasn't always popular with his peers. Somewhere along the line he obviously managed to antagonise Scottish pro Eric Brown. At a golf dinner Brown was asked by Ryder Cup captain Bernard Gallacher what was the best shot he ever saw. Brown described a shot by Bolt in a Ryder Cup match. It was a gorgeous high, floating fade . . . which ended up plugged in the face of an impossible bunker.

Bolt was also routinely foul-mouthed on the course. At one tour event the tournament supervisor, Jack Tuthill, fined him $200 for using abusive language. Before signing the cheque, Bolt insisted on being introduced to whoever it was who had reported him. Tuthill, probably thinking to shame the scatological golfer, took him in a golf cart to where two inoffensive old ladies were standing. Bolt thanked him and made out the cheque. As Bolt began to approach the two ladies, Tuthill pursued him and pointed out that the cheque was made out for $400 dollars, whereas the fine was only half that amount. To which Bolt responded that he wanted to pay in advance for what he was about to say to the two women.

From the "Out of the mouths of babes . . ." department: Bolt was giving a clinic in South America once and he had his son with him. To bolster his credibility as a teacher, at one point during a session Bolt turned to his son and asked him what he had learnt from his Dad. Whereupon the son took a club from his father's bag and flung it as far as he could.

## Lefty Stackhouse

Lefty Stackhouse deserves a niche all to himself in Golf's Hall of Fame, but it should be lovingly trashed before his cremated remains are deposited in it. Lefty devised tortures for himself that even his worst enemy would have baulked at. When he was even vaguely dissastisfied with his performance he would punch himself in the face. When he was extremely unhappy, he would do so very hard indeed. Once he was so pissed off that he actually knocked himself out.

He would have made a wonderful medieval monk or a Christian martyr, so often did he flagellate himself. Once, when he missed a putt his eye lit upon his right hand which he blamed for the lapse. Taking it to a nearby tree, he whacked it off the stump repeatedly, uttering the imprecation, "Take that, that'll teach you."

He was just as hard on his clubs as he was on himself. He used to talk to them a lot and threaten them constantly, like some sort of golfing Thwackford Squeers. Nobody actually saw the clubs cringe and shake, but clubs are only human like everyone else.

Lefty proved he too was human by failing to get in the money in a wartime tournament (the Knoxville Open) which had more prizes (20) than competitors (18). He succeeded in pulling off this seemingly impossible feat by getting totally pie-eyed during the final round. Standing by to present the prizes (War Bonds) was the World War Two hero Sergeant Alvin York. York had never seen the game being played before and he chose to follow Lefty's four-ball around the course. Stackhouse had a Coke bottle with him which was heavily augmented with whiskey in addition to the beverage of origin, and from this he took copious nips. Fatigued and dehydrated, after nine holes Lefty collapsed as he putted out and had to be carried to the locker room. York is supposed to have remarked, "That poor man exhausted himself. I had no idea golf was such a strenuous game." When Lefty came round and realised what had happened, he became energised at the thought of losing the easy prize money. He bolted for the course to complete his round but, like Rip Van Winkle, he'd been kipping for longer than he thought. It was dark, the war was nearly over, the circus had moved on to the next event and Lefty was minus his reward.

It was over some similar blow to his self-esteem (the most pock-marked in the game) that Lefty finally lost his rag with his defenceless Model T Ford motor-car and began to disassemble it as thoroughly as it had been put together by the employees of the Ford Motor Corporation. No one dared go near him as, mouthing curses in a language unknown to any of his listeners, he tore off the doors, dismantled the bodywork and ripped out the seating of the car. To this day, nobody quite knows why the car had to go.

### George Low

George Low was born in 1912 near Baltusrol where his father was the professional. He picked up his indolent habits in the USA ("I was born in the 19th hole, the only one I've ever parred") before going to live in Scotland where he picked up the putting skills which were to ensure that he could lead the life of ease which he mapped out for himself. Before settling on golf as a way of scrounging a living he was a parachute stuntman in an Air Show. ("I didn't exactly jump. I'd open the door, pull the ripcord and let the parachute pull me out of the plane. Who the hell wants to jump if he doesn't know the chute's going to open?" – Very sensible really.) He later branched off into bootlegging illegal liquor by air until the plane he and his partner used crashed unexpectedly. ("The pilot and I escaped but the booze died.") As well as teaching he played golf professionally, and he was the man who ended Byron Nelson's incredible eleven-tournament winning streak in 1945. He didn't actually win the tournament but he got the first prize money because the winner, Fred Haas, was an amateur.

He gave up playing when his reputation as a putter meant he could charge a small fortune for putting lessons and make a mint in wagers on the putting green against young punks who thought they could beat The Man.

He helped Arnold Palmer to his first Masters win in 1960 and the result was an equipment endorsement and the "George Low putter".

As opposition on the putting green began to dry up, he offered to kick the ball into the hole instead of putting it. So proficient did he become at this art that the Foot Joy firm signed him up. Officially he was paid for "testing" their shoes. "I test their $65 alligator models," he observed once, "to see if standing in them for long periods of time in a bar brings them any serious harm." But he became uncomfortable spending his own money and soon reverted to living off other people's. As he put it himself, "I missed the challenge of whether I'd be able to borrow Frank Stranahan's [golf promoter] car and lose it to somebody in a coin flip."

He was famous for his sharp tongue. Once, when he recognised a fellow sponger he remarked, "Loaning you money is like sending lettuce by rabbit." He was acerbic about those who didn't succumb to his charm and pay his way in life. One of those was the thrifty Sam Snead of whom Low said, "When I dine with Mr Snead, he always suggests that I order as if I was expecting to pay for it myself. I have known many great destroyers of money but Mr Snead is not among them."

## Paddy Hanmer

One of the most fearsome spectacles in golf was the sight of Captain PWT (Paddy) Hanmer in full flight. For many years Hanmer was the Secretary of the exclusive Muirfield Golf Club in Scotland, scene of many great Open championship victories (Vardon, Hagen, Cotton, Player, Nicklaus, Trevino, Watson) and some tedious ones (All Hail Alf Perry, victor in 1935 – Alf who?). One of the things about Hanmer was that he didn't much seem to like people playing on his golf course. Unlike the even more vaunted St Andrew's, which is a public course, one can't just march into Muirfield, slap down a green fee and ask, "Where's the locker room and how much should I tip the caddies?" For many years one had to get past Hanmer and few did. Once when Payne Stewart, former USPGA and US Open champion, arrived and presented himself to play he was told that such would, regrettably, be impossible on that particular day. Stewart went instead to Gullane where he was made welcome. Part of Muirfield is visible from Gullane and Stewart expected to see the course thronged. But there was hardly a sinner on it. Hanmer just wanted to show Stewart that his playing credentials didn't guarantee him a round at Muirfield.

He meted out similar treatment to Tom Watson who won the Open there in 1980. Watson and Ben Crenshaw got hold of some old hickory-shafted clubs and went out on to the course, only to be dragged back in by Hanmer. "Young man," he told Watson tersely, "this is no public playground. The Open is over."

Once an American visitor asked to play Muirfield and was told that he couldn't possibly get on the course for hours. Again, there was hardly anybody playing, but Hanmer assumed the nuisance would have the decency to get the message and go away. Instead he waited and waited and waited to be told that he could proceed to the first tee. After a few hours he approached Hanmer again and asked that he be allowed to take the great man's photograph. When Hanmer asked why, he was told by the American, "I just want to show my friends back home a picture of the man who kept me off Muirfield." Hanmer was so amused at this approach that he abandoned the habits of a lifetime and relented.

Members of Muirfield are no inconsequential persons, but they were all the same to Hanmer. On one occasion he watched as a slow-playing member crawled around the course. After he had stood over a ball for an outrageously long time, Hanmer roared at him, "Are you waiting for inspiration or have you suddenly taken ill?"

In response to such stories Hanmer once told writer Michael Bamberger, tongue firmly fastened to his cheek, that wicked tales of people quaking in their boots while addressing him were just so much cant, humbug and hearsay. "I'm not convinced that any of the shaking was genuine at all. They acted the way they thought I expected them to act."

One of Hanmer's successors Brian Evans-Lombe was clearly in the same mould, ably maintaining Muirfield's reputation as "the rudest golf club in the world," (according to journalist Peter Andrews). He was never wrong, even when he was flat-out wrong. He is said to have marched into the Members' Bar on one occasion, strode up to a golfer having a drink and informed him peremptorily that "this facility is for the use of members only" (or words to that effect). The shocked golfer replied, "But I am a member!" To which Evans-Lombe responded haughtily, "In that event you should come here more often, then I would recognise you."

### JF Abercromby

Among the most formidable golf administrators was one JF Abercromby, the designer of the two Addington courses in London. He had a habit of wearing a velour pork pie hat and carrying an old wooden putter with him at all times. (Presumably to fend off "djinns" or green-fee-paying visitors). One day he was standing at the bar of the club he ran as a personal fiefdom when a new member stalked up to the barman and enquired peremptorily, "Where is the suggestion book?" Fixing him with the glare of a gimlet, Abercromby pointed to himself and said, "I'm the suggestion book."

### Dave Hill

Dave Hill, the American pro who had his heyday in the 60s and 70s, had a reputation for being one of the most irascible men on the American tour, and for being reluctant to hide his feelings on many subjects. He seldom lost an opportunity to deflate the pretensions of some of his better-known rivals. He especially disliked the tendency of Gary Player to preach to his peers about fitness and the merit of a good diet. Hill acknowledged that Player ran, lifted weights and ate health foods more than anyone else on the Tour, but what he objected to was Player's constant reminders about his lifestyle. "So what if he has the most perfect bowel movements on the Tour?" growled Hill.

Not that his ire was directed solely at the Politically Correct members of the Tour. He once had a go at the self-confessed "rake" Doug Sanders, he of the new pair of shoes and different woman every day. Hill commented about Sanders's bragging over his many conquests, "Doug Sanders has said he likes to have sex and a hot-tub bath every morning and he's loose and ready to go. Of course, if Sanders had scored half as often with women as he claims he has he'd be dead."

He visited Ireland once and endeared himself to republicans by observing that he had only come to the country because "I heard the Irish hate the British as much as I do." His animosity towards the British extended in particular to the arrival of Tony Jacklin on the American Tour, fresh from his British and US Open triumphs. According to Jacklin, Hill was one of a group of "small-minded guys . . . who didn't like foreigners on their Tour."

One wonders what he made of Lee Trevino!

## Ky Laffoon

Ky Laffoon was a Native American golfer who had an intense love-hate relationship with his golf equipment. In psychological terms he was a classic abuser, at times charming and loving to his clubs, at others vindictive and cruel. At a tournament in Jacksonville, Florida, he tried to strangle a putter which had let him down. Finding himself unable to choke the very last breath from the club, he opted instead to toss it into the nearest lake. This he did, accompanied by the shriek, "Drown, you son of a bitch, drown."

Laffoon drove a yellow Cadillac between tournaments (the driver's door was stained brown from the tobacco juice he would periodically spit out the window) and would often brood while passing away the long tedious hours on the road. Sometimes his thoughts got the better of him and he would stop the car, take out the club which had most recently offended him, tie it to a rear door and drag it all the way along the road to his next port of call. At night he could often be seen approaching, not just by means of the front or rear lights on his Caddy but because of the sparks thrown up by the club trailing behind the car. (He also used this technique, not as a punishment for the clubs, but as a method of grinding down edges of clubs in order to sharpen them, rather in the manner of a downhill skier.)

In his latter years as a club professional, Laffoon gave full vent to his love affair with guns. At 5.30 in the morning, and again in the late afternoon or evening, he would tour the course where he was the professional with a shotgun, seeking out gophers. It was not uncommon for him to loose off a series of blasts in the general direction of members who happened to get too close to some vermin in his sights. (Sadly, on being informed that he was seriously ill, Laffoon eventually took his own life with one of his shotguns.)

Fred Corcoran, sporting entrepreneur and erstwhile organiser of the PGA Tour, once refereed a two-hole golf match between two blind men. The match was played at night, during the Cleveland Open. Corcoran was very taken with the putting method of one of the men, and the following day he happened to meet Ky Laffoon on the practice green and showed him the blind man's stroke. Laffoon liked it and thought he'd give it a try. He duly won the Cleveland. Either he or Corcoran must have said something to the press about the origin of his new putting stroke, because one paper carried a headline the following day: "Blind Man Teaches Laffoon How To Putt".

Ky's wife, tiring of his tantrums on the course, once issued an ultimatum. She said she'd leave him if he ever embarrassed her again with his erratic behaviour. A short time later, Laffoon hit a ball into an inconvenient forsythia bush (have you ever seen a convenient one on a golf course?). He swung at the flora once but failed to dislodge the ball. He tried again, with equal lack of success. Then again. And again. He became unconscious of the presence of his wife as his anger with the bush grew. Finally, entirely bereft of his minimal allocation of reason, he tossed his club aside and wrapped his arms around the bush in an altogether loveless embrace. Then he proceeded to rip it out of its earth-womb. Out of the corner of his eye, he spotted his wife cantering for the parking lot and reason prevailed. Clutching the offending bush he raced after her. When he caught up with her he opened his apology with the immortal line, "It's OK, honey. I wasn't really mad about missing the ball. I just hate forsythia!"

### Peter Teravainen

American pro Peter Teravainen is a well-liked professional. His only real eccentricities, if they can be called that, are that he is a Buddhist and that he is an American playing on the European Tour. He is also an intense, focussed sort of player who finally made his big breakthrough in the Czech Open in 1995. For six months a Boston-based journalist, Michael Bamberger, caddied for Teravainen, in order to gather material on the life of a caddie on the pro Tour. Only once in all that time did Teravainen utter an angry word to his "caddie". That was when Bamberger pushed the wrong button and shouted after a Teravainen ball which looked like it was going astray. His peremptory command to the unheeding ball drew the ire of the professional. Ashen-faced, as he handed him back the club, Teravainen said angrily, "Don't ever talk to my ball again."

### Laddie Lucas

"Laddie" Lucas was one of the best left-handed golfers Britain ever produced. He came out of the Prince's Club in Sandwich and once captained the Walker Cup team. He was also an RAF pilot during World War Two. On one occasion during that conflict he was attacked and hit by a German plane on the way home from France. He managed to cajole his plane across the Channel but knew that he'd never be able to reach his base. He headed instead for Prince's. Using local knowledge and all his considerable flying skills he aimed for the ninth fairway and managed to set down a few yards into the rough. As he stepped down from the plane and surveyed the scene he was heard to remark, "I never could hit that fairway."

### Calvin Peete

Calvin Peete, because he was black, was always a stand-out player on the US Tour. Then he decided to get diamonds in his teeth. Maybe he got tired of always being identified as the leading black player on the Tour and wanted to be known as the leading golf professional with a mouth full of diamonds. Maybe he even wanted a special Tour statistics category. However, after sporting his attractive new smile for a while, Peete decided to get the sparklers removed, insisting that, "I wanted people to recognise me for my character and my quality of play, not as the guy with diamonds in his teeth."

## Charles McDonald

Charles B McDonald was one of the most significant figures in American golf in the early years of the century. He was a millionaire businessman with a passion for the game and the founder of the National Golf Links at Southampton, Long Island. He modelled many of the holes at the National on famous British equivalents. The course, for example, included a copy of the St Andrew's "Road Hole".

McDonald had a house adjacent to the course which commanded wonderful views of the surrounding area. Spurning these vistas, however, McDonald had his windows facing his links. McDonald took criticism of his course to heart. If he overheard a complaint from a member and felt it justified he would see that it was rectified. The bill for the work carried out would then be sent to the complainant. If that person chose not to pay, he was dropped from the club membership list. In this way a bridge room was added to the clubhouse and a pond near the 14th was drained to kill off the indigenous mosquitoes.

One day he was sitting with his nephew, the future shipping magnate Peter Grace, and the younger man saw fit to condemn the course as being "too easy." McDonald would have none of it. Grace pointed out that the first hole was a par-4 but that the green was reachable from the tee.

"Rubbish," bristled his uncle. "No one has ever reached that green with their drive."

"Very well," challenged Grace. "Let's see, shall we?"

The two men decamped from the clubhouse bar to the first tee where, sure enough, with the aid of a following wind Grace launched a huge drive which managed to trickle on to the elevated green. Grace was well satisfied with his effort but McDonald was livid. Without saying a word, he stalked away thunderously. He had the last laugh on his nephew, however. At the earliest opportunity he cut him out of his will. According to Grace, the shot cost him more than a million dollars. He was able to tell the story without cutting his wrists only because he made far more than that himself from his shipping interests.

## Walter Breeze Smith

Towards the turn of the century the president of the newly-established Tuxedo Club in New York was the brilliant gamesman Walker Breeze Smith. Smith was the owner of a glass eye and often carried a box of replacements which allowed him to have a great deal of fun at the expense of others. Playing against the aristocratic New Yorker John C Ten Eyck, he extolled the virtues of a tip he had received on how to play this new game. It was to "keep one's eye on the ball." Standing on the third tee he gave his opponent an example of what he understood the axiom to mean. Having teed up on the little pile of sand players used in those days he took out his glass eye, placed it on top of the ball and drove off, sending the ball into the distance and shattering the eye. He then replaced the eye and did the same thing again on the next tee. He repeated the stunt at every hole, going through most of the box in the process. But he beat his horrified opponent four and three.

## Ivan Gantz

Ivan Gantz, an American professional from the immediate post-World War Two period, was one of the great self-flagellators of golf, following in the Lefty Stackhouse tradition. Don January, one of the more successful players on the American tour in the 1950s and 60s, once spotted Gantz staggering around a wooded area looking as if he'd been attacked by a wild animal. Blood was streaming down his face and he had a faraway look in his eyes. Later January discovered that Gantz had simply missed a putt on the previous green and had smitten himself with his putter.

## Howdy Giles

Howdy Giles, an American dentist, is, thankfully, not as violent as the obsessive fan portrayed by Kathy Bates in the film *Misery*, but he is just as monomaniacal about his particular idol, Arnold Palmer. His fixation began in 1960 when he was given a gift of a set of Palmer golf clubs by his wife. His obsession with Arnie quickly switched to his clothes (from the Arnold Palmer Collection only) and to his cars (Cadillacs from Arnold Palmer dealerships only). To further his obsession he put Arnie's image on his personal stationery and then bought a condominium right beside the Palmer residence in Bay Hill. His porch is positioned so that he can see Palmer at work on his clubs.

Unperturbed by this fixation Arnie himself has befriended his biggest fan, they've played dozens of rounds together and fly to the Masters every year in Arnie's private jet. Invited merely to *watch* a match between Palmer and then US President George Bush the dentist took 220 photographs, many of which now hang in his house. In 1977 Howdy became the Official Palmer Dentist. With the King's approval, he removed a number of gold fillings which he then melted down to make a ball marker.

### Mac O'Grady

Mac O'Grady, former coach to Seve Ballesteros, was a long-time loose cannon on the USPGA Tour and the nemesis of the former Commissioner Deane Beman. O'Grady was something of a slow developer: he holds the record for Tour School attempts, finally making the Big Tour on his 17th try. Having made it, he often looked like he'd be bumped off in about a tenth of the time it took him to get on. Fined by Beman for swearing at a tournament volunteer (he denied the offence), he later accused Beman of being "a liar and a thief" when the Commissioner deducted the fine from his tournament winnings. He subsequently compared Beman to Adolf Hitler. He also attempted to gain entry into the Chrysler Team Invitational as a one-man team. He told the organisers that Mac O'Grady A would play right handed and putt left-handed while Mac O'Grady B would play left-handed and putt right-handed. He once threatened to leave himself a one-inch putt to win the Masters and then turn to the TV cameras and reveal the depths of corruption and depravity on the PGA Tour. In reply to one journalist who had the courage to ask him directly if he was mad, O'Grady observed, "I'm not as bingo, bango, bongo as you think." Clearly Seve agreed because he took O'Grady on as his coach. Their association lasted about as long as Seve's relationship with his caddies.

*Horton Smith*

In a game which abounds in oddballs Horton Smith, winner of the inaugural Masters, stood out because of his very lack of eccentricity. He never touched alcohol, drinking only milk, and always went to bed early. At one function he was invited by a woman to take a drink. He declined. He then turned down the offer of a cigarette. She asked, "Mr Smith, have you no vices?" to which he replied, "I'm often short with my long putts."

# CHAPTER THREE

## *Holes In One*

*"Occasionally, on a par-three hole, a player makes a hole in one, that is, drives the ball from the tee into the cup in one stroke; it has been calculated that the odds against any player doing this are 8606 to 1."*
*(From: Microsoft Encarta)*

Many players go through their lives without achieving a hole in one, but fourteen have accomplished this feat on consecutive holes. None, however, was quite as successful as one Norman L Manley who, on 2 September, 1964, "aced" the par-4 330 yd. 7th hole at Del Valle Country Club in Saugus, California before making it two-in-a-row on the par-4 290 yd. 8th hole. A total of six shots under par for the two holes!

Playing in a match-play competition at Galway Golf Club, a member holed out in one and still managed to lose the hole! Jimmy Duffy aced the thirteenth but, thinking that his ball had gone through the green, searched in vain for it. Five minutes having elapsed, he was forced to concede. The ball was discovered in the hole by the next match coming through. A similar fate befell one Bill Carey, playing a match late in the evening against Edgar Winter at Roehampton Golf Club in July, 1964. Winter's ball pitched close to the hole but darkness interrupted the search for Carey's. It was only after Carey had already conceded that they found his ball in the hole.

The opening of a six-hole golf course at The Country Club, Brookline, Massachusetts in April, 1893 was marked by an exhibition match between three players, including one Arthur Hunnewell. Members of the exclusive club (mainly horsemen and hunters) turned up to see what this new game was all about. Hunnewell explained to the crowd that the object of the exercise was to get the ball in the hole in as few strokes as possible. He then teed up and did just that, scoring a hole in one from a range of about 90 yards. The crowd, who had been expecting just such a thing to happen on the basis of the explanation of the game which had been offered to them, were singularly unimpressed and didn't even acknowledge the achievement. When the other two players failed to hole out in a single shot the spectators began to drift back to the riding, shooting and archery which they had abandoned in order to witness this strange new game.

Seventy-three year old New Zealander Eric Johnston scored his first ever hole in one at the Queen's Park GC, in 1994. But he didn't have much time to bask in the adulation of his fellow members. Shortly after being presented with a tie to mark the achievement, he collapsed and died.

On the 10 October, 1962, Dr Joseph Boydstone "aced" the 3rd and 4th holes at the Bakersfield Ggolf club in California, an exceptional but not unique achievement. However, he then went on to complete his hat-trick by holing out in one at the 9th as well.

Using a driver, Ginny Leyes aced the 9th hole at Morris Park Golf Course in South Bend, Indiana. Not to be outdone, her husband Harold aced the same hole an hour later with a 3-iron.

In 1986 Arnold Palmer became the first Senior Tour player to make a hole in one on consecutive days (and at the same hole!). During the Chrysler Cup at the TPC Avenel course near Washington DC, Palmer aced the 187-yard 3rd hole on consecutive days. The odds against such an outcome are over nine million to one.

Dan Pooley scored an extra special ace at the 17th hole in the 1987 Hertz Bay Hill Classic in Orlando, Florida. As luck would have it, the tournament organisers (presumably with some heavy insurance backing) were offering a one-million-dollar bonus for a hole in one at the 17th. Pooley scooped the lot and with that one shot more than doubled his career prize money earnings.

Joe Lucius of Tiffin, Ohio has aced the 141-yard 15th hole at the local Mohawk Golf Club no less than 13 times! He's only three behind that total on the 10th where he's holed out in one ten times.

American PGA Professional Russ Cochran, one of the few left-handers on the Tour, has scored many holes in one but his particular distinction is that he has used every club in the bag in achieving his aces.

If Robert Taylor had any negative thoughts about the par-3 188-yard third hole at the Hunstanton Golf Club in Norfolk in May, 1974 he'd certainly changed his mind by June. Starting on 31 May, he aced the hole on three successive days.

Harry Gonder, an American pro, decided to initiate an interesting experiment in 1940. He took two witnesses out to a 160-yard par-three hole, along with a supply of helpers to tee up and recover balls for him, and set about seeing how long it would take him to achieve a hole in one. Beginning his attempt at 10.15 am, he reckoned on taking a couple of hours, at the outside, to accomplish the feat. He reckoned wrong. His 86th shot made it to within 15 inches of the flag. His 996th actually hit the flag but settled three inches from the cup. Shot number 1,162 (at 8.10 *pm*) was just six inches short. Twenty-two shots later, he missed by only three inches. His hands beginning to blister, he watched No. 1,750 hit the pin. He must have been getting the hang of it at last, because he hit it again six shots later but the ball stayed above ground by a frustrating inch. At 2.40 am he gave up after 1,817 shots. He'd been trying for 16 hours and 25 minutes without success!

Dontcha just hate it when some young whippersnapper holes in one and you've been waiting all your life for that heady walk to pick the ball out of the cup? If so focus your aggression on Coby Orr of Littelton, Colorado who was all of five years of age when he "aced" the 103-yard. 5th at the Riverside Golf Course, San Antonio, Texas. Grrrr!

But even little Coby isn't the youngest player to have aced a hole. That distinction belongs to four-year-old Scott Statler. His moment of glory came at the 7th hole on the Statler's Par-Three Golf Course in

Greensburg, Pennsylvania on 30 July, 1962. Wonder was he related to the owner?

Anton Shepherd was a positively geriatric eight years of age when he became the third youngest person in Britain to hole out in one. He did it at the 4th hole at the Leeds Golf Centre. Unremarkable, really! But you'd have to take your hat off to the youngster's marketing skills. After his achievement he sold dozens of autographed copies of his photograph for 20p each.

Four holes in one in three rounds – that is the record achieved by Scot Douglas Porteous. He actually averaged a hole in one in every ten holes. On September 26, 1974 he aced the third and sixth holes at Ruchill GC in Glasgow. Two days later, he repeated the achievement at the fifth on the same course. Then, on 30 September, he aced the sixth at the Clydebank and District GC.

David Senior figured he had good cause to celebrate his fortieth birthday when he holed his tee shot at the 15th at Royal Lytham and St Anne's in England. The hole measures 160 yards. But his joy was shortlived. He was playing a match against one Bill Lloyd, who proceeded to stand up and knock *his* tee shot into the hole. To add insult to injury he displaced Senior's ball, although, of course the hole in one stood. No doubt unnerved by this unbelievable half Senior, a thirteen handicapper, went on to lose the match 2 and 1.

Precisely the same thing happened to Albert Wilson, who scored his first ever hole in one during a match with his friend Les Henshaw at the 12th hole at Woodhall Spa in England in 1982. He then watched as Henshaw halved the hole by scoring a hole in one himself. (The odds against such an occurrence are 1,844,874,304 to 1!)

English golfer Graham Salmon hacked up in a "nearest the pin" contest at Cams Hill Course in Hampshire in 1994 when he sank his tee shot. They don't come any nearer the hole than when they're nestling snugly in the cup. An added dimension to the hole in one was the fact that Graham is blind.

Corkman Arthur Powell knows that a hole in one of his was down to luck (or divine intervention) rather than skill. On a 265-yard hole he sliced his ball so far out of bounds that it hit the roof of a house. Powell then watched in disbelief as the ball ricocheted on to the green and dribbled into the cup.

Few, if any, players can boast of an ace at a longer hole than can Larry Bruce. On November 15, 1962 Bruce was playing the 480-yard, par-5 dogleg fifth hole at the Hope Country Club in Arkansas. He decided to cut off the dogleg and go straight for the green. He was rewarded for his risky strategy when he got to the green and discovered his ball in the cup.

Bruce's record stood until July, 1995 when 33-year-old Shaun Lynch shattered it by holing in one in similar fashion at Teign Valley Golf Club near Exeter. He hit a 3-iron across the dogleg at the 496-yard 17th and aced the hole.

Robert Mitera probably holds the record for the longest "straight" hole in one. On 7 October, 1965, when he was 21 years of age he was playing the 10th at the aptly-named Miracle Hills Golf Club in Omaha, Nebraska. The hole is a par-four measuring 447 yards, with a large drop-off from the tee to the green. Mitera had a 50-mph tailwind behind him when he launched into his shot.

Bob Hudson has the unique distinction of being the only player to score back-to-back holes in one in a professional golf tournament. He achieved the feat in the 1971 Martini International in Norwich at the 11th and 12th holes of the host club.

Charles Ward managed to shoot two holes in one at the Open Championship, though not, regrettably, in the same year. He aced the 8th at St Andrew's in 1946, and in 1948 did it again at the 13th at Muirfield.

Perhaps, in the tradition of "birdie," "eagle," and "albatross," they should rename the hole in one a "magpie", in honour of GC Hazen who, at the 105-yard. 2nd at Daylesford, Australia, had a completely bizarre ace. His tee shot hit a tree, ricocheted on to the green and hit a magpie who managed to deflect it into the cup.

Bernard Burkett is probably the only players to have scored holes in one in five different decades. He's only scored six ("Only", what am I saying – I've never even scored one!) but they came in 1937, 1950, 1958, 1961, 1971 and 1980. If he's still alive he's probably due another one soon.

Otto Bucher was a mere seventeen weeks short of his 100th birthday when he holed in one at the 130-yd. 12th hole at La Manga GC in Spain. So never give up hope!

In 1965 Jim Hadderer, aged only 16, scored a hole in one at the Wing Park GC in Elgin, Illinois on a 190-yard hole. What made this particular hole in one interesting was that he was on his knees when he hit the shot.

A hole in one caused Christy O'Connor Sr to stop using two-irons. It happened while playing in a tournament at Moor Allerton in the 1960s. There were hefty prizes for a hole in one at three of the four par-threes but the fourth short hole was in fact so long, at well over 200 yards, that the tournament organisers considered the possibility of an ace remote in the extreme. So when Christy actually holed out with a two-iron and won only a bottle of whisky, he was so disgusted he never used the club again.

While on holiday in South Carolina in 1978, an American, Ben Thomas, holed out in one. So what? He's blind, that's so what!

Scott Palmer from San Diego, California is the acknowledged hole in one "ace". He holds almost every conceivable record in the book. He is the only golfer to have scored more than 100 holes in one. In one year, between June 1983 and June 1984, he scored no less than 33 aces. In October 1983 he had holes in one during four consecutive rounds. Figure out the odds on that little lot!

Mark Law is almost unique among the annals of golfers in that he was intensely displeased at scoring a hole in one at Goring and Streathley, Oxfordshire. Unfortunately, at the time Mr Law was taking part in a long-driving competition!

Hubert Pressley, of G1lendale, Arizona was 55 years old when he scored a hole in one at the Glendale 500 club. He used a five-iron at the fifth hole, playing on the fifth of May (the fifth month, in case you hadn't noticed).

When it comes to unusual holes in one that of George Wegener (aged 14) of Portal, North Dakota, beats most. Not because he was a mere teenager, but because he was playing the ninth hole at the Gateway GC which straddles the US-Canadian border. The tee is in the US and the green is in Canada. Which means that your Master Wegener teed up in one country and holed out in another.

An American, Marie Robie, from Wollaston in Massachusetts holds the distinction of having hit the longest hole in one ever by a woman, 393 yards. She was playing the first hole at the Furnace Brook golf club in Wollaston on 4 September, 1949 when she really connected with her driver on the par-4 hole and watched the ball fall into the cup.

One of the great "sentimental" holes in one was that scored by Gene Sarazen during the British Open at Troon in 1973 at the age of 71. His ace came at the famous "Postage Stamp" hole, notorious for its small green. He thus became the oldest player to hole in one during an Open championship.

Bob Stallcup aced the first hole (150 yards) playing in a four-ball competition in Bramblewood Country Club in Holly, Michigan in June, 1993. A few minutes later his son Tim, in the following four-ball match, emulated his father's achievement.

An unusual prize was once offered for a hole in one in a professional tournament. In the 1985 New South Wales Open in Canberra a local sponsor, mortician Paul Smith, offered a full funeral service to anyone who might ace the 8th hole at the host course. He may have been influenced by the knowledge that, in the event of a tie, the eighth would be the first hole of the "sudden death" play-off.

At the tender age of 75, Harold Snider from Arizona had the distinction of scoring three holes in one in a single round of golf. His great good fortune befell him on the 8th, 13th and 14th holes at the Ironwood Golf Course in Phoenix. on June 9, 1976. There is no record of whether he then went on to beat his age, but he only needed to shoot 71 or better over the other 15 holes to have achieved that distinction as well.

Art Wall has probably the most successful professional record for shooting holes in one. His career lasted over forty years and in that time he averaged virtually an ace a season. Between 1936 and 1979, he holed in one 42 times.

Wall's record didn't impress at least one Southern golfing fan, an acolyte of the great Georgian Bobby Jones. In his collection of articles "Fairways and Greens", the endlessly amusing and provocative writer Dan Jenkins recalls talking to Wall when "an overbeveraged Southerner in an ill-fitting blazer" strolled up to them. He recognised Art Wall and asked, "Ain't you the fella who's supposed to make all them holes in one?" Jenkins confirmed that the fan was not mistaken. "Thirty or forty of the suckers," the Southerner persisted. "It's up to thirty-four now," Wall corrected him politely. "Thirty-four?" queried the good ole boy, his brow furrowed as if he was trying to solve some complicated calculus problem, before adding, "Boy, who are you tryin' to kid? Bobby didn't make but *three*."

In September 1993 Ryan Procop (a forbidding name if ever there was one) sank the longest putt of his life, all of 168 yards, for an ace at the par-3 15th at Gleaneagles GC, Twinsburg, Ohio. He'd been having a bad time at the previous hole, a par-5 where he'd just taken a 12. So when he stood up on the 15th tee, he angrily took out his putter and lashed away at the ball. "I figured I couldn't hit any of my other clubs straight," he commented afterwards, "so I might as well use my putter."

Karen Disabella got a skewed impression of how easy the game of golf is when she stepped up to the first hole she had ever played on a golf course, in 1984, and aced it. Afterwards she explained that she may have been prompted to this extraordinary feat by the fear of delaying the players behind her by playing too slowly.

40

Playing the 120-yard 1st hole at the Hill course of the Lake Spivey, GC in Jonesboro in Georgia, an airline pilot, Larry Rankin, dumped his tee shot into the water in front of the green. Using the same eight-iron he teed up again and made his par with an ace. Rankin, who had been playing golf for 35 years, had never scored a hole in one. Four holes later he was on the tee of the 135-yard fifth hole when his playing partner bet him he couldn't repeat the ace. Taking the same eight-iron he had used at the first, Rankin duly scored the second ace of his life within an hour of the first.

Jo Ann Washam is the only woman pro to have hit two holes in one in the same tournament. At the Women's Kemper Open in the Mesa Verde GC in Colorado, she aced the 16th during the first round. During the final round she repeated the achievement at the 17th.

US Tour pro Neal Lancaster can never forget his first ever hole-in-one. It happened when he was fifteen and, as bad luck would have it, he was on his own. Wildly excited by what he'd done, he looked around to find someone he could tell. So he ran to the next tee where another singleton was playing his round. The man, a Mr Creech, happened to be lying next to his golf cart when the animated Lancaster began to gush with wild excitement. Slowly it dawned on him that the man was not responding to his enthusiasm . . . in fact, he wasn't responding to anything . . . in fact, he was dead. "They found he'd had a heart attack and died," Lancaster recalled as a 33-year-old touring pro. "So here I was, just a kid shooting his first hole in one and the first person I tried to tell was dead."

During his National Service in 1954 Ray Woodhouse lost an arm but it didn't stop him playing golf. In June 1994, at the par-3 8th hole of the Mapperley GC in Nottinghamshire, he holed out in one and, by his own account started "jumping around like a ten-year-old. It was wonderful."

John Parkinson, secretary of Penwortham GC in Lancashire, dodged the bullet when he scored the first ever hole in one at the new Pryors Hayes Golf club. He didn't have to buy drinks for everyone in the bar afterwards, because there was none; the club didn't have an alcohol licence.

In September 1993, a charity golf tournament in Rancho Santa Fe, California offered $10,000 for a hole in one at the par-3 fifth hole and a Thunderbird LX car for one at the par-3 16th. One of the competitors, a Joe Szeles, managed to make an ace but did so at the par-3, 163-yard 14th. This hole was sponsored by a local dentist who generously awarded Mr Szeles a toothbrush for his efforts.

A "Grand Slam" of holes in one on any course is an unusual enough achievement but 12-handicap Dick Nicols managed it within a nine-month period at his home course, the Lake Charles Country Club. On 20 January, 1993 he aced the 152-yard 3rd hole. The very next month it was the turn of the 157-yard 14th. In August he aced the 185-yard 6th and then completed his own personal Grand Slam by acing the 175-yard 16th on 9 September.

How about this for performance under pressure? Robert Trent Jones, whose course designs have tormented professionals the world over, was asked to make some adjustments to Baltusrol for the 1954 US Open. The changes certainly made the course a tougher test of golf for the pros, but club members were reported to be in revolt at how difficult the course had become. There were particular complaints about the par-3 fourth, measuring 194 yards, most of which was across water. To satisfy himself that he had not set an impossible task, and to pacify the members, Jones organised a four-ball with the club pro and two members. Coming to the fourth, Jones was up last. The three players preceding him had all found the green when Jones, using a long iron, flew the ball across the water and hopped it into the cup. Putting the club back in the bag, satisfied that he had ended all arguments on the subject, he said, "Gentlemen, I believe this hole is eminently fair."

During the 1989 US Open Championship at Oak Hill, the par-three sixth hole proved a pushover when no less than four players aced it. All four (Tom Weaver, Jerry Pate, Nick Price and Mark Wiebe) did it with seven-irons.

The first hole in one in the history of the Open was in 1878 at Prestwick. James Anderson needed some heroics to beat the score of 161 which had been posted by JOF Morris, the son of Old Tom and the brother of Young Tom. He got what he needed at the seventeenth. He overshot the hole at the par-three but his ball struck a mound before slowly trickling back down the slope and into the hole. Anderson won that year and captured the two Opens which followed.

In November 1993, a young chemistry student from Pennsylvania, Jason Bohn, won one million dollars after he holed out in one in a charity golf tournament in Tuscaloosa, Alabama. As a consequence, he lost his amateur status. Now, before you start thinking "what shall it profit it a man that he gain the whole world but loseth his soul", bear in mind that the kid got paid $5,000 a month for the next twenty years!

In Japan, getting a hole in one can be a costly experience. The successful "ace" golfer is expected, in many clubs, not just to tip his caddie and buy a round of drinks for everyone in the clubhouse but to throw a party for all the members and present them with a bottle of malt whiskey each. He must also plant a commemorative tree on the course at his own expense. The total bill for an ace has been known to come to as much as £4,000 before all the bills are paid. In fact, so expensive is an "ace" in Japan that a trade union there actually offers its golfing members a special insurance policy against ever achieving one.

US President Dwight Eisenhower, shrugging aside two Presidential election victories, the D-Day landings and V-E Day claimed February 6, 1968, as the happiest day of his life. Playing at the Seven Lakes Country Club, Palm Springs (he was aged 77 at the time), Ike took a 9-iron at the par-3, 104-yard 13th hole and watched the ball pitch into the cup for the only hole in one of his life.

# CHAPTER FOUR

## *Some of the World's Worst Golfing Jokes*

QUICKIES

Old golfers never die; they just putter away.

A labourer stands watching a club member attempting to extricate himself from a bunker. After five futile efforts the golfer loses his temper and screams at the onlooker, "The club is for golfers only."
    "I know," replies the navvy, "but I won't tell them if you don't."

A true golfer is one who shouts "fore", shoots a seven and marks himself down for five.

"Right," said the pro, "Just swing normally. Don't hit the ball."
    "But that's what I came here to cure."

A beginner excavates an enormous divot from the ground after playing a risible shot. "What do I do with this?" he asks the caddie.
    "Take it home and practise on it."

"I've just got a great new set of clubs for my husband."
    "Terrific, that's a really good trade."

GOLFER: "I think I dropped a bottle of Scotch out of my bag somewhere around the tenth, was anything handed in?"
STARTER: "Yes sir, two of the members of the four-ball following you."

Night is drawing in and a golfer hits a ball off into the gloom. "Did that go straight?" he inquires of his partner.

"I didn't see it but it sounded crooked," comes the reply.

The bright imaginative child is caddie for her father for the first time. She spends nine holes observing and ruminating before asking the obvious question. "Daddy, why must you keep the ball out of the little hole?"

"Did you know," he said, "that the Dutch claim to have invented a game that bears a vague resemblance to golf."

"Oh yes," she replied, "I know. My husband's been playing it for years."

GOLFER: "Caddie master, this caddie you've given me is a mere child."
C'MASTER: "Indeed sir. But remember, he hasn't learned to count up to ten yet."

A conversation is overheard at a golf club after a mixed foursome. Husband is berating wife for her performance. "You drive me out of my mind," he finally explodes.

"That would be a putt, dear," comes the tart riposte.

The novice decides that a philosophical front is the best approach after yet another dismal failure. "Funny old game, golf," he observes, with a meaningful sigh.

"It's not meant to be," replies the longsuffering caddie.

DOCTOR: "Do you want the good news or the bad news first?"
PATIENT: "The bad news."
DOCTOR: "I'm afraid you can't play golf."
PATIENT: "How do you know? You've never even watched me."

A golfer .is someone who blames anyone but himself for his own mediocrity but claims personal responsibility for a hole in one.

GOLFER: "Why do you keep looking at the sun?"
CADDIE: "Compass bearing, sir!"

Two women approach the pro in his shop and strike up a conversation which doesn't seem to be getting anywhere. Finally he asks one of them, "Were ye wanting to learn a bit of golf?"

"Oh no!" came the reply. "It's my friend here who's interested. I learned yesterday."

Bill and Bob are playing in not unfamiliar conditions at Lahinch. A storm-force gale is howling in from the Atlantic and is buffeting everything on the treeless links. Bill is lining up a putt when he asks Bob, "How do we stand?"

"I don't know," comes the shouted reply. "Gravity?"

Sam eyes his ball in the depths of a water hazard. It's a balata and he's loath to part with it.

"Go on in after it," encourages Gordon.

"It looks rather deep," says Sam warily. "I might drown."

"No chance. You'll never be able to keep your head down."

Peter has just hit a few balls on the practice range. Proudly he turns to the pro and says, "I'm sure you'll have spotted a major difference since the last time we met?"

"Absolutely," replies the pro. "But I don't think the beard really suits you."

SOME HOARY OLD CHESTNUTS

The teenage caddie was having a bad day. It was his first job as a bag carrier at the local country club and because of his inexperience he'd been dumped on one of the worst hackers in the club. Teeing off on the first the caddie sneezed violently just as his "bag" swung the club back. The result was a topped shot which barely made the women's tee. The hacker then took seven more shots to get down and open his account with a quadruple bogey. Standing on the second he glared balefully at the caddie as he addressed his drive. This time the nervous teenager dropped the clubs and the result was a vicious hook into some bushes. Through his own pathetic efforts the hacker took another nine shots to get down. After putting out he turned to the caddie and told him, "You're fired. You can't keep quiet, you can't keep still. You must be the worst caddie in the world."

"I don't think so, sir," the caddie responded, "that would be too much of a coincidence."

A Established Member of a snooty Country Club was appalled to behold what he took to be a new member playing his ball from in front of the tee markers. He stormed up to the cheat, demanded his name, and insisted that he return the ball to its proper position. The player studied the Established Member sardonically for a moment before remarking, "I am playing it from its proper position, this is my second shot."

"If I died," she asks archly, "would you remarry?"

"Probably, darling!"

"And would you let her play golf with you?"

"Probably, darling!"

"And would you let her use my clubs?"

"Definitely not! She's left-handed."

A tourist in Africa decides he wants a game of golf so he drives to a course he's heard good reports of, which is situated on the edge of a jungle. The club's secretary manager, having ascertained that the tourist's handicap is a more-than-competent ten, allocates a caddie and sends him off. The tourist is intrigued to see the caddie insert a rifle into the bag of hired clubs.

Playing the first, a low-index par-four, the tourist is on the green in regulation and is lining up his first putt when a lion bounds out of the jungle and leaps for his jugular. Quick as a flash the caddie reaches into the bag, grabs the rifle, aims and fires. The lion falls dead at the golfer's feet.

"Phew," the golfer exclaims to the caddie. "Thanks, you saved my life there."

"All part of the service, sir," replies the caddie.

They go on to the second, another low-index par-four with a green surrounded by water. Once again the tourist is on target with his approach shot but when he lines up his putt he is close to the edge of the water. As he studies the line, a crocodile emerges from the water and snaps at his leg. Once again the caddie comes to his rescue with the rifle. The crocodile is despatched with a single shot.

Nothing daunted, the intrepid golfer, despite these two brushes with death, decides to continue his round.

The third is a high-index par-five which poses no real challenge, the tourist is on the green in two but as he lines up his eagle putt he fails to notice a poisonous snake approaching. His preoccupation with the eagle proves fatal. The caddie fails to come to the rescue, the snake strikes and finds its target. As the golfer lies dying he looks accusingly at the caddie and pleads, "Why didn't you kill him?"

"Sorry sir,'" replies the caddie, "Index twelve, you didn't have a shot."


Both bored and intrigued by the fascination her husband has for the game of golf the professor of physics decides she will learn something about this strange game. She decides to take some lessons.

On the practice ground the professional asks her to address the ball and take a swing.

"That won't be necessary," she responds haughtily. "Please just explain the theory to me and I'll put it into effect."

The professional launches into a lengthy discursion on the dynamics of the swing. His pupil listens intently, making copious notes and occasionally jabbing on the buttons of a pocket calculator.

When the professional finishes the professor demands, "Right, my good man, take me to one of these golf holes." So the pro brings her to the tenth, which happens to be free, and tees up the ball for her. The professor takes out a tape, makes a few measurements, selects a club, stands up to the ball and makes a picture-perfect swing. The ball comes to rest about a foot from the hole.

The pro is dumbfounded, the professor blasé. "Now what?" she asks.

"Well," replies the pro, "we just go down to the green and you hit the ball into the hole."

"*Now* he tells me!"

Max, nearing seventy-five years of age, is forced to the conclusion that he is going to have to give up the game he loves because of advancing short-sightedness.

"No, no, no," wheedles his sexagenarian friend Angus. "You can't do that. Look, why not play with old Collins?"

"Collins! But, for God's sake, he's in his late eighties. He needs a Zimmer frame to get round the course," argues Max.

"OK, so he's a bit old and he suffers from most of the usual maladies of age. But he has one advantage, perfect eyesight."

Max concedes that playing with Collins is going to be the only way of playing regularly. The two men arrange a game. When they meet on the first, Max steps up and hits his ball. Within a few yards of it leaving the tee he loses sight of it completely. Confidently he turns to Collins. "Did you see that?" he asks.

"Yes! Very good indeed!"

"Yes, I know. But did you see where it finished?"

"Indeed I did. Saw it all the way."

"Where is it?"

At this, Collins's face clouds over. "I don't remember," he admits.

A wealthy businessman is trying out a new and very expensive golf course with membership in view. The marketing manager is being obsequious in the extreme. He meets the fat-cat as he troops back into the clubhouse.

"So, how was the golf?" he asks, in his most ingratiating tone.

"Bad," replies the millionaire. "Seventy-five."

"Really. Seventy-five. That's damn good, actually."

"Why, thank you. I'm hoping to do a little better on the back nine."

A priest was added at the last moment to a three-ball as it prepared to tee off. Not all of the golfers were delighted at the addition. The doctor was renowned for his salty tongue. Sure enough, on about the second hole he missed a fourteen-inch putt for par. "Shit!" he screamed. "I missed."

The priest was shocked at the profanity but let it pass.

On the very next hole, however, the doctor topped his approach shot and repeated the curse. "Shit, I missed again," he roared.

In order to avoid a constant repetition, the priest decided to admonish him. "My good man," he cautioned, "The Lord does not hold with profanity. Please keep a civil tongue in your head or the Lord will exact retribution."'

The doctor was chastened, but only briefly. At the very next hole he missed another tiddler and danced around the green in a scatological frenzy firing epithets to the heavens. Suddenly, there was a flash of lightning followed by a crash of thunder. The priest, struck directly by the lighting, fell dead at the doctor's feet. From the heavens an angry voice was heard. "Shit, I missed," it intoned.

The laird, the brigadier, the group captain and the consultant anaesthetist are having their weekly round at the local club. As usual, the course in front of them is deserted as they drive off after an extremely unhealthy lunch. No one ventures out on Mondays at 2.00 pm because the four-ball has become notorious throughout the length and breadth of the men's and women's locker rooms. However, as the four-ball approaches the fifth hole, a small figure can be seen in the distance. Someone is on the course in front of them! Worse, that person is a woman! The laird, appalled by this barefaced effrontery, laces into his drive with venom and watches with satisfaction as it catches the woman full in the back, having expended only half of its force. The woman turns round, rubbing her back, and gallantly waves the four-ball through. As the four men pass her in silence, she reaches into her bag and produces a sign which reads "DEAF AND DUMB, PLEASE PLAY THROUGH". Not at all abashed, the Fearsome Foursome sail past the woman and stand by their balls. The laird is to play first. As he stands over his ball, all four men become aware of the "swish" of a club being swung rhythmically behind them and the click of a ball taking off. But it is too late for the laird, who crashes to the ground as the ball smacks him solidly in the back of the head. The other three rush towards their fallen friend. As they do so, they look indignantly back down the fairway at the woman behind them. She is smiling apologetically and holding up the four fingers of her right hand.

"Why don't you ever play golf with Dr Simmons these days?" asks Mavis.

"Would you play golf with a habitual cheat who sneezes when you're putting, taps down spike marks in his line and *always* seems to find his ball, even in the deepest rough?" her husband replies.

"No, I certainly would not!" says Mavis indignantly.

"Well, neither will he!"

The small Dorset village had, for sixty years, tried in vain to win a regional inter-club competition. Then, joy of joys, playing on its home course, its ten-man team found itself in the final against the hot favourites. With only one match still out on the course the sides were level. Playing in the anchor position on both teams were the respective captains. Their game came right down to the eighteenth, where the captain of the win-less village faced a six-foot birdie putt to win the match and the competition. A large gallery waited, tense and breathless, as he lined up the putt. Having made up his mind on the line, the captain then addressed the ball. Just as he was about to draw back his putter, a funeral cortege passed by. Incredibly, the captain stood back, took off his cap and waited until the hearse and mourners had passed. The tension could now be cut with a knife. Coolly, however, he stood over his ball and slotted the putt as if it was of no consequence. The crowd around the green went berserk. The losing captain stepped up to shake the hand of the "victor ludorum."

"I just want to say," he observed, "that I was most impressed with your demeanour. Moving away from that putt at that moment to honour the dead was a lesson to us all."

"Thank you," responded his adversary. "But it was the least I could do. She'd been a good wife to me for the best part of thirty years."

Taking a short cut to the beach for a swim, Paddy and Dinjo wandered by accident on to a golf course. Both men heard a shout of "Fore" but, not being golfers, continued to walk. A ball whistled by Dinjo's head. Both men ducked. "Jaysus, Dinjo," said Paddy, "shtay shtill, will ya, there's three more of them missiles to come."

Sam is almost ready to pounce but he knows this new girl, Jill, is interested in sport, so he decides to apply the *coup de grace* first.

"You know, I'm a pretty good golfer. All the guys at the club are afraid to play with me. Guess what my handicap is?"

"I don't know," says the longsuffering Jill, "Flatulence?"

A Sunday four-ball was putting out on a blind par-three when, out of the blue, a ball trickled on to the green. A mischievous member of the group tapped the ball into the hole with his putter. Shortly afterwards, the waiting four were rewarded by the arrival of a tiny man struggling under the weight of a large bag of clubs.

"Sorry about that. I didn't realise you were still here," he apologised sweatily. He surveyed the green before asking in bafflement, "Did anyone see my ball?"

"Yes, it went straight into the hole as a matter of fact," claimed the practical joker.

"It did what? Wow!" he exclaimed. Turning to his partner, who had by now caught up with him, he shouted excitedly, "Hey, Bob. Guess what? I got an eight!"

Somehow the vicar found himself playing in a four-ball and partnering Chris, the most obnoxious and overbearing person ever sent to try the patience of a man of the cloth. Chris managed to criticise everything about the vicar's golf. He started by going through almost every club in the cleric's bag and pointing out how his own equivalent was vastly superior.

Then, after observing the vicar tee off, he started to giggle. "You've been watching your wife beating the carpets too much, Reverend, if you don't mind my saying so."

When they got to the first green he had a go at the vicar's putting grip, his stance and finally his stroke. This constant carping continued throughout the round. Afterwards, in the locker room, Chris approached the reverend gentleman and offered to partner him again.

"Assuming you take a few lessons first, of course. Listen, why don't I show you a thing or two? Come along next Monday at 11.00 and bring your clubs."

The vicar swallowed hard. "That's very kind of you. Incidentally, one good turn deserves another. Bring your parents along while you're at it. I can marry them for you."

Coming down the eighteenth, needing only a par for 40 stableford points for the round, Alan was feeling extremely pleased with himself. But, to his chagrin his approach shot to the green was viciously sliced over the boundary wall of the club. He took his penalty but the experience had rattled him and he had to content himself with 37 points for his round.

Later that evening, sitting at home, he was summoned to the door and greeted there by a large policeman. The officer of the law produced a golf ball. "Would you, by any chance, sir, have hit this ball over the boundary wall of the golf club at about 3.30 pm this afternoon?"

Alan examined the ball. It was a Maxfli with his distinctive markings on it. "Yes, officer, that's mine all right. Is there a problem?"

"I'm afraid you could say that, yes. Your ball hit a cyclist, causing him to veer across the road into the path of a car. The cyclist was killed instantly by the impact. The car then ran out of control and was hit by a bus coming in the opposite direction. The two people in the car, two nuns, in fact, were mangled beyond recognition but the bus continued on for about two hundred yards before hurtling down an embankment into the path of a passing train. Twenty seven of the passengers of the bus were killed instantly, twelve more died on their way to hospital and seventeen are in a critical condition."

"Oh, my God," muttered an ashen-faced and horrified Alan.

"I'm afraid that's not all, sir. The train was derailed on impact with the bus. Five passenger carriages were crushed together like a concertina. It was awful. So far they've managed to dig thirty-five bodies out of the wreckage."

"But this is just too horrible . . ."

"I'm afraid there's more, sir. Because the rescue services were completely preoccupied with the train/bus accident they were caught on the hop when a Boeing 767 crash-landed in fields near the local airport. They couldn't get to the scene in time, and at least fifteen people died while awaiting attention, in addition to the forty-seven killed outright by the crash itself."

By now all the blood had drained from Alan's face. "This is like a terrible nightmare. What can I do?"

"Well, I'm not an expert," observed the policeman, "but shouldn't you close the face of the club more at address?"


## DODGY ONES

Three golfers, one Irish, one English and one Scottish, travelled to France on a golfing holiday. Overnighting in Paris, they decided to test the services of a local brothel. All three were very taken with one of its employees, the young Fifi. A side bet was laid. The winnings would go to the man who could, for the same financial outlay, retain the services of Fifi for the longest period. Jock, the Scot, went first and returned, well pleased with himself, half an hour later. George, the Englishman went next and forty minutes had elapsed before he reappeared, smirking to beat the band. Finally Paddy followed Fifi upstairs. Half an hour went by. Then three-quarters of an hour. Just after sixty minutes had elapsed, a red-faced Fifi emerged from her room and approached the brothel madam. "Madame," she inquired, "quest-ce que c'est un Mulligan?"

Two golfers are having a drink in the bar after their round.

"Have you heard about George?" asks John.

"No, what happened?" replies Peter.

"He lost in the club matchplay by a whopping six and five and, because he finished early, found his wife in bed with another man when he went home. So he shot them both. Isn't it dreadful?"

"It could have been worse."

"How, for God's sake?"

"If he'd finished early in the Sunday Medal he'd have shot me."

A woman member comes running into the pro shop, clearly upset and disturbed about something.

"I've just been stung by a bee," she howls.

"Where?" inquires the pro.

"Between the first and second holes."

54

"Tut, tut," replies the pro. 'We're going to have to work on your stance."

The enthusiastic amateur is attempting to hack his ball out of deep woods adjacent to, but far removed from, the ninth fairway on his local nine-hole course, when who should stumble across his path but a leprechaun.

"Well I suppose ye'll be wanting a wish now," observed the lugubrious leprechaun.

"I will, aye," replied Michael.

"And what will you be wanting?"

"Do ye know what, I'd love a longer penis."

"All right, whatever you want," said the leprechaun, eyeing Michael malevolently.

Michael had hardly hacked back out on to the fairway before he felt the stirring in his member. By the time he'd begun his back nine, he would have walked away with the Member's Prize. At first he was proud of his ever-growing penis but as it grew and grew it became an irritant. He found it impeded his putting and chipping. By the time he'd got to the seventeenth it was interfering with his backswing. He decided something had to be done. With little difficulty, he managed to slice his ball back into the woods where he'd met the leprechaun. The little fellow was not difficult to find second time round, in fact he'd anticipated Michael's discomfort and allowed himself to be caught so he could enjoy it.

"I suppose you'll be wanting another wish," he repeated the routine.

"I will aye," concurred Michael.

"I bet I know what you want, too."

"Aye, you're right there. I want longer legs."

Simon was lining up his putt when, suddenly, a seagull swooped low and crapped on his head. Almost simultaneously, another one crapped right on his line.

"Will I get some toilet paper?" asked Ned.

"Not much point," observed Simon philosophically. "They'll be miles away by now."

The enthusiastic but lately deceased golfer presented himself at the Gates of Heaven without, as he fervently believed, a stain on his character. St Peter, however, didn't exactly concur.

"Sorry. This will take a little while but we have a record of your having used foul language and taken the name of the Lord in vain. It was on a golf course . . ."

". . . in September, 1970. Yes, I must admit I did get rather het up on that occasion."

"Do you have anything to offer in extenuation or mitigation before I consign you to Purgatory so that you may purge your sins?"

"Well, I was rather provoked. You see, I had come to the eighteenth with a chance to break eighty for the first and only time in my life. I only needed a par four to finish for a 79."

"So you topped your drive and bogeyed the hole, hence the blasphemous utterance."

"No, actually my drive was perfect. But when I got up to it, I discovered it was in a divot."

"Tricky,' said St Peter. "Been there myself. So what happened, you pulled the shot left of the green in an effort to dig it out?"

"No. I actually caught it quite cleanly. But it took a vicious kick as it approached the green and it ended up in a bunker . . ."

"Which, of course, it took you two shots to get out of, and that's when you lost your rag . . . blaspheming and cursing."

"Well . . . no, as a matter of fact. I managed to hit an almost perfect explosion shot to within twelve inches of the flag . . ."

"Jesus Christ," exclaimed St Peter angrily. "You're not trying to tell me you missed the fucking putt?"

Four youngish women members were about to tee off when a man blithely walked across the fairway about twenty yards in front of them. When he got close to the tee he suddenly parted the flaps of the raincoat he was wearing and flashed at the four golfers. After he'd fled the four women got around to discussing the incident.

"Well, I never," said Jill. "We must report that man to the Secretary-Manager."

"Indeed we must," agreed Cynthia. "Did anyone get a good look at his face?"

Shamefacedly, all were forced to acknowledge that they had not even looked at the man's face.

"Never mind," asserted the ever-practical Dorothy. "Process of elimination. I can swear on the evidence of what I saw that he wasn't my husband."

"Nor mine,"' nodded Fiona.

"Nor mine," asserted Jill.

"Actually," whispered Cynthia conspiratorially, "he's not even a club member."

A golfer strayed into the woods to follow his erratic drive. There he encountered a witch who made him an offer he couldn't refuse.

"I'll make all your drives long and straight. I can make you a winner,"' she cackled.

"What's the catch?" asked the golfer, taken aback at her appearance.

"Well, there's no such thing as a free lunch. Your drives will be long and straight but your sex life will be lousy."

The golfer thought for a moment. "OK ! It's a deal," he said.

A year later, he found himself in the same wooded area. His drive, as was the case with each and every one of his shots, nestled on the lush grass in the middle of the fairway. He'd just nipped into the woods for a quick pee. As he zipped himself up, he noticed a movement over his shoulder. It was the witch.

"How's the golf?" she asked.

"Great. Just like you promised. Every shot is sweet and straight. I've been winning all round me and I've been cut by ten shots in the last year," he responded.

"Good. How's your sex life, though?" She cackled maliciously.

"Great!"

"Great? How many times have you had sex in the last year?"

"Twice."

"Twice? You call that great?"

"Perhaps I should introduce myself. My name's Doyle . . . Monsignor Doyle!"

# CHAPTER FIVE

## *Lists*

BYRON NELSON'S STREAK
*(His eleven consecutive victories in 1945)*

| | | |
|---|---|---|
| Miami Four-Ball | March 8–11 | With Harold (Jug) McSpaden he beat Denny Shute and Sam Byrd 8 and 6 in the final. |
| Charlotte | March 16-19 | Beat Sam Snead in 36-hole play-off |
| Greensboro | March 23-25 | Won by 8 shots |
| Durham | March 30-Apr 1 | Won by 5 |
| Atlanta | April 5-8 | Won by 9 |
| Montreal | June 7-10 | Won by 10 |
| Philadelphia | June 14-17 | Won by 2 |
| Chicago Victory | June 29-July 1 | Won by 7 |
| PGA Championship | July 9-15 | Beat Sam Byrd in the final by 4 & 3 |
| Tam O'Shanter | July 26-29 | Won by 11 |
| Canadian | August 2-4 | Won by 4 |

MAJOR LOWS
*(No player has ever shot a 62 in a Major championship. But the following 15 have all shot 63s)*

| | | | |
|---|---|---|---|
| Johnny Miller | 1973 | US Open | Oakmont |
| Bruce Crampton | 1975 | USPGA | Firestone |
| Mark Hayes | 1977 | Open | Turnberry |
| Tom Weiskopf | 1980 | US Open | Baltusrol |

| | | | |
|---|---|---|---|
| Jack Nicklaus | 1980 | US Open | Baltusrol |
| Isao Aoki | 1980 | Open | Muirfield |
| Raymond Floyd | 1982 | USPGA | Southern Hills |
| Gary Player | 1984 | USPGA | Shoal Creek |
| Nick Price | 1986 | Masters | Augusta |
| Greg Norman | 1986 | Open | Turnberry |
| Paul Broadhurst | 1990 | Open | St Andrew's |
| Jodie Mudd | 1991 | Open | Birkdale |
| Nick Faldo | 1993 | Open | Sandwich |
| Payne Stewart | 1993 | Open | Sandwich |
| Vijay Singh | 1993 | USPGA | Inverness |

(Despite the superb scores only Miller, Nicklaus, Floyd and Norman went on to win.)

## MOST MAJOR GOLF TITLES

| | | | |
|---|---|---|---|
| The Open | Harry Vardon | 6 | 1896, 1898-'99, 1903, '11, '14 |
| The Amateur | John Ball | 8 | 1888, '90, '92, '94, '99, 1907, '10, '12 |
| US Open | Willie Anderson | 4 | 1901, 1903-'05 |
| | Bobby Jones | 4 | 1923, '26, '29-'30 |
| | Ben Hogan | 4 | 1948, 1950-'51, '53 |
| | Jack Nicklaus | 4 | 1962, '67, '72, '80 |
| US Amateur | Bobby Jones | 5 | 1924-'25, '27-'28, '30 |
| US PGA | Walter Hagen | 5 | 1921, 1924-'27 |
| US Masters | Jack Nicklaus | 6 | 1963, 1965-'66, '72, '75, '86 |
| US Women's Open | Betsy Earl-Rawls | 4 | 1951, '53, '57, '60 |
| | Mickey Wright | 4 | 1958-'59, '61, '64 |
| US Women's Amateur | Glenna Collett Vare | 6 | 1922, '25, '28-'30, '35 |
| British Women's | Charlotte Leitch | 4 | 1914, '20-'21, '26 |
| | Joyce Wethered | 4 | 1922, '24-'25, '29 |

## THE TEN BEST KNOWN ANTICLOCKWISE GOLF COURSES IN BRITAIN AND IRELAND
*(In alphabetical order)*

Ballybunion
County Louth (Baltray)
County Sligo (Rosses Point)
Killarney
Mount Juliet
Royal Birkdale
Royal Lytham
Royal St George's
Royal Troon
St Andrew's

## SIXTY-DOWN
*(USPGA Tour players who have shot 60 or less)*

| | | |
|---|---|---|
| 59 | Al Geiberger | (Memphis, 1977) |
| | Chip Beck | (Las Vegas, 1991) |
| 60 | Al Brosch | (Texas Open, 1951) |
| | Bill Nary | (El Paso, 1952) |
| | Ted Kroll | (Texas Open, 1954) |
| | Wally Ulrich | (Virginia Beach, 1954) |
| | Tommy Bolt | (Insurance City, 1954) |
| | Mike Souchak | (Texas Open, 1955) |
| | Sam Snead | (Dallas Open, 1957) |
| | David Frost | (Northern Telecom Open, 1990) |
| | Davis Love | (Hawaiian Open, 1993) |

## SOME OF MULLIGAN'S LAWS
*(Thomas Mulligan, 4th Earl of Murphy, is the man who – according to golf writer Jim Murray – gave the world the Mulligan, God bless him and keep him safe)*

1. If you really want to get better at golf, go back and take it up at a much earlier age.
2. When your shot has to carry over a water hazard, you can either hit one or more club or two more balls.
3. A ball will always travel farthest when hit in the wrong direction.
4. A golf match is a test of your skill against your opponent's luck.
5. Always limp with the same leg for the whole round.
6. A two-foot putt counts the same as a two-foot drive.
7. Never wash your ball on the tee of a water hole.
8. If there is a ball on the fringe and a ball in the bunker, the ball in the bunker is yours.
9. You can hit a 200-acre fairway 10% of the time and a two-inch branch 90% of the time.
10. The odds of hitting a duffed shot increase by the square of the number of people watching.


GOOD YEARS

*(The following players have won at least one Major and finished in the top ten of all four Majors in the same year)*

|                    | Masters | US Open | Open | PGA |
|--------------------|---------|---------|------|-----|
| 1960 Arnold Palmer | 1       | 1       | 2    | t7  |
| 1971 Jack Nicklaus | t2      | 2       | t5   | 1   |
| 1973 Jack Nicklaus | t3      | t4      | 4    | 1   |
| 1974 Gary Player   | 1       | t8      | 1    | 7   |
| 1975 Jack Nicklaus | 1       | t7      | t3   | 1   |
| 1975 Tom Watson    | t8      | t9      | 1    | 9   |
| 1977 Tom Watson    | 1       | t7      | 1    | t6  |
| 1982 Tom Watson    | t5      | 1       | 1    | t9  |


THE MAJOR MEN

*(All-time career total of Major Top Ten finishes)*

| Jack Nicklaus | 72 |
|---------------|----|
| Sam Snead     | 46 |

| | |
|---|---|
| Gary Player | 44 |
| Tom Watson | 41 |
| Ben Hogan | 39 |
| Arnold Palmer | 38 |
| Gene Sarazen | 36 |
| Walter Hagen | 32 |
| Byron Nelson | 29 |
| Ray Floyd | 27 |

## SOME NOVELS WITH GOLF AS THEIR SUBJECT

1. *Dead Solid Perfect* by Dan Jenkins (the antics of amoral golf pro)
2. *Golf in the Kingdom* by Michael Murphy (tale of golfing mysticism set in Scotland)
3. *Operation Birdie* by Willie Rock (The IRA plan to disrupt the Open at Turnberry)
4. *The Duke* by Peter Alliss (Showdown between ageing superstar and new kid)

## THE THIRTEEN-POINT PLAN

*(HS Colt and Dr Alister Mackenzie's prospectus for the design of a golf course)*

1. Two loops of nine holes are preferable.
2. At least four short holes, two or three drive-and-pitch holes and a large preponderance of good two-shot holes.
3. Short walks only from green to following tee, preferably forward to leave elasticity for future lengthening.
4. Undulating greens and fairways but no hill climbing.
5. A different character to every hole.
6. Minimum blindness for the approach.
7. Beautiful surroundings and man-made features, indistinguishable from nature.
8. Sufficient heroic carries from the tee but alternative routes for the shorter player if he sacrifices a stroke or a half-stroke.

9. Endless variety in shot-making.
10. No lost balls.
11. Playing interest to stimulate improvement in performance.
12. High-scoring golfers should still be able to enjoy the layout.
13. Perfect greens and fairways, approaches equal to greens and conditions just as good in winter as summer.

## 80 AND OUT!

*(A list of 54 hole leaders in the US Open who shot eighty or higher in the final round)*

| | | |
|---|---|---|
| 1898 Fred Herd | 84 | (He won anyway) |
| 1900 Harry Vardon | 80 | (So did he!) |
| 1901 Willie Anderson | 81 | (It was starting to become a pattern by now, he won also) |
| 1903 Willie Anderson | 82 | (Guess what?) |
| 1904 Fred MacKenzie | 80 | (Only managed third) |
| 1907 Jack Hobens | 85 | (Fourth) |
| 1911 Fred McLeod | 83 | (Fourth) |
| 1919 Mike Brady | 80 | (Second – playoff) |
| 1967 Marty Fleckman | 80 | (Tied 18th) |
| 1992 Gil Morgan | 81 | (Tied 13th) |

## GOLFERS AND THEIR MIDWIVES (AKA CADDIES)

*(Check out this list in two years from now and see how many are still together)*

| | |
|---|---|
| 1. Nick Faldo | Fanny Sunesson |
| 2. Colin Montgomerie | Alistair McLean |
| 3. Nick Price | "Squeeky" Medlin |
| 4. Ian Woosnam | Phil "Wobbly" Morbey |
| 5. Greg Norman | Tony Novarro |
| 6. Phil Mickelson | Jim Mackey |
| 7. Bernhard Langer | Pete Coleman |
| 8. Seve Ballesteros | Are you kidding? |

## THE RICH AND THE FAMOUS
### *(Ten wealthy or titled golfing nuts)*

1. The Sultan of Brunei – the world's richest man/golfer with a modest fortune of $35 billion.
2. Warren Buffet – American industrialist and Augusta member.
3. Yoshiaki Tsutsumi – Japanese billionaire who doesn't have to play his golf under floodlights.
4. Sheik Mohammed bin Rashid Al Maktoum – swings a bit when he isn't studying horseflesh.
5. King Hassan of Morocco – hosts his own tournament.
6. Galen Weston – Supermarket king.
7. Mark McCormack – has made half a billion from the start he got in golf management.
8. Jamie Ortiz Patino – owns his own golf course – it's called Valderrama.
9. HRH the Duke of York – probably not as rich as any of the others but the No. 1 British Royal golf fan.
10. Arnold Palmer – one of the two golfers (the other is Nicklaus) who can go dollar for dollar with some of the above.


## McCORDISMS
### *(Statements on TV and elsewhere by CBS broadcaster Gary McCord)*

1. "I don't think they cut them out here, I think they use bikini wax on them." (The line that got him canned/banned by the Masters Committee.)
2. "I applaud their decision. In the contract with CBS, they have the right to evaluate the announcers and decide who personifies the muted rituals of restraint. I am a loud wail." (His unusual reaction to the ban.)
3. "It's DOA down there." (Advising Jose Maria Olazabal not to overshoot a green.)

4. "That's down there with the body bags." (His reaction when Olly did overshoot.)
5. "Fuzzy's science project." (His description of the relationship between Fuzzy Zoeller and John Daly.)

LOCAL WARTIME RULES, ST MELLON'S GOLF CLUB, MONMOUTHSHIRE, 1940

1. Players are asked to collect the bomb and shrapnel splinters to prevent their causing damage to the mowing machines.
2. In competition, during gunfire or while bombs are falling, players may take shelter without penalty for ceasing play.
3. The positions of known delayed-action bombs are marked by red flags at a reasonable but not guaranteed safe distance therefrom.
4. Shrapnel and/or bomb splinters on the fairways or in bunkers within a club's length of a ball may be moved without penalty, and no penalty shall be incurred if a ball is thereby caused to move accidentally.
5. A ball moved by enemy action may be replaced or, if lost or destroyed, a ball may be dropped without penalty, not nearer the hole.
6. A ball lying in a crater may be lifted and dropped not nearer the hole, preserving the line to the hole, without penalty.
7. A player whose stroke is affected by the simultaneous explosion of a bomb may play another ball under penalty of one stroke.

SOME HOLLYWOOD MOVIES ABOUT GOLF (IN NO PARTICULAR ORDER)

1. Tin Cup (1995) *The movie that forced Kevin Costner to take up golf*
2. Follow the Sun (1951) *Glenn Ford as Ben Hogan in his comeback after the car crash*
3. Caddyshack (1980) *Enlivened only by Bill Murray's war with the gophers*
4. Caddyshack II (1988) *The time lapse between original and sequel speaks volumes*

5. The Caddy (1953) *Dean Martin and Jerry Lewis as golf coach and aspiring champion*
6. Dead Solid Perfect (1988) *Far from perfect and not even solid adaptation of Dan Jenkins's novel*
7. Banning (1967) *Robert Wagner as a pro in a sleazy but posh LA golf club*
8. The Golf Specialist (1930) *Another WC Fields vehicle*
9. Follow Thru (1930) *Two women in pursuit of the same golf pro*

## SOME HOLLYWOOD MOVIES IN WHICH GOLF FIGURES PROMINENTLY

1. M.A.S.H. (1970) *Gould and Sutherland as the "Pros from Dover"*
2. Bat 21 (1988) *A shot-down Vietnam flyer uses golf code to get home*
3. You're Telling Me (1934) *WC Fields classic which incudes a golf game*
4. Pat and Mike (1952) *A Hepburn/Tracy movie which allowed Hepburn to show her golfing abilities*
5. Goldfinger (1964) *Connery and Gert Frobe cheat their way through a round*

## HOLLYWOOD MOVIES NOT ABOUT GOLF

1. Caddie (1976) *An Australian movie in which an abandoned wife (not a golf widow) takes off with her two children*
2. Don Camillo's Last Round (1955) *Adapted from the books about the rivalry between an Italian priest and the Communist Mayor of his town*
3. How Green Was My Valley (1941) *Welsh mining movie rather than a Country Club drama*
4. The Driver (1978) *He (Ryan O'Neal) drives a car*
5. Putting on the Ritz (1930) *Nothing to do with that "game within a game"*
6. The Masters (1975) *Actually an Italian film about a teacher getting involved in politics after a Mafia murder*

GOLF ON THE INTERNET
*(Some golfing Web Sites and Newsgroups)*

1. Golf Web: http://www.golfweb.com
2. ESPNET sportszone: http.//espnet.sportszone.com/TV news – charges a subscription fee
3. iGOLF: http://www.igolf.com/
4. The Masters: http://www.cris.com:80/Masters/
5. The 19th Hole: http://www.sport.net/golf/
6. GOLFplex: http://www.directnet.com/wow/golf/index.htm
7. Unisys: http://www.unisys.com/
8. GolfData Web: http://www.gdol.com/
9. Callaway Web page: http://www.callawaygolf.com/callaway.html
10. Shell's Wonderful World of Golf: http://www.shellus.com
11. email address – Golf digest: Golfd@ix.net-com.com
12. Usenet Newsgroup: rec.sport.golf

# CHAPTER SIX

## Caddies – A Breed Apart

*"Real golfers, whatever the provocation, never strike a caddie with the driver . . . the sand wedge is far more effective."*
*Unattributed quote (borrowed from* A Good Walk Spoiled *– with no intention to return it)*

Mary, Queen of Scots, took the game to France, where she was educated. The young men who attended her on the golf links were known as cadets, "pupils"; the term was adopted later in Scotland and England, becoming caddy or caddie.

Most top pros, even when they travel over and back across the Atlantic, take their regular caddies with them. Perhaps they'd be better off leaving them at home. When Canada sprung a surprise win in the Dunhill Cup at St Andrew's in 1994, two of the players used local caddies.

Up until the 1970s, the USPGA had a rule that professional caddies couldn't work on the Tour between June 1 and September 1. This period was kept free for college students to earn money by carrying the bags of the pros. And, until quite recently, the field for the Masters was not allowed to bring their own caddies, the players were forced to use the local (black) caddies. By his own admission Fuzzy Zoeller worked this to his advantage in 1979 when he won the event on his debut appearance. He had so little acquaintance with the course that as he stood over each ball he simply held out his hand and hit whatever club his caddie put into it.

One of the best-known Scottish caddies, often seen at Open

championships, is known to one and all as Turnberry George. He is, to say the least, corpulent and he made up half of a wonderful Laurel and Hardy act during the 1995 Open championship at St Andrew's. He was caddying for the tiny Japanese player Katsuyoshi Tomori who spoke not a word of English. Not that it stopped the two men conversing animatedly with each other, each probably unconscious of the fact that the other couldn't understand a single syllable of the chatter. When it came to reading the greens, Turnberry George adopted an improvised technique for keeping his "bag" informed as to the break. If the putt had no borrow whatever, he would put his arm straight out in front of him. If it had break either way, George would indicate how much with thumb and index finger. It worked for the first two rounds: Tomori led after 36 holes!

St Andrew's caddies were (are) an assertive lot. One oft-told story concerns a caddie who interrupted his master at the top of his backswing with a cry of "Stop! We've changed our mind. We'll go with an iron."

One of the legendary caddies at St Andrew's in the first half of this century was one Patrick McAnespie, alias Patsy "Pickford". His *nom de guerre* derived from his nocturnal activities as a burglar. Because he had spent most of his adult life in prison he knew little or nothing about golf, despite being a native of St Andrew's. On one occasion he was carrying the bag of an inept American who took an unmentionable number of shots to traverse the approach to the first green. He was still about 250 yards away from the flag on what is a relatively short hole when he turned to "Pickford" and asked him, "How far is it from here to the flag?" The swagman turned bagman studied the distance and replied in an accent one hopes the American found impenetrable "About another hour and a half's walk."

St Andrew's caddies are no respecters of rank or status. Arthur Balfour, one-time British Tory Prime Minister, was playing the course one day and faced a long, difficult birdie putt on the short eleventh. His caddie gave him specific instructions to "Hit the ball a-yard to the left of the cup." Balfour, clearly dubious at this advice, went for speed and distance and hit it straight at the flag. To his consternation and the disgust of the caddie, it finished pin high exactly a-yard to the *right* of the hole. Game, set and match to the caddie who muttered loudly enough to be heard "And these are the bastards that run the country."

This loathing Scottish caddies had for players who did not do precisely as they were told was equally true at Muirfield. The American Bobby Cruickshank got a taste of their autocratic tendencies in his first practice round for the 1929 Open Championship when he thumped a drive at the first hole. Standing over his ball in the middle of the fairway, he turned to his seventy-five year old caddie, Willie Black and asked him for a two-iron. "Look here, sir," Black responded, politely but with a firmness of tone that brooked no argument. "I'll say what club, you play the bloody shot."

Frank Stranahan, the useful American amateur, consistently defied the Brotherhood during a British Amateur championship at Muirfield and paid the penalty. He hired and fired a caddie a day as one argument over club selection followed another. Finally he got his comeuppance when he had to play a blind shot to a green. Caddying for him was a man he probably intended to fire as soon as the round was over; they had fought all the way round and Stranahan had found it difficult to concentrate on his game. He sent the caddie up to the brow of the hill with instructions to stand in a position where a shot hit over his head would make the target. The caddie did as instructed and Stranahan let fly. When he got to the ridge, however, he saw where he'd actually been aiming; at a large clump of gorse about twenty yards to the left of the green. He had little enough chance of finding the ball, no chance whatever of playing it. He was about to bawl out the caddie for this basic error when the man dumped Stranahan's golf clubs at his feet, grinned at him crookedly and vindictively and, before turning for the clubhouse, said, "Now, sir, as you know so much about it, let's see you get yourself out of there."

Caddies, not given to complete silence on the course, are often prone to verbal solecisms. One of the best recorded examples comes from Henry Longhurst, the great broadcaster. On an extremely windy day, he was playing at a London course and facing a drive into the breeze on a long par-four. His caddie, after surveying the scene for a few moments, commented, "It'll take three damn good shots to get up in two today, sir."

The great Harry Vardon put up with quite a bit from irascible caddies. At the Open in Prestwick in 1893, Vardon's caddie was so disgusted at his rejection of clubbing advice that he started to turn his back and hold out the golf bag for Vardon to choose from. On another occasion, Vardon hit into an absolutely unplayable lie. He studied his predicament for a while and then consulted his caddie. "What will I take?" he asked. "I'd recommend the 4.05 train," came the petulant reply.

For a brief period in the 1960s, Arnold Palmer had a caddie who was a former Marine Corps Colonel on the run from a wife who was trying to find and sue him. He figured that the life of a caddie was sufficiently nomadic and anonymous to offer him an interesting concealment. The strategy worked until he started carrying Palmer's bag and started to get ideas above his station. He lasted until he was discovered signing Arnie's name to cheques.

For years Lee Trevino has relied on the services of Herman Mitchell as caddie. Mitchell is a huge, rotund black man who spars constantly with his employer. Trevino will routinely snap at Mitchell, "Herman, you can't add," when he leaves shots short or overhits greens. To which Mitchell will respond, "No, you just can't play golf." Because of his enormous girth (Mitchell's that is; Trevino is but a Mexican sylph in comparison), Trevino likes to tell his partners in a pro-am when they are lining up putts that they will all automatically fall towards Herman.

A man should trust his caddie. During the 1995 Walker Cup match at Royal Porthcawl, the young American prodigy Tiger Woods was playing Gary Wolstenholme of Britain and Ireland in the anchor singles match. Out of sorts with himself and his caddie, Woods ignored the bagman's advice completely. This may or may not have had something to do with his being out of bounds three times (no, not "in the woods" – Porthcawl is a links course). The final insult came at the eighteenth where he rejected his caddie's offer of a six-iron to the green, grabbed a five and pulled the shot well wide of the green. He lost by one hole!

Possibly the most unusual caddies in the world are to be found at the Talamore Golf Club in Southern Pines, North Carolina. They are llamas, those rather aloof and condescending-looking animals. They've been in service at the club, along with their human handlers, for the last five years. They will carry two golf bags each without complaint but won't give you the distance to the flag or recommend what club to use. Sensitive souls, vulnerable with the putter perhaps, who wish to avoid that perpetual look of contempt which seems to adorn their faces should carry their own bags.

In the 1960s, Jack Nicklaus used to have an old caddie nicknamed "Pappy". After a win in one tournament, "Pappy" took his earnings to the crap tables at Las Vegas where he went on a stupendous roll. He made $22,000 in a short space of time and seemed set either to win more or lose everything. Somehow, Nicklaus got to hear about what was going on. He appeared in the casino, walked up to Pappy's table and demanded that the caddie hand the winnings over. The bagman reluctantly obeyed and Nicklaus let him keep $2,000. That was soon lost, but the rest Nicklaus invested in Arnold Palmer's equipment company. If he's still around, Pappy is probably sitting pretty, thanks to the Golden Bear's invesment *nous*.

Dubliner Paul Cuddy spent just over a year (1990/91) on the European Tour as a caddie for English pro Stephen Bennet. Like many caddies, he is an accomplished golfer and on one occasion was filling in some time on the practice ground hitting balls with Bennet's clubs. The celebrated coach David Leadbetter happened to be passing and stopped briefly to watch the considerably chuffed Cuddy in action. Before moving on he asked the Dubliner, "What do you play off?" Cuddy, metaphorically thrusting his chest forward, proudly acknowledged that he played off four. To which Leadbetter responded caustically, "You must be a really good putter." Collapse of Dublin caddie. But Cuddy had the last laugh. Three years later, now a teaching pro, Cuddy ended up working for the expanding organisation of . . . David Leadbetter.

During the final round of the 1991 Balearic Open, Stephen Bennet found himself coming down the 18th hole in the unaccustomed position of leader out on the course, albeit with any number of players capable of catching him on the run-in. Bennet and Paul Cuddy were equally unaccustomed to the dizzying heights of the higher reaches of the leaderboard. Like many of his fellow Dubliners, Cuddy has a problem with the pronunciation of the letters "th". Thus . . . "this, that, these and those" becomes "dis, dat, dese and dose" and "thirty-three" becomes "tirty-tree". Add to this knowledge the fact that English people seem utterly incapable of understanding their own language unless it is spoken in their particular dialect and you have a recipe for confusion. As luck would have it, Bennet's drive on the 18th at Santa Ponsa in Mallorca finished exactly 233 yards from the flag, which, as luck would have it, was thirty-three yards from the front of the green. At the back of the green were three trees which, given the prevailing wind on the day, provided Bennet with a perfect line for his shot.

Standing over his ball the nervous pro, asked the tense Cuddy for the yardage. The following dialogue took place.

CADDIE: Two hundred and tirty-tree yards.

PRO: What?

CADDIE: Two hundred and tirty-tree yards.

PRO: What?

CADDIE: Between two hundred and tirty-two and two hundred and tirty-four yards.

PRO: Right. How far is the flag from the front?

CADDIE: Tirty-tree yards.

PRO: What?

CADDIE: Tirty-tree yards.

PRO: What?

CADDIE: Between tirty-two and tirty-four.

PRO: Right. What club?

CADDIE: The wind's against . . . a tree-wood.

PRO: A what?

CADDIE: (Giving in early) Between a two and a four.

PRO: Right. What's the line?

CADDIE: The tree trees at the back of the green.

PRO: The WHAT?

CADDIE: You see those bushes . . . aim at them.

(For the record, Gavin Levenson birdied four of the last five holes to win the Balearic Open.)

Communication difficulties more often than not emanate from player and caddie speaking different languages rather than different versions of the same language. Such was the case in the Caliente Open in Tijuana, Mexico in the late 1950s when a local Mexican caddie was carrying the bag of American professional Joe Zackarian. Each had a skimpy knowledge of the other person's mother tongue. At one point, seeking the yardage to the green Zackarian asked "Eduardo, quantos yardos?" The caddie, squinting towards the hole in an attitude of intense concentration replied. "Eet ees one hundred and feefty . . . or two hundred."

The great Irish amateur Joe Carr once revisited the scene of some of his many successes, Co. Louth Golf Club at Baltray, where he had won no less than fourteen East of Ireland championships. He found himself assigned a callow young caddie who, to the amusement of all, including Carr himself, clearly hadn't a notion of whose bag he was privileged to be carrying. As Carr prepared to tee off at the first the youth asked him had he ever played Baltray before. Carr avowed that indeed he had. As the round progressed the caddie, no doubt impressed by the great man's prowess, asked him had he ever played in the East of Ireland. Carr admitted that indeed he had. A few holes later, the caddie asked had Carr ever won the East of Ireland. Carr responded that he had indeed carried off the honours on no less than fourteen occasions. On the very next hole, as luck would have it, Carr did the unthinkable and topped his drive. At which point the caddie observed, "It must have been a lot easier in those days."

Maybe there's something about flamboyant pros which attracts strange and bizarre caddies. Max Faulkner's bag was carried for a while by a man called Mad Mac who always wore three ties but never a shirt. What he did wear constantly was an overcoat. This he never removed, hail, rain or shine. Around his neck he wore a pair of binoculars with the lenses missing. He would peer through these with an air of studied concentration whenever Faulkner was lining up a putt and as often as not the advice he would proffer would be the same, "Hit it slightly straight, sir."

An American arrived at the great Lahinch course in Co. Clare determined to test his mettle on the championship links. The problem was that the weather was of the sort that even Lahinch serves up only occasionally. It was the filthiest of filthy days. The rain was descending diagonally with the impact of railway sleepers driven by a wind which would reveal the secret of what Scotsmen wear under their kilts were any idiotic enough to step outside. But the American insisted, against all available advice, that he was going to play and, accordingly, he requested a caddie. There was none to be had, they had all long since made their excuses and left for the nearest pub. Finally, one was routed out to accompany the intrepid golfer from the New World. As it transpired, however, his skills were no match for his gritty resolve. His golf stank worse than an abattoir. After four hours of soaking rain and penetrating wind during which the pitiable caddie had gone a variety of different shades of blue, the American tapped in for an 18-hole total of 129. He turned to the caddie and asked, "What do I owe you?" "You owe me an apology!" growled the caddie.

It is rumoured in some officious circles that one or two of the estimable caddies at Lahinch draw unemployment benefit while being in constant remunerative employment carrying the bags of the many thousands of players visiting the course annually. This might explain a decision by a group of Inspectors from the Social Welfare Dept. to pay the course a surprise visit and have a chat with one or two of the caddies. Half a dozen of these zealous civil servants secreted themselves around the course maintaining contact with each other by means of walkie-talkies. When they struck, however, the element of surprise had already somewhat dissipated. Word of their arrival spread like wildfire and golfers all over the course were left to shunt their own bags as caddies headed for the sand dunes. One or two individuals were too slow on their feet and were unable to escape the interrogation of the officials. In one case a caddie, seeing the inspectors approach, thinking rapidly, handed the bag he was carrying to its owner, took the club he had been about to hand over and addressed the ball. Another, when quizzed about what he was doing, indicated the owner of the bag and insisted, "This is my friend Jake from New York. When he's in Lahinch, I always caddie for him and when I'm in New York, he caddies for me."

Similar enterprising, if over-optimistic, caddies were in evidence at a course in Portugal which shall remain nameless. On one occasion an American four-ball, each member with a caddie, was playing a blind par-three. Only a marker on top of a mound indicated the line to the hole. All four men drove off and, to the great delight of one of them, when he approached the green he saw his caddie walk past the pin, stop in disbelief, stoop down and pick the ball out of the hole. After the whooping and hollering had died down, he reached into his pocket and handed his caddie a one-hundred-dollar bill.

The following day, the four Americans returned and hired the same caddies. This time when the four-ball came to the blind hole the men's caddies handed out the required clubs and carried the bags forward to the green.

The four Americans drove off. All four balls cleared the mound which blocked their view of the green. When they got to the putting surface, however, there were no balls in evidence. All four were nestling, like round duck eggs, in the cup.

Bob Goalby once fired his caddie, nicknamed the Baron, three times on the same hole. The first time, Goalby asked Baron for the yardage to the hole. When the caddie gave it to him, Goalby looked at him sceptically and said, "You're fired." He then made a mess of the shot and, realising that his bagman had been right, he rehired him. He then missed the next shot to the green and fired Baron again but instantly rehired him when the caddie dropped the bag and headed for the ropes. Finally, on the green, when Goalby ignored Baron's read on a putt and proved his own illiteracy by making a pig's dinner of it he fired him again, probably for being right. This time Baron headed straight for the clubhouse. Goalby's wife had to run after him and plead with him to go back as the only alternative to Baron carrying the bag was that she do it herself. He agreed . . . for her sake only.

The great Gene Sarazen was making one last effort to qualify for the US Open, in 1960. As he got further and further into the round, it was clear that his chance was slipping away. The final catastrophic act came when he topped his drive. As he watched the ball settle a few short yards in front of him he turned, dejectedly, to his caddie and apologised. "I'm sorry, Joe," he said mournfully, "I went to church last Sunday and I prayed and I prayed that I'd qualify for this championship just one more time." The caddie sighed and said, "Well, boss, I don't know how you folks pray when you go to church, but when I pray I keep my head down."

Northern Irish pro David Jones likes to recall the occasion on which his regular caddie Kenny Savage bested a student in the pub in Maynooth, Co. Kildare. The tall, languorous Jones was sitting in a pub with his tiny ferret-like caddie as Kenny pored over his yardage chart and made various alterations and calculations. A young man walked over to where they were sitting and asked Kenny politely and curiously what exactly he was doing.

Kenny explained to the young man that the tall member of the company was a golf professional and that he, the caddie, needed to be able to give him yardages to the hole from any point on the course and that he was working on his yardage chart.

"That's very interesting," replied the young man, "because I'm a maths student at Maynooth College. Do you know that sometimes we have to do complicated calculations to within .000000001 of a decimal point?"

"Really?" replied Savage. "Is that so? Mind you, that would be no good to a caddie. You see, we have to be spot on."

Caddying for Tommy Bolt, famed hurler of clubs, could be a hazardous occupation, particularly if you couldn't duck fast enough. Bolt once had one of the most celebrated caddies on the American tour carrying his bag, a man known only as Hagan, but widely respected by his peers. On one occasion, Bolt sought Hagan's advice on a shot. "It's a six-iron!" Hagan proffered confidently. "No, it's a five." Bolt contradicted. "It's a six, and a soft six at that," retorted Hagan. His employer, however, insisted on the five and proceeded, as Hagan knew he would, to knock the ball twenty yards through the green. Typically, Bolt responded by breaking the club over his knee. So Hagan, disgusted at the sloppy decision, affronted by Bolt's antics and still holding a six-iron in his hand, broke *that* club over *his* knee, dropped the bag and strode towards the clubhouse. A chastened Bolt had to pursue him down the fairway and beg him to resume his duties.

Bolt's regular caddie was known to one and all as "Snake". Bolt, who was renowned for his short fuse, once had a short-lived compact with Snake that the caddie was never to talk to him on the course. "Don't say a word," Bolt had commanded, "even if I ask you a question." The arrangement went swimmingly until a tournament in LA when Snake took his instructions too literally. Bolt's ball was next to a tree and he had to negotiate a low branch first, while at the same time giving the ball sufficient elevation to get over a lake and on to the green. Bolt was having difficulty taking his stance without improving his lie and was unsure about club selection.

"What do you think, Snake? A 5-iron?"

"No, Mr Bolt," replied the caddie.

"What do you mean, no? Watch this."

"No, no, no, Mr Bolt," warned Snake.

Unimpressed by his caddie's apparent lack of confidence, Bolt took out his 5-iron and hit a miraculous shot to within three feet of the flag. He looked smugly at his caddie.

"Now, what do you think about that?" he inquired triumphantly.

"It wasn't your ball, Mr Bolt."

Archie Compston, the English pro who was in his heyday in the 1920s, employed no less than three caddies simultaneously. One carried his clubs, the second carried any spare articles of clothing he felt he might need out on the course while the third looked after the chain-smoking Compston's cigars, cigarettes and pipes.

American pro Bill Kratzert's caddie did his master no favours on July 11, 1986 in the Anheuser Busch Golf Classic in Williamsburg, Virginia. It was a hot, sticky Southern kind of a day and the caddie was trying to keep down the weight of the bag he was carrying. Calculating that his pro would only change his ball twice in the course of the round the caddie brought three balls with him. But Kratzert had one of those days and lost all three. When he put his hand out for a fourth the caddie told him (gulp!) that there were none left. Kratzert was forced to withdraw from the tournament.

Francis Ouimet was a humble caddie when he shocked the golf world by winning the 1913 US Open. He only entered the competition in the first place because it happened to be taking place at the Brookline club near Boston in Massachusetts right across the road from where he lived. More surprising than his victory was the nature of it. He defeated the two great British golfers Harry Vardon and Ted Ray in a play-off.

Ouimet's caddie throughout the Open was ten-year-old "Little" Eddie Lowery. But when it came to the play-off, some of Ouimet's friends decided that he needed a more mature bagman. One of them, Francis Hoyt, suggested to Ouimet that he should caddie for him over the final 18-hole strokeplay play-off. Hoyt was told to consult Lowery, who refused to give up the bag, so Hoyt appealed to Ouimet's better judgement. However, after a short discussion, Ouimet looked across at Little Eddie. The child was close to tears and, anyway, had been a talisman for Ouimet during the tournament so far. He told Hoyt he was going to stick with Lowery. The kid obviously did whatever was required of him.

The small-of-stature "Squeaky" Medlin (if you've ever heard him speak, you'll know why he's called Squeaky) has the distinction of winning back-to-back USPGA Championships with different "bags". In 1991, John Daly borrowed him when Nick Price withdrew because his wife was having a baby. The following year he carried Price's bag to *his* first Major victory. Just for good measure, he was at Price's shoulder when he won it for a second time two years later. (In between he'd added a fourth Major when Price won the British Open.)

Porky Oliver was an American pro who made a living for himself in the 1950s and 60s. He had the widest feet on the Tour, but it was his caddie who was often more noticeable. He had a habit of depositing his share of any stake money, not in a bank or similar financial institution, but in his right shoe. What this meant was that, if Porky Oliver was playing well and was regularly in the money, his caddie (this is true!) would be seen to walk with a pronounced and ever-worsening limp.

Just to show that caddies are not infallible, Raymond Floyd was playing in a tournament in Memphis one year and was having a miserable time with his clubbing. His caddie, Adolphus Hull, nicknamed Golf Ball, thought it might be because he'd been having too good a time with his nightclubbing. Floyd had missed the first four greens on the course. Sometimes his ball was yards short, at other times well through. A series of miraculous saves meant that he was still level par after four. On the fifth, he hit a huge drive which Golf Ball told him left him with a 7-iron to the pin. The ball was struck perfectly and sailed 20 yards over the green into some bushes. Floyd couldn't believe it. He grabbed Golf Ball's yardage book and looked at it. The hole bore no resemblance whatever to the one they were playing. "What is this?" Floyd asked angrily. "This isn't the book for Memphis." "Memphis. Are we in Memphis?" inquired Golf Ball. "I thought we were in Fort Worth."

According to the *Golfer's Handbook* the record rebound for bouncing the ball off the head of a British caddie (I kid you not, it's in the book) is 42 yards, 2 feet, 10 inches – as measured with a tape measure. What happened was that one RJ Barton was approaching the green of a blind hole measuring 354 yards at Machrie, on the Isle of Arran in Scotland, on September 1, 1913. He hit his shot to the green, not realising that a caddie from the previous match, John McNiven, was still on the green. The ball hit him on the head as he was replacing the flag. Barton and the other members of his group, astonished by how far the ball had rebounded, got out the measuring tape (You mean you don't carry one in *your* golf bag?) and came up with the above computation. There is no mention of whether they ordered an ambulance for poor John McNiven or ministered to him in any other way. And, in case you think this is the kind of puerile record people didn't attend to at the time, Mr Barton's effort beat the *previous* record of 34 yards (obviously not measured quite so scientifically and therefore suspect) which had been set in August, 1908 at Blairgowrie. The world record (which still stands) was established just four weeks after the British one. It was achieved by Mr Edward W Sladward at the 7th hole of the Premier Mine Golf Course in South Africa. A full-blooded drive, described as a "hard raking shot", was intercepted by the head of a native caddie after travelling for about 150 yards. It caught the unfortunate man just above the right eye and travelled backwards for seventy-five yards. The name of the caddie was not recorded (well, this was South Africa in 1913, so what else did you expect?) but his injuries were recorded as minor and he was able to continue the round. One wonders if he was given any choice in the matter.

In the late 1980s Brett Upper, hardly a household name on the USPGA Tour, was playing in the AT & T Pro-Am at Cypress Point. When he came to the treacherous par-3 16th, perched on the edge of a cliff, he pulled his tee shot over the green and into the ocean below. At least, it should have been in the ocean, but the tide happened to be out at the time so the ball was perched invitingly on the sand when he and his caddie DJ Murphy (nicknamed "Father") got to the green.

Upper went down with his wedge to play the shot, Murphy stayed aloft to give him a line to the flag. Just as Upper was about to hit, "Father" Murphy stopped him to allow one of the amateurs to play a chip shot. Upper waited for Murphy's signal to play. As he did so, he failed to notice a huge wave approach. It splashed over him, not only drenching him from head to toe but sucking up his ball and taking it to Hawaii. Upper had to take a penalty and slosh round the rest of the course. To make matters worse, he'd begun his round on the 10th and still had eleven holes to go.

Orville Moody was the surprise winner of the 1969 US Open championship. Surprise, because in 15 years on the USPGA Tour Moody had only one win to his credit. He owed a considerable amount of the success he did achieve to a caddie who can be seen as a perfectionist or another "touched" member of the "Brotherhood of the Bag". This bag carrier was so intent on accuracy that, when he was pacing out yardages, he would walk right through water hazards with Moody's golf bag over his head.

US President Woodrow Wilson was an enthusiastic if ineffective golfer (a real "14 Points" man when it came to Stableford). One day he was playing the Bannockburn course in Maryland when he was astonished to see a man run on to the course, grab his young caddie and begin to haul him away. If that sort of thing happened today, he would have had 10% of the Secret Service wrapped around him within seconds. As it was, Wilson remonstrated with the man, who explained that the caddie was playing truant from a nearby school. It can't have done the boy much harm. His name was Al Houghton and many years later he became Vice-President of the PGA.

In 1981, Sally Farmer became the first woman caddie in the history of the British Open Championship. She carried the bag of her husband Lawrence Farmer, a club pro from West Middlesex.

Caddies have long since learned never to trust an endorsement from a pro. In 1994, after caddying for Seve Ballesteros for nearly two years, the young Scot Billy Foster (a 6-handicapper himself) carried the Spaniard's bag to his first tournament victory in an age in the Benson and Hedges at St Melion. Ballesteros had not been forking out much in the way of prize money percentages to Foster during that time, a fact he acknowledged after the win when he said, "Caddies have to make a living . . . he was just about broke. It was nice of him to stick with me." Indeed it was. But the following year, Seve sacked him, anyway!

Greg Norman's caddie Tony Novarro was getting really irritated. He was carrying his man's bag during the 1994 World Series of Golf in Akron and the ever-impatient John Daly was in the grouping behind. Repeatedly he hit into Norman's group, incensing golfers and caddies. Finally Novarro lost his temper and shouted back at Daly, "You're hitting into us on every hole," – or words to that effect. To which Daly responded, "If you'd move your asses, maybe we could play some golf." Novarro may have had his next barb prepared, because it was a good one. "What?" he hollered, "You can't shoot 80 fast enough?"

The great English golfer Henry Cotton was surprised, as he lined up a putt at the last hole of a Dunlop Masters tournament, when someone stepped out of the crowd on to the green. However, the spectator had no interest in Cotton; instead, he approached his caddie and served him with a summons. The caddie, known to one and all as Barnes, had been falling behind with his alimony payments.

Bruce Lietzke is the "Invisible Man" of the US Tour. He plays only when it suits him but has still made more than six million dollars in prize money from a small number of tournaments. He prefers fishing and car racing to golf and doesn't bother with a regular caddie any more. The last bagman he had was veteran Tour caddie Al Hansen who decided to test one of Lietzke's claims, that he never ever even touched a golf club during the close season. One October, in Florida, Hansen put a banana inside the headcover of Lietzke's driver. Twelve weeks later, at the start of a practice round for the Bob Hope Classic in California Lietzke unzipped the cover and the sickly smell of the rotten banana made him, and Hansen, gag. After that, the caddie never doubted Lietzke's ability to put the game of golf well behind him.

During the 1940s, caddies at the famous Pinehurst Country Club, North Carolina went on strike. Scottish course designer and professional Donald Ross was the club administrator at the time and adopted an interesting approach to industrial relations. He met the caddies and asked which of them was speaking on behalf of the group. Noticing a 5-iron in his hand, one of the older and bigger caddies stepped forward a mite nervously and admitted that he was to be the chief negotiator. As if the words "conciliation" and "arbitration" were not in the dictionary (they certainly weren't in his), Ross gripped the club, hopped it off the caddie's shoulder a few times and said menacingly, "If you don't get back to work, I'll bounce this 5-iron off your *head*." Industrial action ceased forthwith.

US Pro Loren Roberts, still smarting after the defeat of the USA by Europe in the 1995 Ryder Cup match, was outraged when he heard on the grapevine that his caddie "Dirty" Dan Stojak had placed a bet of $1,000 on the Europeans to win at odds of 10–1. Stojak had been so proud of his neat little *coup* that he had bragged about it once too often. Stojak quickly found something to spend his windfall on (his mortgage) when Roberts fired him.

South African pro Simon Hobday will be familiar from other pages of this book as a wonderfully eccentric human being. But he more than met his match during a practice round for a tournament at Wentworth. By the time Hobday got to the course, there was only one caddie left. It was apparent to Hobday immediately why no one else had chosen to allow this man to carry their bag. He was unclean, unkempt (even to Hobday, whose nickname was "Scruffy") with waist-length hair, and had clearly been abusing his body with some sort of foreign substances for years. But he was a caddie and Hobday didn't feel like carrying his own bag. The trouble began on the first fairway. The caddie had to negotiate a large mound, carrying the South African's bag. He marched up the hill perfectly adequately, but on his way down the other side collapsed in an ungainly heap and rolled all the way to the bottom.

By the time they had got to the seventeenth tee, by Hobday's calculation, his caddie had fallen over thirteen times, he had sand on his face and in his hair and the bag was also full of sand, further weighing down the already overburdened bag carrier. Hobday issued instructions to the unfortunate that on no account was he to attempt the short cut from the seventeenth green to the final tee. This involved descending a steeply sloping bank. Precedent told Hobday that his caddie wouldn't make it to the bottom without some mishap. And so it proved. Determined to make one last effort to remain vertical while descending an incline, the caddie grabbed the flagstick and used it like a staff to support him on his way down. Unfortunately it was made of fibreglass and was not designed to take such a strain. It snapped, precipitating the caddie forward and sending him on his fourteenth downward spiral of the day. He landed on his face at the bottom of the winding pathway which he would have been better advised to have taken in the first place. As he hit the track, Hobday's bag landed on him, the clubs cut into the back of his head and blood began to pour from the resulting gash. After the round, the South African paid him off and advised him to try another line of employment.

(And there is a postscript to the above. In the bar that evening, Hobday listened to a succession of irate players as they recounted the tales of woe which had befallen them at the seventeenth. Almost all had drastically overclubbed and sent their shots scurrying through the green. Then the penny dropped: the broken flagstick. It had been replaced in the hole but, of course, at half its normal height, it would have totally altered the appearance of the green and caused a distorted view of the distance. Hobday, wisely, kept his counsel on who had been responsible.)

# CHAPTER SEVEN

## Courses

*Things you never ever needed to know about . . .*

### Augusta National

Augusta National exists largely because Bobby Jones wanted a course where he could play with his friends without the presence of onlookers. After Jones had retired from competitive golf his lustre was, if anything, enhanced: with the result that, even when he played a weekend four-ball with his buddies, dozens of people would turn up to watch. (On the basis that The Great Man was hardly likely to top or shank, I'd feel sorry for the buddies.) The site he chose for his venture (co-designed by the great Scottish architect Alister MacKenzie) was the site of the Fruitlands Nursery in Augusta, which had, at one stage, been an indigo plantation. He and his partners paid $31,000 for the land in 1931. Jones was the club's first and only President. After his death he was declared President in Perpetuity.

Incidentally, the lowest recorded score for Amen Corner (11th, 12th and 13th) at Augusta didn't come during the Masters, neither did it come from a professional. It was the 2-2-4 recorded by George Bush's nephew "Hap" (sic) Ellis. He began at the eleventh by holing a 100-yard wedge shot and then birdied the next two holes. The best score by the pros is nine, recorded by players like Nick Price, Mark Calcavecchia, Ben Hogan, Gay Brewer and Maurice Bembridge.

US President Dwight D Eisenhower was an enthusiastic golfer and a member of Augusta National. The tree which comes into play on the left-hand side of the 17th fairway was the bane of his life. Over the years, because of the number of times he ended up in or behind it, it became known as "Ike's Tree". Eventually, in frustration, he wrote to the Chairman of Augusta, Clifford Roberts, and asked if it might be possible for the tree to be chopped down. Roberts's response was pithy. "Not a chance," he wrote. "You run the country, we'll run Augusta."

War hero and golf patron the late Lord Derby (once President of the PGA European Tour) was invited to become a member of Augusta National and set a date for his first visit on a day when Clifford Roberts, the celebrated chairman of the club, couldn't be there to welcome him. Instead he designated another founder member, Charlie Yates, to do the needful. But when the appointed day arrived, Yates discovered that he too was unable to be there. He contacted a member who actually lived in Augusta and asked him to welcome their distinguished new addition. The problem was that the local Augustan had no idea what Lord Derby looked like. He was, however, put at his ease when a majestic Buick purred up Magnolia Drive and a man emerged from the rear who was clearly the product of centuries of correct breeding. The Augustan launched into a vivid southern welcome whose flow was staunched by a dismissive wave from the aristocratic creature who had just emerged from the Buick. "I am Lord Derby's valet," he informed his southern host. "His lordship is following in the other car."

### Saint Andrew's

So celebrated is St Andrew's and so associated is the town with the game of golf ("you mean they do other things there?") that the following letters were actually delivered by the British Post Office to the addressees at the 1995 Open Championship. They were addressed simply, "Jack Nicklaus, the Home of Golf," "The Great Arnold Palmer, Scotland," and "Colin Montgomerie, Player, St Andrew's."

In 1922, Prince Edward (Later King Edward VIII) became captain of the Royal and Ancient and arrived, amid much fussing, for the driving-in ceremony. Traditionally, the captain was offered a tincture before the nerve-wracking experience. The Prince must have been crippled with nerves, because he managed quite a number of tinctures before he stepped up to drive off. In any event, the Prince's drive was less than successful. He caught it somewhere on the heel of the club and managed to hit it behind him. As it rolled down into the infamous Valley of Sin in front of the 18th green, some disloyal subject, who in different times might have risked losing his head, was heard to mutter, "God, if he sinks that one we'll have a new course record."

The 18th green at St Andrew's has seen triumph and tragedy (insofar as losing a golf tournament can, in the scale of things, be deemed tragic). But the one single putt everyone seems to remember (even people who weren't born at the time) was also one of the shortest. In 1970, Doug Sanders came to the eighteenth needing a par to win the Open championship by a shot from Jack Nicklaus. He left himself a two and a half foot putt for his par. It was slightly downhill with a left to right break. Sanders seemed to stand over the putt for hours. Then he stepped back and bent down to flick away a speck of grass. He lined himself up again, took back the putter, moved on the shot and missed. The following day he lost an 18-hole playoff to Nicklaus. Sanders never won a Major, though he missed the Open, the US Open and the PGA by one shot and the Masters by two. He is constantly asked the question, "Do you still think about *that* putt?" His stock response is, "Do I ever think about it? I remember going as long as five minutes without thinking about it." He still has *that* putter around his house in Houston, Texas. It's in two pieces!

The Road Hole at St Andrew's is probably the single most famous and feared hole on the course. Ignoring the danger posed by the out-of-bounds (and would that one could), the Road hole bunker must be negotiated on the second (or subsequent) shots. In avoiding that entrance to the Seventh Level of Hell by overclubbing, the wall behind the green beckons. And so on and so forth. Ronan Rafferty, who has played the hole many times in Open Championships and Dunhill Cup events, says he walks on to the tee hoping he won't make ten. Arnold Palmer once did and commented, "I should have played the hole in an ambulance."

The Road Hole Bunker has also been dubbed "The Sands of Nakajima". At the Open in 1978 Tommy Nakajima, the Japanese pro, was on the green in regulation (no mean achievement), but his putt towards a pin perched close to the edge of the bunker took off on him and plopped into Dante's Inferno. It took him four shots to get out of the bunker and he then two-putted. On in two . . . down in nine!

We can blame the size and extent of the well-named Hell Bunker at St Andrew's (near the 14th green) on an unidentified player and a conversation with Old Tom Morris in 1882. The golfer, after having completed his round, complained to Morris about the condition of the course, claiming that he had had only one good lie all day. That had been in what is now the Hell Bunker. He had been able to play out with a wooden club. Old Tom, professional and greenkeeper at St Andrew's at the time, immediately despatched a work crew to the area and within a short time the bunker was reconstructed so that only an imbecile would ever think of playing a wooden club out of it (bar a "Heavenly Seven", perhaps).

## The Rest

Tuctu Golf Club in Peru, at 14,335 feet above sea level, is the highest course in the world. It's a mere 13,000 feet higher than Leadhills GC in Strathclyde, which is the highest in Britain. The lowest course in the world is Kallia GC on the shores of the Dead Sea; it's 1,250 feet below sea level.

The biggest bunker in the world is the infamous "Hell's Half-acre" on the 535-metre 7th hole at the Pine Valley course in New Jersey, USA. Some might argue that the sand traps adjoining many of the fairways on the Pete Dye-designed course at Kiawah Island, which staged the 1991 Ryder Cup match, are even bigger but, as players are allowed to ground their clubs in these hazards, they don't constitute bunkers in the accepted sense of the word.

The longest golf course in the world is believed to be the International

Golf club in the USA. Redesigned by Robert Trent Jones (who else?) in 1977, it measured 8325 yards from the back tees. It has a par of 77.

The longest golf hole in the world is the 7th hole at the Sano Course, Satsuki GC in Japan. It's a par-7 and measures 909 yards.

The longest hole in American golf is the par-6 841-yard 12th at Meadow's Farms GC in Locust Grove, Virginia.

The largest green in the world awaits those who manage to get to the end of the par-6 695-yard 5th hole at the International Golf Club in Boston, Mass. Don't celebrate too wildly if your third shot makes the green. An eagle could be a long way off, as the green has an area of 28,000 square feet (or .64 of an acre).

Anyone who has played the beautiful Jack Nicklaus-designed Mount Juliet course in Co. Kilkenny may be familiar with that tense feeling you get if your ball goes into the water which runs along a goodly part of the left side of the eighteenth fairway. The uneasiness comes from the presence of a number of swans, any one of whom could decide to pounce as you play your (third/fourth?) shot to the green. Spare a thought for the members of a club in Kenya. It has a local rule which stipulates that, if your ball comes to rest near a *crocodile*, you may move the ball a club's length away. Those with the surname Dundee and the skills to match can also decide to move the crocodile.

Torrey Pines in San Diego has a pond adjoining the 18th green which bears a plaque naming it "Devlin's Pond". The reason is the visit paid to it by Australian pro Bruce Devlin during the 1975 San Diego Open. In a commanding position in the tournament he followed an errant ball into the pond in the hope of playing it out. After much splashing and cursing he finally got it out six shots later. Spotting the plaque some time later, Devlin suggested that, given his nationality, the pond should be called "Devlin's Billabong".

The tiny "Postage Stamp" in Troon is famous not just for yielding up a hole in one to the great Gene Sarazen during the Open championship but for being mightily unyielding to many others. Take the experience of a German amateur, Herman Tissies, who was attempting to qualify for the 1950 British Open. He was bunkered off his tee shot and then splashed from bunker to bunker in an attempt to get the ball on the green. Finally, after fourteen attempts he managed to get the ball to stop on the green. He then sank the putt for a 15.

The Championship tees at Carnoustie are known as "Tiger" tees. Those for lesser mortals are known as "Rabbit" tees. In the immediate post war years, the British Armed forces made use of land adjoining Carnoustie for artillery exercises. This meant that there was a fence alongside the sixth fairway which carried a sign reading, "Do not touch anything, it may explode and kill you."

Oak Ridge Golf Club in Wellesley Island, New York is more than a little different. For a start it has 19 holes, largely because its owner, Jack Webb, doesn't play very well himself, "So I needed one hole I could throw away." His mission, to make the course as unchallenging as possible, means that it measures barely 5,000 yards, has no sand traps, yet has a par of 74. The only cloud on the horizon is a water-bearing one; water comes into play on 12 of the 18 (sorry, 19) holes. Webb also likes to make the round more memorable by inviting golfers to pluck some of the vegetables he has planted in various places around the course. These include pumpkins near the sixth hole!

Don't be put off by the name Lucifer's Anvil Golf Course at Reno, Nevada. Well, on second thoughts, maybe you *should* be put off. It's laid out over a parched desert, has no grass (but no rough either) and the greens are distinguished from the fairways by being painted vivid colours

Remember John DeLorean? He won't be forgotten in Belfast for quite a while after his sports car factory closed down, costing the Northern Industrial Development Board millions of pounds. Subsequently he was convicted of drug dealing, which he engaged in in an attempt to save the DeLorean Motor Corporation. Now he wants to build a golf club in his Bedminton, New Jersey estate and charge $90,000 for memberships, to help him pay off the $6.3 million he incurred in legal fees defending the drugs rap. An interesting move that, from coke to grass.

St George's, Sandwich can be a nightmarish place to try to visit when the Open is being staged there. Once, holder of the "Most Famous Husband in the World" title, Denis Thatcher, a keen golfer, was asked by a friend what was the best way to avoid the traffic during Open week. He replied, "Fly from Heathrow to Paris, take the train to Calais, hovercraft to Ramsgate, then walk down the beach." Of course that was in the days before the Channel Tunnel, which makes travel between Britain and France much more . . . on second thoughts, it's probably best to stick to his original advice.

At the Golf Club of Jacksonville they introduced (albeit for one day only) the "Play First, Pay Later" concept. To those of us in this country who are used to being told, "sure, you can settle up in the bar afterwards," this is hardly a revolutionary concept. But the idea was somewhat different than the easy-going approach to green fees on some Irish courses. In Jacksonville you got to play first and then *you* decided how much to pay, based on what you thought of the course. 236 players showed up, which represented a 150% increase over the normal green fee traffic. All but two cheapskates paid something, while the money from the other 234 averaged $18 a round, which is only $2 a round less than the normal green fee..

For 105 years, the Lundin Ladies Golf Club in Fife, in Scotland, has continued to treat male golfers in pretty much the same fashion as thousands of golf clubs worldwide treat women. It is an exclusively female club as far as membership is concerned. Men can only play when accompanied by a woman, and there are a mere three Gentleman Associates on the council of the club, but they attend in an advisory capacity only and have no voting rights. (Sound familiar?)

Members of the Ganton Golf Club in England got a bit of a fright in 1991. The course once hosted the Ryder Cup and regularly stages events like the British Amateur. A letter circulated to members informed them that the club was about to be acquired by a consortium of Japanese businessmen. They were invited to renew their memberships but were warned about some changes which would be taking place. A modern hotel complex would replace the clubhouse. A massage parlour employing local women would be opened. Sushi would replace steak on the menu and, while sake would be available in the bar, there would be no beer on tap any more. Members, used to wearing ties and jackets, would be asked to change to kimonos and sandals. The Secretary of the club was quick to issue a denial that such a move was contemplated. "I'd like to assure the membership," he wrote, "that we have never talked to the Japanese and have no intention of talking to them." The original letter, of course, had been an elaborate and highly entertaining hoax.

They have a sign at the Woomera Golf club in Australia which is utterly redundant. It reads "Keep off the Grass". Its redundancy is not derived from the futility of observing such an injunction on a golf course, but because there is not a blade of grass anywhere to be seen. Woomera is probably the biggest sand bunker in the world masquerading as a golf course. The only green spots on the course are the thick brush trees and the portable mats the players carry, off which they play their balls. When they get to the putting surfaces ("greens" would be a complete misnomer), members are advised to putt with gloves on in case they are stung by scorpions when retrieving their balls from the holes. The motto of the club is appropriately Australian: "Eat My Dust".

There used to be a small golf course in the Phoenix Park in Dublin, but golfing activity came to an abrupt end there for political reasons. The Chief Secretary for Ireland (and future Prime Minister), Arthur Balfour, nicknamed "Bloody Balfour", used to defy the type of political activist who had murdered Cavendish and Burke in the infamous "Phoenix Park Murders" by playing the course with very little in the way of personal protection. But Parnell's Land League, though committed to non-violent methods of political action, were no respecters of the leisure pursuits of the man who was putting dozens of their members in jail. So one night, in an appropriately agrarian gesture, they dug up the course.

Pillar Mountain Golf Course has to be one of the most challenging anywhere. First of all, it isn't so much a golf course as an obstacle course. Secondly, it's in Alaska. It only has one hole and it's a par-70. The course is 2,000 yards long and rises 1,400 vertical feet. Beginning to get the picture? The "fairway" is a rocky, rutted 4WD pathway, frequently under snow, lined by trees with a sheer drop on the far side. It comes into play once a year for the Pillar Mountain Classic and is described as "treacherous, fast and life-threatening". USGA rules are observed, where possible, but with the following local exceptions:

a) Hazardous weather conditions may postpone play by one week.

b) Two-way radios, dogs or guns aren't allowed. (For some reason, USGA rules don't include any specific reference banning these outside agencies.)

c) Spruce trees or power pylons must not be sawn down to confer an advantage or improve a lie.

d) Cursing officials will incur a $25 fine. (I assume that means that *players* cursing officials will be fined, but I could be wrong.)

Players are allowed not only a caddie but a spotter who goes ahead and tries to locate the ball as it lands. Any implement can be used to locate a ball (how about a snowplough or piste-basher?) and dig it out.

The tournament started as a drunken bet, but has developed into an annual event which raises a lot of money for charity. No fatalities have resulted so far, though frostbite and hypothermia are not uncommon. The course record is a stunning 25, or 45 under par.

The southernmost course in the game has to be the Scott Base Country Club. With a name like that, it would have to be in Antarctica. In fact, it's just 13 degrees north of the South Pole. The club (where golfers favour orange balls) is run by the New Zealand Antarctic programme and the playing season is short. Golfwear in such a climate is not of the type produced by Pringle or Scott and Lyle. Virtually obligatory are mittens, insulated jackets and trousers and massive insulated boots called mukluks.

Among the hazards faced by members are the difficulty of keeping track of the ball in the air (the glare is painful) and of finding it once it has landed (it tends to bury itself in the snow). Then there are the predators . . . the ones who find orange golf balls curious and interesting items. These are mainly skuas, seagull-type scavengers who will try to steal balls (presumably for resale).

The quaint local rules provide for skua attacks. If the bird interferes with the ball it may be replaced, but if he steals it the tracker who accompanies each golfer is deemed to have failed in his duty and a penalty is incurred. Likewise, melt pools in the sea ice constitute water hazards.

On the plus side, divots need only be replaced if they are more than one mukluk deep and as the greens (whites??) are not Augusta-smooth (though they are bikini-wax fast), a ball is deemed to have been holed if it finishes within one body-length of the pin – which clearly confers an advantage on the taller player.

But the most encouraging local rule, more a custom really, is the injunction against not drinking on the course. As this is essential for keeping warm the final club rule reads, "The use of artificial stimulants during play, whilst not compulsory, is strongly recommended."

The La Cantera course in Texas became the new home of the Texas Open in 1995 and features at least one rollercoaster of a hole, the 7th. The hole is called "The Rattler" because of its backdrop – the massive rollercoaster of the neighbouring "Fiesta Texas" theme park next door.

# CHAPTER EIGHT

## Murphy's Law

*"Anything that can go wrong will."* Murphy

Golfers were a tough and indefatigable breed in 1912, and none more so than the unknown doughty warrior who took 166 strokes to complete the 130-yard par-3 16th during the qualifying round for the Shawnee Ladies Invitational in Shawnee-on-Delaware, Pennsylvania.

Her tribulations began when she carved her tee shot into the water and watched as the current took her ball downstream. Most of us tenderhearts would simply have given the ball up for dead and played three off the tee. Not this heroine. Instructing her husband (as the story will reveal, they can't possibly have been very long married) to grab a nearby boat and start paddling she pursued the ball swishing at it with her club from the prow of the boat every time she got close. To no avail, she failed to make contact and her tally rose inexorably as her husband kept count.

Eventually she managed to get the ball ashore, one and a half miles away from her original objective, but was then forced to hack the ball as best she could through a forest. 165 strokes later, she was faced with a putt for a 166 and duly slotted it. Had she been playing in a Stableford competition, her astronomical score on that single hole would have been a mere tremor on her card but, as it was medal play, the effect was more like that produced at the epicentre of an earthquake.

American professional Paul Farmer incurred a record 18 penalty shots during the third round of the 1960 Texas Open at the Fort Sam Houston Golf Course in San Antonio. Farmer made the mistake of a) not knowing the rules, and b) changing his putter between the front and the back nine. After nine holes he switched blades, and it was only after completing his round (and before signing his card) that he learned he could only change putters if the one he started with was broken. He was penalised two shots for every hole on which he had used the illegal putter and his round of 70 became one of 88.

Leonard Crawley scored Great Britain and Ireland's solitary point in their 8-1 drubbing by the USA in the 1932 Walker Cup at Brookline, Massachusetts. But he also left another personal mark on the occasion. As he played the 18th, the trophy had been left behind the green ready to be presented to the American team captain. Crawley overshot the green and struck the cup, leaving a dent in it.

Bernhard Langer, as is pointed out by some commentator almost every time he stands over a putt with his self-designed method, has conquered the putting "yips" three times. But he never had the yips like one AJ Lewis. In 1890, Lewis putted no less than 156 times on a single green in Peacehaven in Sussex without getting the ball into the hole. He finally gave up and went on to the next tee.

In India, cows are sacred and often wander untrammelled all over the place. On golf courses they are profane, and often wander untrammelled all over the place as well. Playing the tenth hole on a Guernsey golf course in 1963, Mr SC King was unwise enough to leave his ball in the middle of the fairway in order to assist his playing partner Mr RW Clark to search for his ball in the rough. When he returned to his own ball he discovered that a cow had eaten it. The two friends played again the following day. This time, no doubt because he was psychologically scarred by the events of the previous day, King's tee shot ended up in the rough while Clark's landed on the fairway. Mindful of previous events, Mr King wisely covered his ball with a straw hat before generously assisting Mr RW Clark to search for his. When he returned, he found that the same cow had eaten his straw hat!

Raymond Floyd has hit many great and many accurate shots in his long and successful career, but none was hit so unerringly as one in the 1987 Tournament Players Championship at Ponte Vedra Beach in Florida. On the 11th hole, he whacked a drive 250 yards down the fairway. Unfortunately for Floyd, his caddie had left the golfer's bag lying in the longish grass in the rough adjoining the fairway. Floyd's ball sought out the bag like a dimpled homing pigeon and the resulting impact cost the pro a two-shot penalty.

Andy Bean lost the 1983 Canadian Open by making a putt with the grip of his putter. Bean had left one short and, instead of tapping in with the head, showed his annoyance by putting the ball into the hole from a couple of inches with the handle of his club. This was adjudged to have been an illegal stroke and he was penalised two shots. The following day he shot a 62 but missed out on a play-off by . . . two shots!

The quest for the 1922 Amateur Golf Championship at Prestwick in Scotland ended early for one competitor. He boarded a train at Ayr which he assumed would stop at Prestwick. But his assumption proved incorrect as the train sailed on through the station, bound instead for Troon. He alerted competition officials to his difficulty by the ingenious device of rolling down his compartment window as the train hurtled past the first hole, which lay adjacent to the railway track. His efforts were in vain, however; despite hotfooting it back from Troon he missed his start time and was disqualified.

It could hardly happen to a sweeter guy. Displaying his inadequacies as a golfer, (one can say that now only because he's dead), Al Capone once managed to shoot himself in the foot while playing the game. It happened at the Burnham Woods Golf Course (very "Scottish Play", really!) near Chicago. In circumstances that are somewhat murky, a gun he carried in his golf bag for protection went off, injuring the noted tax evader.

Never line up a shot while your ball nestles behind you! A golfing axiom ignored to his cost by Roger Wethered, in the 1921 Open at St

Andrew's. During the third round, he stepped backwards at the 14th on to his ball and incurred a one-stroke penalty. That one shot would have been enough for Wethered to have avoided a play-off with the American Jock Hutchison, a play-off which the American won.

American Seniors Tour player Al Chandler will have unhappy memories of the 15th at the Canterbury Country Club near Cleveland, Ohio. In the 1986 Senior Tournament Players Championship there, he had three fresh air shots at the par-4 hole. He hit an approach shot close to an oak tree and took two "whiffs" while trying to chip on to the green. Then, unbelievably, as he went to tap his ball into the hole a little later, he missed it completely.

We've all experienced that "here-comes-my-dinner-back-up-again" feeling as our tee shot, followed by a large divot, is pulled by the combined forces of gravity and ineptitude towards the lake guarding the green. Playing in the final round of the 1934 US Open at Merion, Bobby Cruickshank watched with that "ole familiar feeling" in the pit of his stomach as his second shot to the 11th headed for the $H_2O$. Waiting for the inevitable "plop", Cruickshank was overjoyed instead to hear a determined "clunk" as his ball hit a rock and bounced on to the green. Jubilantly he tossed his club into the air in celebration at this miracle, only to have it hit him solidly on the head as it descended while he danced a celebratory jig. Cruickshank was knocked out cold. He continued his round half-concussed and finished third.

Eight years earlier, something similar had happened in the far less exalted surroundings of an amateur tournament at Harrogate. A competitor who had sunk a 60-foot putt threw his club in the air in sheer delight. Unconscious of the effect of gravitational forces, he did a jig around the green as the club sailed ever onwards, ever upwards. When it came to rest it landed on his *partner's* head and knocked him out cold.

Suzanne Parker, playing in a round of the 1979 Carlsberg Women's Professional Golf Tournament in Wolverhampton, had an undistinguished front nine. She took a 45. Unfortunately, she made things even worse for herself by writing the nine hole total in the box allocated for the recording of her score on the *ninth* hole. Neither she, her caddie, or her playing partner noticed this error and she signed the card as it stood. Officials informed her at the end of her round that, as she had put herself down for a 45 on the 9th and signed the card, she had recorded an eighteen-hole total of 121.

The ebullient Brian Barnes looked well set up as he approached the 8th green in the 1968 French Open at St Cloud. He was three feet from the pin and within easy reach of a birdie. Then things started to go askew. He missed the putt. Annoyed with himself, he went to tap in the ball, but it was still moving. He incurred a penalty of two shots. He also stood astride the line of the putt, thus incurring another penalty of two shots. By the time he left the green he had added 12 shots to the three it took him to get on board, thus chalking up a 15 for the hole!

Christy O'Connor Jr fell foul of the ninth green at Crans-sur-Sierre during the final round of the European Masters in September, 1995. The green is constructed in three tiers which, to Christy, must have looked like the first three levels of Dante's Inferno. His ball pitched to within three feet of the flag, set on the top level for the final round. But it then spun backwards down the hill to the front of the green. To the amusement of the crowd, and the chagrin of the normally jovial Irish pro, he made three unsuccessful attempts to get the ball back up the hill to the sanctuary of the flat area around the hole. When he finally got the ball to stick, the crowd gave an ironic cheer and Christy holed out for a triple bogey eight after taking five putts. Seve Ballesteros, through his Amen Corner company, commissioned to re-design the Swiss Alpine course, has said he has no plans to tamper with the ninth green which he believes is "very exciting for the crowd". Christy Jr will not be adding his "Amen" to that.

A 222-yard par-three is a tad long for most amateurs, but could you envisage taking 19 shots to complete the hole? Hans Merell racked up just such a score at the par-3 6th in Del Monte California, during the 1959 Bing Crosby Pro Am. If you work it out, you could advance the ball (in a forward direction) just under 15 yards per shot and still have four putts to get down in 18 to beat his score!

Jim Meade, an English pub landlord, has experienced golf as a contact sport. He was playing in a society outing one day when he was knocked out twice in a matter of minutes by two errant golf balls.

The first one hit him while he was searching for his own ball in the rough. It came from an adjoining fairway and hit him in the eye via the branch of a tree. As his playing partners lifted the dazed Jim from his prostrate position in the rough, he was hit in the back by a drive from the tee behind, lurched forward and fell to the ground unconscious. When he came round he needed four stitches to his forehead.

When he plays now he says that his friends ". . . want me to hold the flag on every hole so they can be sure of hitting the target."

During the 1965 US Amateur Championship, Bob Dickson noticed that he was carrying 15 clubs in his bag. He'd started out with fourteen, he was sure of that, but now he had fifteen. Being an honest upstanding young man, he told a rules official and was penalised four shots. It later transpired that one of his opponents had put the club into his bag by mistake. Neat trick, though! Try it next time you're a few holes down to someone you really detest.

One of the most feared competitors at pro-am competitions in the 1970s was US Vice President Spiro Agnew. Feared, not because of his abilities, but because of his waywardness off the tee. Bob Hope once said that he could find Agnew on a golf course simply by following the trail of prostrate spectators. At one tournament, however, he actually hit Doug Sanders on the head. A short letter of apology followed and with it was enclosed a silver tray on which was engraved the simple legend "FORE". He probably had them custom-made!

During the 1989 Australian Tournament Players Championship, Bob Emond had a bad day at the office. The office in question was a par-five where he might have anticipated a birdie. But after four visits to the water on the hole, he had already given up on that idea even before he incurred a penalty. That was for allowing the ball to hit his shoe on one of the penalty drops. When he finally took the water out of play he'd accumulated a score of eleven on the hole. Shortly thereafter, he had his second stroke of bad judgement when he picked up his ball and marked it. No problem if you're on the green, but he wasn't! Now he was playing his seventeenth shot. Doubtless a bit upset by it all, he three-putted for a grand total of 19.

Driving off the 17th tee at Lyme Regis Golf Club in Dorset in England, Mr Derek Gatley had the misfortune to snap the shaft of his driver in two on what can only have been an exceptionally fast backswing. His bad fortune didn't end there, however, as the head of the wooden club broke off and hit him, knocking him unconscious. Afterwards Mr Gatley admitted that, "It was the first thing I had hit all day."

Armando Saavedra probably isn't entitled to much of our sympathy for what happened to him. Playing with the colourful Mark Roe in a European Tour event, Saavedra missed a short putt on the 6th green. Rather displeased with himself, he took his putter and dealt himself a blow on the forehead with it. The man obviously possesses a skull composed of equal parts marble and petrified resin, because the putter broke. He putted with a 3-iron and a headache for the rest of the round.

A spot of bad luck for the club professional at St Margaret's at Cliffe, in Kent, WJ Robinson, proved very unlucky indeed for the cow who was grazing 100 yards up the fairway as he prepared to drive off at the 18th. Assuming he would clear the cow, Robinson teed off, half topped the shot and sent it booming straight into the inoffensive quadruped, who dropped to the ground stone dead. It is not recorded whether Robinson was more put out by the death of the cow or by the tricky nature of his second shot.

Wayne Grady is hardly the sort of player one would associate with an identity crisis, but he was disqualified twice in the same year for playing someone else's ball. In 1986, he made an early exit from the Phoenix and Los Angeles Opens.

Mark Roe will not remember the final round of the 1995 Scandinavian Open with any nostalgia. Suffering from an unusual condition which causes his knee to lock, he took a 10 at the 12th hole of the Malmo course where the event was being staged. He took another ten at the 13th and added a third at the 16th. He finished the round with an eight for an inward half of 58 strokes and an eighteen-hole total of 95! But that wasn't all. He'd signed for a mere ten at the 12th when in fact he'd taken an 11, because he should have penalised himself for hitting a moving ball. That *still* wasn't all. His playing partner, Mark Litton, complained to the European Tour about what he alleged was Roe's unprofessional conduct. When compiling his ten, (the one which turned out to be really an eleven), Litton claimed that Roe had deliberately whacked a six-inch putt 20 yards off the green which had taken him four shots to reach. Roe was disqualified for signing for a wrong score.

A few years back, a group of Irish golfers from a club in the west of the country jetted off to the USA to play a number of American courses. But their trip had a secondary purpose: they almost all intended to purchase sets of clubs and bags in the USA which were prohibitively expensive at home. Many had similar orders from other club members who had not made the trip. Naturally, the golfers did not want to add to the cost of their purchases by paying duty on them when they returned to Ireland. Allegedly they approached a customs official, a golfer himself, who would be likely to be sympathetic to their plight. He agreed that his back might well be turned when the golfers trooped through the Green channel carrying anything up to fifty brand new bags and sets of clubs. The return of the merry group was timed to coincide with the shift of the complaisant official but, horror of horrors, he fell ill on the appointed day and a completely unsympathetic functionary awaited the smugglers as they wafted through the "Nothing to Declare" area. The result was the confiscation of about fifty brand new sets of clubs, which could only be redeemed upon payment of the duty owed.

Twice US Open winner Cary Middlecoff was in a good position to win the 1952 Palm Beach Round Robin tournament teeing off on the 16th at Wykagil Country Club in New Rochelle, New York. But his errant tee shot bounced near a spectator and hopped into his pocket. In his surprise and consternation, the spectator threw the ball out of his pocket and ran away. Unfortunately for Middlecoff, he didn't throw the ball on to the green but into the deep rough. Middlecoff took a double bogey at the hole and lost the tournament.

Big-hitting Swede Jarmo Sandelin won't forget the 10th hole at the Campo de Golfe in Madeira. During the last round of the 1995 Madeira Island Open, he decided to have a blast at reaching the downhill 408-yard tenth hole with his drive. Now, Sandelin may have John Daly's length off the tee but, as far as direction is concerned, he is even more erratic than the American. His first effort was accurate all right but, unfortunately, it bounced viciously on the green into a ravine behind. Unable to locate the ball, Sandelin was forced to go all the way back to the tee and reload. His second finished up in some trees and yet again he had to go back to the tee. He put his third into a bunker in front of the hole but at least he was in play at last. He carded an eight, but had taken almost half an hour to play the hole and caused his infuriated playing partner Eamon Darcy to three-putt for a bogey. Shortly afterwards, the pairing was warned for slow play. Sandelin shot an 80 but the experience didn't seem to bother him too much, because the next week the novice pro won his first tournament, the Turespana Open de Canarias.

Watching US Presidents play golf can be a hazardous pastime. In February 1995 Bob Hope, aged 91, played with President Clinton and former Presidents Bush and Ford in the Bob Hope Classic at Indian Wells in California. President Ford had a well-earned reputation for inaccuracy. Hope once said of him, "They have 57 golf courses in Palm Springs and he doesn't know which one he is going to play until after his first drive." He didn't let Hope down; his first tee shot was duck-hooked straight into the crowd, though no one was maimed. George Bush's second shot ricocheted off a tree and struck a spectator on the nose, breaking her glasses. His drive at the 14th struck another fan on the thigh but drew no blood. President Ford, anxious not to be left out of some macabre side-bet, proceeded to hit a woman on the knuckles with one shot, while President Clinton kept up the honour of the baby boomers by lofting one shot into a neighbouring garden.

Afterwards, asked by a reporter what was the attraction of golf, Mr Clinton responded emotionally, "it's a peaceful, beautiful thing."

In the second round of the 1994 French Open, Swedish pro Anders Forsbrand threw away a perfectly good chance to be the first European Tour player in 16 years to complete his round without breaking 100. In fact, had he not run out of golf balls on the 18th and walked off the course without finishing the hole (he was disqualified for not returning a card), he would easily have achieved that distinction. He was already 27 over par when he disappeared, 35 shots behind the tournament leader Malcolm McKenzie.

Approaching the 18th, Forsbrand had already lost seven balls, five in water and two in waist-high rough. During his relatively successful outward half of 43, he'd carded an eight at the 7th hole. He took five putts to hole out for a nine at the 12th. He went 10-6-8-3-7 for the next five holes. At the eighteenth, having already taken 93 strokes to get that far, he put two more balls in the water and, when he went to reload, discovered he had run out of ammunition. This presumably gave him the excuse he needed to go somewhere quiet and work on his game. Had he had another ball in his bag, he would have needed a birdie from it to have avoided a three-digit single round total. Truly there is hope for us all.

Scot George Russell hit a unique 300-yard drive in the 1913 Braids Tournament. What was marvellous about the shot was not the distance the ball travelled, though a 300-yard drive with 1913 equipment was indeed exceptional. Much more noteworthy was the fact that it went backwards. He was standing on an elevated tee and managed to catch the ball flush on his backswing. By the time the ball stopped rolling down the hill, it was three hundred yards away from the tee.

Otto Guernsey is probably unique in the annals of golfing disasters in that he is the only recorded player to have driven off in one golf club and seen his ball finish in a different club in a different city. It happened on the 11th at Apawanis GC in Rye, New York. He managed to shank his tee shot and watched it land in the adjoining Green Meadows GC. As the metropolitan boundary runs between the two courses, his drive had started in Rye and finished inside the city limits of Harrison, New York.

When Hale Irwin hit a shot during the 1973 Sea Pines Heritage Classic at Hilton Head, SC which lodged in the bra of a female spectator, he was faced with a dilemma. According to the rules the ball could be removed from this . . . obstruction and the player granted a free drop. The only problem was that the rules specify that the player himself remove the ball from the obstruction. After some debate on the subject, the woman was allowed to take the ball out of her own bra.

Elain Johnson, a Canadian amateur, went one better than Irwin. She actually hit one incredibly errant shot into her *own* bra. She thus incurred a two-stroke penalty but, as she is recorded as having said at the time, "I'll be damned if I play it where it lays."

Tony Lema, known to one and all as "Champagne Tony" because of his Walter Hagen-type lifestyle, once came a cropper after an over-the-top celebration sent him, quite literally, over the top. During the 1957 Bing Crosby National Pro-Am at Pebble Beach, he hit a spectacular shot at the ninth hole. He jumped in the air by way of celebration. He'd unfortunately forgotten the reason for his excitement: he had made the shot from perilously close to the edge of a cliff. His rapture took him down a steep embankment from which he was fortunate to escape with only minor cuts and bruises.

In 1931, Bayly McArthur's ball found the "Sand Trap From Hell". Playing in a tournament in New South Wales he hit a shot into a sand trap and, cursing his luck, went in after it. As he stepped into the "bunker" he realised, too late, that it was quicksand. (Yes, I wondered as well why he bothered getting into the bunker when it had obviously already swallowed up his ball.) This quicksand seems to have been especially quick, as his head was about to go under when his shouts alerted his playing partners, who managed to pull him out.

Occasionally ignorance of the rules causes golfers to be disqualified from competitions but John McMullin, an American professional, managed to get himself disqualified twice in the one round. It happened in the 1960 Motor City Open in (guess where?) Detroit. On the seventh hole he was penalised for *taking a practice swing in a sand bunker*. (I kid you not!) Then, on the fourteenth, he incurred another penalty for striking a moving ball. He added a one-shot penalty in each case and signed his scorecard. He then discovered that he should have docked himself two shots in each instance. He was disqualified for recording the wrong score on two different holes.

As long as people like TJ Moore continue to play golf, companies like Titleist and Maxfli need never worry about turnover. Moore, at a single hole, accounted for most of the declared profits of quite a few ball manufacturers when he knocked no less than 20 consecutive balls into the water on the 18th hole at the Port Arthur Country Club in Texas, during the 1978 Dryden (how inappropriate!) Invitational. By the time he got aboard and putted out, which to be fair to him he actually did, he had carded a score of 45 on the hole.

Australian Golfer Jack Newton underestimated the power of the lowly African Formicidae family (the African ant) when it comes to defending its patch. Newton was leading the Cock o' the North Tournament in Zambia when he got to the penultimate hole. He hit a shot just too near one of their nests for comfort and, as he shaped up to hit his ball, he was attacked by a swarm of ants which ran up his legs and stung them repeatedly. Newton ripped off his clothes and fled the area. Surprisingly he came back, got himself together and actually won the tournament.

One bad turn deserves another. Signing an incorrect scorecard lost Jackie Pung the US Women's Open. She was tied with Betsy Rawls after 72 holes but failed to spot that her playing partner Betty Jameson had put her down for an incorrect score on the fourth hole. As soon as she signed the card, she was disqualified. But Pung had no cause to be angry at Jameson, because she marked her playing partner down for a wrong score as well, with the result that Jameson too was disqualified.

Here's one of those "Why the hell didn't I just take the penalty shot?" stories. Phil Rodgers was challenging for the 1962 US Open, which was being staged at Oakmont. But his tee shot on the 17th went straight into a tree and didn't come out. Rather than declare the ball unplayable, Rodgers climbed the tree to play the ball where it lay. But it took him four shots to dislodge his ball, he had a quadruple bogey 8 on the hole and he lost the tournament by two shots.

Sweden's Michael Krantz grew too immediately fond of some of the local Irish alcoholic brews when he played in the 1990 Carroll's Irish Open. He arrived at the practice ground somewhat the worse for drink and, according to his caddie, "he was hitting his divots further than the balls." After one swing, he teetered for a moment before falling forwards on top of the caddie. When he got to the first tee, he became tired and emotional all over again and had another collapse. He shot an 82, quite an achievement under the circumstances really.

In case you've never played in an event with a shotgun start, it is a mechanism used to get teams to start and finish at the same time. All teams are assigned a tee and make their way there, awaiting the firing of a shotgun to indicate that it is time to start. Just such an event drew an interested crowd to the Kershaqua GC in New York recently, except it was after the shotgun had sounded and they were, members of the law enforcement community. It wasn't so much the shotgun they objected to but the location of the shot. Kershaqua GC is situated in the grounds of a minimum security prison.

The colourful JC Snead's Panama hat cost him two shots at the 1977 Tournament Players Championship. Snead was as well known for the headgear as Payne Stewart is for his plus-fours. It was a windy day at the TPC Sawgrass course at Ponte Vedra, Florida and Snead had just watched his shot land on the green of the fourth hole. As he approached the putting surface the wind gusted and blew the hat off his head. It travelled more than thirty yards and hit his ball. He was adjudged to have putted with the hat and penalised two strokes.

The great "Slammin'" Sam Snead was "Uncle Sam" to JC, and his famous uncle (the oldest player to have won a US Tour event at the age of 52, the best player never to win the US Open etc., etc.) once managed to hit his ball into a men's toilet and lose the Cleveland

Open. A stray shot went sailing in the open door of the men's locker room and finished in what the Americans like to call "the bathroom". Snead dropped two shots as a result and lost the championship by only a single stroke.

Paul Azinger, in his days as a struggling young professional, used to travel around the country with his wife Toni in a motor home. At the 1982 Disney Classic he parked the camper in the parking lot of the golf club. At about 2.00 am, he was woken up by an unsympathetic security guard and told to move the van. Appeals that he was taking part in the tournament and that he had an 8.00 am tee time fell on deaf ears. On another occasion, having missed a 36-hole cut, Azinger was asleep in the back of the van when, with his wife at the wheel, it got stuck in a tollbooth. Eventually Toni was forced to back out, pulling the canopy off in the process. It's a great life on the USPGA Tour!

What could possibly go wrong with the shot to the green John Cook faced on the fifth hole at Muirfield Village Golf Club, during the second round of the Memorial Tournament in 1995? His ball was 100 yards from a soft green with a generous flag position. Cook badly needed a birdie on what was his fourteenth hole in order to make the cut. He hit the ball well, only to watch it bounce on to the green and then spin back off into casual water. Annoyed, as he approached to mark his ball he attempted to scoop it out with a swipe of his right hand. But he missed! Instead of cupping the errant ball in his palm, he sent it flying into a lateral water hazard to the left of the green. Cook had to finish the hole with the same ball he'd put into play on the tee so he and his caddie went fishing. But they never did find the ball and Cook finished up with a triple bogey 8. He missed the cut by two shots.

Obviously almost everything went wrong with Nick Faldo in the first round of the Players Championship in 1995. He shot an unprecedented 80. In other years, Nick might have been able to blame jet lag, but in 1995 he'd committed himself to the US Tour and had moved to America. Instead blame lay with an anonymous representative of his golf ball company who had, mistakenly, left 100-compression balls in Faldo's locker. He uses 90s.

In the "When You're Hot . . . Dept", Ian Baker-Finch registers somewhere in the depths of the Alaskan winter. The 1991 Open Champion has been having a dreadful time since that victory. In 1995, he had already missed the cut in every single tormented tournament of the year before he got to the Open at St Andrew's. Then, on the first tee, looking at the widest fairway in golf, his visor blew off on his backswing. He snatched at the shot and sent it scuttling out of bounds to the left. He shot a 76. The next day he added a 77. Guess what?

In the summer of 1994, a Bristol golfer, Gerry Dacombe, drove off at the 2nd hole at Trevose in Cornwall and watched as his tee shot hooked . . . hooked and hooked some more. Then, having long since left the confines of the golf course it smashed through the upstairs window of the Sea Spell guest-house, into a guest's bathroom, where it bounced around for a while before disappearing into a toilet bowl on which a now twice-relieved woman had been sitting moments before.

Playing in the 1994 Cannes Open, Ronan Rafferty, with his second shot to the par-5 14th hole, tried to bend the ball around a tree. But the ball didn't bend (or the tree moved?) and it bounced back hitting Rafferty painfully in the leg. "I've got Spalding imprinted on my leg forever now," he commented afterwards. The shot also hurt him in the pocket, as he incurred a two-shot penalty and missed the cut.

"Pride cometh before a fall" should be the motto of all golfers. Jeff Sluman was reminded of the accuracy of the old adage in 1988 immediately after winning his first Major, the US PGA Championship. The following week, at his next tournament, Sluman was introduced on the first tee, with great ceremony, as the new PGA Champion. Acknowledging the warm applause of the crowd Sluman teed up, swung and thundered his drive all of 30 yards off the tee-box.

American woman pro Amy Alcott has been waiting a long time for her 30th LPGA Tour victory. She's been stuck on 29 since 1991. She had no idea how many people were aware of this fact until a tournament in 1994 in Nashville. She had an early tee time, so at 5.45 in the morning she got up and wandered out, stark naked, to get her morning paper on the corridor outside. Given the time, she figured there would be no one around. She figured wrongly. As she opened her door, a passing guest (male) spotted her and remarked, "Hope you win your 30th soon". "Thanks," she replied coolly. "How did you know it was me?" "Oh, I'd recognise you anywhere," came the response.

In the final round of the 1991 Catalan Open, England's Roger Chapman got a bit miffed with his tee shot at the par-3 13th at the Bonmont Club in Tarragona. He badly wanted to take his anger out on something and the nearest available object (his caddie had wisely stepped backwards) was a concrete tee marker. So Chapman, as you might, took a swipe at it with his 7-iron. Only it wasn't concrete and it performed a wonderful imitation of the Big Bang by exploding into fragments. Chapman was embarrassed, but there were no PGA officials or referees around so he figured he'd get away with this particular bit of petulance. But he was wrong, wasn't he? The following week he was fined £100 by Tournament Director John Paramor. Someone had diligently collected all the pieces of the deceased tee marker and sent them to Paramor with a note appended which read, "Love from Roger Chapman".

European Tour pro Paul Way can be a little accident-prone at times. He was forced to withdraw from the European Open in September, 1993 after he pulled a door frame down on top of himself and required two stitches in his face. You might well wonder what he was doing, demolishing door frames. Actually, he was practising his pull-ups in a local bar and the frame of the door wasn't as up to the strain as Mr Way. In 1990, he broke two toes playing soccer in Tobago. Twice he hurt his ribs badly. On the first occasion, he foolishly allowed fellow pro Peter Mitchell to practise karate on him, then he hurt them again in a go-karting accident. Not all the accidents which befall him are entirely his own fault. In 1992, his partner in a pro-am hit him solidly in the back with a 3-wood shot.

An expensive game of golf cost an aide to President Bill Clinton his job. David Watkins used the Presidential helicopter to go on a golfing trip. He was probably showboating because he was not short of readies himself (Watkins is a millionaire friend of the President), but he was forced to resign when the trip was exposed and had to reimburse the US Treasury Dept the $13,130 the journey had cost.

While playing from the ninth tee at Inglewood Country Club, Seattle the shaft of Mr Edward M Harrison's driver broke and the jagged end penetrated his groin. Bleeding copiously, Mr Harrison managed to drag himself for 100 yards in a futile effort to get help. Unable to move any further, he bled to death.

Australian pro Brett Ogle was lucky not to lose an eye at the 1995 Hawaiian Open in Waialae Country Club. Defending the championship he had won the previous year, he pushed his tee shot at the par-5 13th and wound up behind a tree. Playing a 5-iron recovery shot, he connected with the tree on his follow through. The shaft came apart in his hands, the clubhead rebounded off the tree and hit Ogle above his left eye. A piece of the shaft sliced off part of his left forearm, another piece cut his right forearm and a third hit him on the back. Had he not been wearing wraparound sunglasses at the time, the impact of the clubhead would probably have caused him to lose the sight of his left eye.

Zimbabwe's Tony Johnstone was a lot luckier than both Ogle and Harrison. His putter head merely dropped off in the middle of the Zimbabwe Open when, in the intense heat, the glue melted on it.

You might say he got what was coming to him, and that he had his share of luck at the venue, but, when local boy Larry Mize hit a bad tee shot at Augusta's famous 15th, the crowd reacted badly when they saw him take out an iron to lay up short of the water. Feeling guilty for not providing them with sufficient entertainment, Mize changed his mind and took out a wood instead. This move earned him a great ovation as the jeers and catcalls turned to cheers. The encouragement didn't do Mize any good, however; his overly ambitious shot ended up in the water.

Ping putters have stood up to a number of exacting tests over the years, but during a recent trial in the USA their distinctive shape and appearance proved crucial in putting away a murderer. A man had killed his wife of thirty years by brutally beating her to death with his putter. He was convicted on the basis of a forensic examination of the wounds to her head which revealed that they matched the outline of her husband's Ping putter.

A Spanish wind known as a *cierzo* wreaked havoc with the 1996 Catalan Open at Bonmont, near Tarragona. It gusted at 60 mph and caused the tournament to be cut to 36 holes. PGA Tour promoter Jamie Birkmyre didn't need to be convinced to abandon two rounds after he tried a little experiment of his own on the 15th green of the Bonmont course. He placed a ball two feet from the flag. The wind started the ball rolling and kept it going until it finished up in a bunker 60 yards away.

In March 1993, a 68-year-old golf nut, Ken Bullman, nearly froze to death while queuing for hours in sub-zero temperatures just so that he could book a game of golf at a municipal golf course in Altrincham in England. He is diagnosed as suffering from hypothermia.

Jasper Parnevik should have suffered a similar fate when he dived into a freezing cold lake at St Melion in Cornwall. His action was not prompted by natural exuberance, but by the fact that he had just shot an 86 in the third round of the Benson and Hedges International, the worst score of his professional career.

Two bank robbers had cause to regret their brief flirtation with the game of golf in 1993. Having stolen $20,000 from a Bank of America in Newport Beach in California, they made their getaway, but their car was spotted and chased. They dumped it near the Newport Beach Country Club and grabbed a golf cart to try and outdistance the pursuing police. They failed miserably. With a top speed of about 5 mph, the bad guys could have been caught by an overweight cop on an afternoon stroll. They were overhauled before they got as far as the fifth green and arrested.

African golf tournaments have a magic of their own, though sometimes the spell may be woven in bizarre ways. In 1986, for example, a pro called Paul Burley was playing in his first tournament on the Dark Continent, participating in the Phalabowra Open. As he teed up on the third, he heard an almighty crash of undergrowth behind him and became conscious of his playing partners scattering as he reached the top of his backswing. Wisely deciding to abandon the stroke, Burley looked behind him to see a hippopotamus bearing down on him, looking as if Burley had kidnapped its baby. Burley made his second sensible decision that day when he ran for his life. He didn't stop until he got to the clubhouse. It was hours before he could be persuaded to leave the sanctuary of the locker room to resume his round.

In one Nigerian Open, Philip Walton's caddie showed his dedication to duty by being fully prepared to sacrifice his man to ensure an important shot was played properly. Walton had to play a shot from under some trees. He was concerned about clipping a branch with his club on his backswing. He hit the shot well, but as he watched it in flight a spectator inquired whether he had been aware that the branch about which he had been so anxious was the temporary home of a snake. Walton checked out the branch, confirmed the presence of the reptile, and then rounded on his caddie. "Why didn't you tell me?" he roared, with the pent-up anger of a man whose entire life has just flashed before his eyes. "If I'd hit the branch, that thing could have landed on the back of my neck." The caddie shrugged his shoulders and replied, "I wanted you to hit a good shot, so I didn't want you worrying about it."

Your average mugger is just not up to coping with a women's four-ball. So discovered one hapless practitioner of the thieving art in a club in the USA in 1994. Armed with a baseball bat, he approached a group of ladies and instructed them to hand over their valuables. They demurred, in the most forceful fashion possible. One of them flattened him with a blow and the rest of them sat on him immediately. The boxer then sat on his face (I kid you not) so that he could barely breathe. Help soon arrived (for the mugger, the four ladies were having no problems at all) and the failed thief was overjoyed to be delivered into the arms of the law.

Byron Nelson was cursed with accuracy at the 1957 US Masters. Mishitting his tee shot to the par-3 sixteenth, Nelson saw his ball plop into the water guarding the green. Reloading, he was unerring with his second shot. It hit the flagstick. Unfortunately, it did so with such force that the ball bounced backwards . . . into the water.

# CHAPTER NINE

## Players and Others

### The Professional

There is no such thing as a "typical" pro. Some are superstars, some are "rabbits" fated to play over the early morning dew. But it is still possible to give a general idea of some of the trivia of the life of an "average" pro, i.e. one who fits into neither of the above categories. He's probably been a professional for 9/10 years, and has been on the Tour for 7/8 years. He's probably got one or two Tour wins to his credit and plays in about 27 tournaments every year. In the course of his professional duties he will (if he's lucky) walk 750 miles a year on the golf course and will probably hit at least 20,000 balls in practice. He will (or should) spend 140–150 hours a year on the putting practice green, and will visit the Media Interview room 10–12 times a year if he's having a halfway decent season. If he has a stroke average of 72.00 over the season he will win between £120,000–130,000, but will also incur annual expenses of around £30,000. In addition, he will pay his caddie a retainer of about £300 a week as well as 5–10% of his winnings. He will get three dozen balls (usually balatas) from his sponsors for every tournament and will mark each of them with his own distinctive mark. All going well, he will use 3–6 balls a round. He will be likely to lose 15–20 balls a year by hitting them into water hazards or out of bounds. He will go through about 100 gloves each year (3–4 per tournament), probably giving away the used ones to young fans who clamour for them during each tournament. His sponsors will supply him with 60–70 shirts a season and 30–35

115

sweaters. He will go through anything between 6 and 12 pairs of shoes a season.

Professionals on the US Tour are better known for their born-again Christianity than they are for their social consciences. Few modern professionals come from very impoverished backgrounds and, when the Democratic President of the United States, Bill Clinton, invited the 1993 American Ryder Cup team to the White House prior to their departure for Europe, many of the players simply did not want to go. None had voted for him in 1992 and all were opposed to his plans to impose increased taxes on the wealthy. As Lee Janzen put it, "Where I grew up you were better off telling people you were a garbage man than a Democrat." Paul Azinger is reputed to have said, "I don't want to shake hands with a draft dodger." However, at the insistence of team Captain, Tom Watson (who had voted for George McGovern in 1972, before reverting to type and plumping for Reagan and Bush in the 1980s), the Ryder Cup team duly made the trip to the White House.

Golf pros didn't always have it easy (some of them still don't). There was a time when they were at the beck and call of rich country club members. In 1899, for example, Willie Davis, designer of the original Shinnecock Hills course, took some time off from his duties in the Newport Club to play in the US Open which was being held in Baltimore. Before he could actually get into the competition, an irate message came from a Newport member summoning him back to play a game at his own club. Davis had no option but to obey the summons, which he duly did. But his stay at Newport was not protracted. The first thing he did when he returned was to hand in his resignation.

### Tommy Armour

A Scot, Armour was a good enough player to have won all three Major championships which existed in his heyday. He claimed the US Open in 1927, the PGA in 1930 and the Open in 1931, all without the aid of an eye. He had lost it during World War 1, in the course of which he was reputed to have strangled a German soldier with his bare hands.

As a teaching pro in later life at the Medinah Country Club, host to a number of US Opens, Armour would take his mind off the inadequacies of his pupils by practising his shooting (courtesy of his good eye) with a .22 calibre rifle. One day, he drew a really short straw and was forced to waste his teaching talents on a player incapable of taking advantage of them. To the pupil he seemed to be spending most of his time taking pot shots at the local fauna. Finally his patience snapped and he petulantly inquired of Armour, "When are you going to take care of me?" With the gun still cocked, Armour turned towards the member and muttered, "Don't tempt me."

## Seve Ballesteros

Since reaching his thirties Seve's form has been chequered. His lapses have been as frequent but his ability to escape from them with a display of Mephistophelean trickery has not been as apparent. Despite his often seething anger with himself at his failures, he can still demonstrate his sense of humour. Having missed the cut for the Scottish Open at Carnoustie in 1995 with two awful rounds, Seve travelled early to St Andrew's to practise for the Open. He was followed around by a small crowd delighted with this bonus, among which was Observer journalist Derek Lawrenson. To his amazement Seve asked him would he like to play, offering to let Lawrenson use his clubs. Unfortunately Lawrenson is left-handed and had to decline but, before he did so, Seve asked, "What do you play off?" "Eight," replied Lawrenson. "Eight!" said Seve. "Well, I played off ten at Carnoustie so it should be a good match."

Because of his inability in the 1990s to reproduce the form which won him three Open championships and two Masters titles Ballesteros sought advice from many sources before settling on the maverick pro Mac O'Grady as his coaching guru. In early 1995 O'Grady performed, with Ballesteros, a bizarre ritual of exorcism. As the Spaniard explained, "We collected all the photographs taken over the years which show my bad swing habits and we put them in an old shoe box. Then we drove out into the desert near Palm Springs, dug a grave and buried them. I now have only my good habits left." Maybe

117

the juju worked, because Ballesteros made the Ryder Cup team on merit that year. But it didn't last. By the end of the season Mad Mac and Seve had parted company and Ballesteros had announced that he was quitting golf for five months.

## Ben Crenshaw

"Gentle Ben" brought a lump to millions of throats with his 1995 US Masters victory. It came a few days after the death of his mentor and guide Harvey Penick. Throughout the tournament, Crenshaw had felt the presence of the spirit of his old coach and it was enough to sustain him as he rediscovered form which had all but deserted him. Times had been difficult for Crenshaw in the years prior to his second Masters triumph. In 1992 he had to pre-qualify for the British Open, as he had lost his exempt status. After a disastrous first qualifying round he shot a 79 and had lost his chance of making the Open proper in Muirfield. That night, he hoisted himself gloomily on to a barstool at his hotel. The bartender asked politely, "What can I get you, sir?" To which Crenshaw glumly replied, "Arsenic".

## John Daly

Big-hitting American pro John Daly has had a well-publicised relationship with Mr Jack Daniels and others of his ilk, and he seems to have been suspended more often than a Christmas stocking. He used to hit the bottle as hard as he hit the ball. But after being threatened with expulsion from the game by USPGA Tour Commissioner Deane Beman, he went on the wagon. On one occasion he was finding the wagon an unpleasant vehicle on which to hitch a ride, so his good friend and fellow pro Fuzzy Zoeller took him out to dinner. Driving by a cemetery *en route* to the restaurant Zoeller pointed out the gravestones to Daly and remarked, "You think *you've* got it bad, what about those guys?"

Daly's personal problems have included very public rows with the women in his life, sometimes reaching the level of pure soap opera. When he made his breakthrough at the 1991 PGA Championship at Crooked Stick, by his side was Bettye Fulford. Later that year, after the Johnny Walker World Championship, she got her marching orders when he discovered that she was ten years older than she had ever admitted to (39 as opposed to 29), that she was married and that she had a child.

Daly recently designed his first golf course. The appropriately named Wicked Stick Golf Links in Myrtle Beach, South Carolina (a place badly in need of new courses) was opened in October 1995. As befits Daly's style, it features two 300-yard-plus par-three holes. (Only kidding!)

1995 was a typical year for John Daly, except that he didn't fall foul of the USPGA. (In previous years he'd been suspended for picking up his ball and walking off a course, and "voluntarily" took a lay-off after fighting with a fellow-pro's father in a club parking lot.) He won a Major (the British Open), during which his presence attracted a colourful streaker clad only in a cap and carrying a set of toy clubs. He shaved his head on a semi-regular basis. He was ignored for Ryder Cup selection by Lanny Wadkins, despite winning a Major. And he appeared on the NBC *Tonight Show* with Jay Leno wearing a leopard-skin coat and tossed doughnuts at members of the audience. All pretty jaded really.

The successful American Seniors Tour player Bob Brue once observed that, "the good thing about the Senior Tour is that I won't have to play against John Daly until I'm 82 years old."

### Ernie Els

The young South African was only 24 when he won his first Major, the US Open, in 1994 in an error-prone play-off. However, his best round that year was not at Oakmont but in the Dubai Desert Classic, where he shot an 11-under round of 61 which included 12 birdies and only 21 putts.

After playing with Els in the first two rounds of the 1994 US Open, the two-time champion Curtis Strange said of Els, "I think I just played with the next God."

### Nick Faldo

The taciturn Englishman, playing in the US, had some trouble with an over-zealous marshal who insisted on raising his "Quiet Please" sign even though it cast a shadow across Faldo's line. Twice the Englishman asked him to drop the sign, but the marshal insisted in raising it again just as Faldo lined up his putt. Finally Faldo turned to him and observed tartly, "You'll have to excuse me. I've only been in America for a short while. Perhaps my English isn't good enough." The marshal finally got the message and the sign was lowered.

Faldo's aversion to the press is legendary. In the mid-eighties he became a front-page tabloid story because of his divorce from his wife Melanie and his marriage to his second wife Gill. He hit the headlines again ten years later with his separation from Gill. His most famous and graceless dig at the press hounds was after his victory in the Open at Muirfield in 1992 when he made his victory speech and, in front of 25,000 fans and a huge TV audience, said, "I'd like to thank the press from the bottom of my . . . well, from the heart of my bottom, anyway."

One of Faldo's rare exhibitions of humour on the course was at the 1992 US Open at Pebble Beach. During the second round of the tournament, at the 14th hole his shot to the green ended up in a tree. Climbing up to identify his ball, he was perched precariously on a branch. He saw the funny side of his situation and hollered, "Where the hell is Jane?" But Faldo being Faldo we can assume that he didn't find the triple bogey eight he took at the hole to be very amusing.

Partnering Faldo during the 1995 Open at St Andrew's the Australian player Steve Elkington (who would win his first Major, the USPGA, later in the year) was walking down the first fairway when a scantily-clad female spectator broke through the ropes and came towards him. Elkington, by his own account, was extremely upset by what happened next. She ran straight past him, kissed Faldo and presented him with a rose.

The prevailing image of professional golfers is of a group who, while they might practise their craft, are also overweight, smoke too much and drink far more than is good for them. That may well be true in certain instances, but it is not the case with Faldo. A battery of tests were performed on him in 1993 at the British Olympic Association's medical centre. They found that he had the leg strength of an Olympic downhill skier, the wrists of a top rower and the aerobic capacity of a 1,500-metre runner. In one test, he was able to touch a point seven inches below his toes while keeping his knees straight.

In 1992, Faldo realised an ambition and met with Ben Hogan. Given the reputation both men have for taciturnity you might wonder what they found to talk about but, off the course, Faldo can actually be quite an amiable soul, especially in comparison with Hogan. Over lunch at Hogan's Shady Oaks club in Fort Worth, Texas, Faldo asked if he could watch Hogan hit some practice balls. The request was denied. The Englishman tried a different tack. He told Hogan he badly wanted to win the US Open Championship and asked him what was the secret (Hogan being a four-time winner). Hogan's response was positively Buddhist: "Shoot a lower score than anybody else". Sensing that the Great Man was being playful, Faldo repeated the question. "Just score lower than anybody else." This invaluable piece of advice having been passed on, Hogan made his excuses and left.

### David Feherty

David Feherty has always been good copy for the members of the noble Fourth Estate. He's one of the few players who will be sought out for a comment even after a mediocre round, because he's always apt to come up with the sort of apposite quip about a tournament, a player or a course which the less quick witted scribe would not manage to produce in an average working life. Feherty often reserves his most caustic comments for the work of golf architects (he runs his own golf design company in partnership with golf pro and commentator David Jones). But he usually keeps his powder dry until he plays a good round, lest he be accused of sour grapes. On one occasion, he was wheeled into the press tent after a fine round on a Robert Trent Jones course. One of the gentlemen of the press popped the first question. In response, Feherty stared vacantly into space as if on another planet. He was then quizzed about his bizarre behaviour. He replied, "Sorry, guys, I was just thinking about the Apollo 11 astronauts. It must have been very discouraging for them, getting to the moon, hopping out of the lunar module, looking around at all those craters and realising that Robert Trent Jones had been there before them."

Feherty was standing in the lobby of a Spanish hotel once when he was approached by a man, who asked him, "Are you Severiano Ballesteros?" Feherty confessed that he wasn't, but the following day he went out and shot a round of 66. "Imagine," he told Dai Davies, "me having a 66 just because someone *thought* I was Seve."

A nonplussed Feherty once watched Bob Tway in the clubhouse tearfully celebrating his first tournament win since his USPGA triumph against Greg Norman. (The win came shortly after a right-wing terrorist bomb killed nearly 200 people in the Federal Building in Oklahoma City.) "Tway was in tears," recalled Feherty. "Everyone was in tears. And I'm thinking: hell, this man's from Oklahoma City. The Oklahoma bombing should have you in tears. But winning a golf tournament?"

1Feherty's regular caddie Rod Wooller followed him to America when he joined the US Tour. The Irishman's efforts in the USA were not crowned with conspicuous success and he missed a lot of cuts in his first season. On one occasion when he did make a cut, to the delight of Wooller who was starting to miss his percentage of the prize money earned by his "bag", he approached the caddie with a long face and told him to pack his bags. When Wooller asked why, Feherty told him that he'd been disqualified for failing to sign his card. As the stunned Wooller began to bemoan this latest piece of bad fortune, Feherty referred him to the calendar. It was the first of April!

Once, in the course of a round on one of his least favourite courses, St Melion in Cornwall, a peckish Feherty had sent his caddie off to buy them a couple of hamburgers. Feherty stood munching his while he waited on the tee to drive off. When his turn came, Feherty had only taken a bite out of his burger and he was reluctant to hand it over to Wooller whom he was not convinced wouldn't eat a second one. In order to protect his lunch he put it on the tee-box, plunged a tee through the middle of it, popped his ball on top and drove off without damaging the burger!

Feherty moved to the US Tour in 1994. Nick Faldo followed in 1995, apparently intent on winning more Majors. But Feherty had other ideas about Faldo's motivation. "He just couldn't bear to be separated from me," opined the Ulsterman.

Feherty, who keeps himself extremely fit, was once told that the veteran player Jerry Barber, then in his mid-seventies, did likewise by walking five miles every morning. To which Feherty responded, "Why? Doesn't he sleep at home?"

### Raymond Floyd

He of the inelegant but oh-so-effective swing was making his way to a British Open championship in Scotland one year when he flew over the Firth of Forth. (Travelling first class, one presumes, which he always does.) Looking down, he asked, "What's that below?" "That's the Forth," he was told. "Hell of a carry," Floyd quipped.

### Walter Hagen

Walter Hagen, "The Haig", was one of the first great characters of professional golf. He did for golf in the teens and twenties what Palmer was to do for it at the dawn of the TV era. His philosophy of life was to "stop and smell the roses". He enjoyed life to the full, drank like a fish, womanised as if he'd been celibate for years and was making up for lost time, and had a healthy contempt for his "betters". He was also an inveterate gambler, a man who would have a wager on anything. The bet would be all the more attractive if it involved the testing of his own skill. One bizarre wager that he lost was in Tijuana in 1928. He was playing in the Tijuana Open when a fellow competitor, the Australian professional Joe Kirkwood, bet him $50 that he could hit his ball back to the hotel and into the toilet bowl of his room before Hagen could. So the two men set off through the streets of Tijuana hitting a golf ball as they went. Hagen got back to the hotel first but was stymied by the toilet bowl. He just couldn't get his ball into it. Kirkwood, however, potted his at the first attempt.

In a typically flamboyant gesture in 1923, Hagen struck a blow for golf professionals. In 1914, during the US Open at Midlothian in Chicago, professionals were admitted to the clubhouse by the members for the first time. But Britain was slow to follow that precedent, so that in 1923, when Hagen travelled to Troon to play in the 1923 Open championship, he discovered that professionals were still denied access to the clubhouse. With characteristic aplomb, Hagen decided to show the establishment what he thought of it. Arriving at the clubhouse in a limousine, he had his chauffeur set out a table on the lawn outside the club dining-room. The chauffeur then proceeded to unpack lunch, including a bottle of champagne, which Hagen sipped while the members looked on, in varying degrees of admiration and horror, from inside the clubhouse.

Hagen was the great master of one-upmanship. He would burn the candle at both ends, rationalising that, while potential opponents might be safely tucked up in bed they wouldn't be sleeping, as their minds turned over the prospect of challenging him. In the 1919 Open championship he tied with Mike Brady for first. As the two waited on the tee for the play-off to begin, Hagen remarked to Brady, "Mike, if I were you I'd roll down my shirtsleeves." Brady bristled, assuming some put-down was in the offing. When he asked for an explanation of the remark, he discovered he'd been right. "The way they are now," observed The Haig, "everyone can see your forearms quivering." In a match with Jim Barnes (an Open, US Open and PGA winner), Hagen was unable to shake his opponent over thirty-six holes. At the first tie hole, a par-3, Barnes had the honour. As he prepared to select his club, he noticed Hagen ostentatiously practice swinging with a 6-iron. Barnes had been contemplating taking an 8-iron, but when he saw Hagen's apparent choice of club he reached instead for a 7-iron. He then watched, nonplussed, as his ball flew over the green and down a steep bank on the far side. Annoyed, he stepped back to watch Hagen get himself into even more trouble. But the Haig merely grinned at him, put the 6-iron back in the bag and took out the 8-iron he'd intended to play all along.

The Haig would be unlikely to prosper in the politically correct 1990s: part of his philosophy for dealing with the opposite sex was, "Call every woman 'Sugar' and you can't go wrong."

## Ben Hogan

Thinking to divert the young Hogan's attention away from the silly game he seemed to spend all his time playing, Hogan's Ma once told him, "You'll never get anywhere fooling around those golf courses." And they say a mother knows!

Gary Player was an inveterate seeker of advice and tips from both great and gross alike. Once he made the mistake of seeking the good counsel of Mr Hogan, unaware that the latter had none to offer. When Player put some question to him, Hogan fixed him with a withering stare and asked, "What equipment do you play with?" "Spalding, Mr Hogan," Player replied uneasily. "Well, then, why don't you ask Mr Spalding?" was the terse reply.

So obsessed was Hogan with his own game (or so much a gamesman was he) that he once walked off the 12th at Augusta and said to fellow competitor Claude Harmon, "You know, Claude, that's the first time I've ever birdied that hole." Harmon had just aced the hole!

Hogan is credited with winning the US Open on four occasions, but claims a fifth victory (his first) in 1942. In the first year after US entry into World War Two the US Open, scheduled for Interlachen, was cancelled. Instead, something called the Hale America National Open Golf Tournament was played at Ridgemoor Country Club in Chicago. Hogan won. He didn't win the US Open "proper" until 1948. On the basis that a wartime Masters was played that year (Byron Nelson won and is officially credited with the win), ditto a wartime PGA Championship (won by Sam Snead), Hogan has always claimed that the Hale America (co-sponsored by the USGA and the PGA) was the national Open for that year. To support his claim, he was awarded a gold medal for this triumph which is identical to the other four which adorn his trophy room at Colonial Country Club in Fort Worth.

## Bobby Jones

The great amateur had, as his long-time teacher and mentor, the dour Scottish pro at East Lake in Atlanta, Stewart Maiden. In 1925,

Jones was preparing for the US Open at the Worcester GC in Massachusetts and things were not going well. Like a Nick Faldo urgently sending for David Leadbetter, word was despatched to Maiden that his greatest pupil needed him. The Scot came all the way from the south, by train. Out on the practice ground he watched Jones for a few minutes before observing tartly, "Why don't ye hit the ball with yer backswing?" Having said his say, he trotted off the practice area and took the next train home. (Jones slowed down his swing, tied for first and lost in a play-off to Willie McFarlane.)

Jones did what he did because of his outrageous talent and his ability to overcome chronic nervousness. He was so anxious during tournaments that he would be physically ill and was often unable to eat while he was playing in a competition.

As a precocious youth, Jones lacked the calmness which he brought to his performances in his more mature years. He played in his first national championship in 1916, when he was only fourteen years of age. Jones, a distinguished club-hurler, was drawn against one Eben Byers in the first round. Byers, though considerably older than Jones, had similar propensities as regards cruelty to golf clubs. The match was surreal. Both players were unable to control their tempers and the members of the small gallery following their match frequently found themselves having to dodge flying projectiles. At one hole, Byers actually threw his club all the way out of bounds in a prodigious effort and ordered his much put-upon caddie to leave it where it was. Jones won the match 3 and 1, claiming that victory had been his because Byers had run out of clubs first.

Jones almost missed out on his great 1930 Grand Slam, thanks to the bane of many lives, an over-zealous security man. He was due to play with Al Watrous in the final round of the Open at Royal Lytham. After the third round, with Watrous holding a two-stroke lead, both men agreed to retreat to Jones's hotel room and order up lunch. However, when they returned to the course Jones discovered that he had left his player's badge back at the hotel. No amount of argument would get Jones in so he was forced to send Watrous ahead, go around to another entrance and pay the admission charge (seven shillings!), in order to get in and compete in the final round of the Open.

Jones had his fair share of luck in that banner year of 1930. During the US Open at Interlachen he was playing the par-5 ninth, going for the green with his second shot, across water, and was already into his backswing when two children ran across the course behind him. Losing concentration he topped the shot and watched in horror as the ball headed, like a bullet, straight for the lake. However, its trajectory was so shallow that, in the manner of a stone pitched across a lake, it skidded once across the surface of the water before climbing on to land thirty yards from the pin. Instead of a possible bogey, Jones managed to get up and down for his birdie. (That same year, Jones was also lucky to survive a lightning storm with his life.)

Jones's latter years were a tragedy for a man who had been one of the great athletes of his generation. He was diagnosed in the 1950s as suffering from syringomyelia, a wasting disease which leaves its victims in constant pain. Jones bore the disease publicly with all the class and dignity people had come to expect of him. But the pain and the enforced inactivity depressed him in his private moments. Towards the end of his life he remarked poignantly, "When it first happened to me I was pretty bitter and there were times when I didn't want to go on living. But I did go on living, so I had to face the problem of how I was to live. I decided I'd just do the very best I could." In 1971 Jones, probably the greatest natural golfer who ever lived, died at the age of 69.

### Robert Trent Jones

Robert Trent Jones, one of the great course designers of this century, was not altogether popular with all professional golfers, a fact which probably caused him considerable satisfaction and led him to conclude that he was doing his job properly. One of his detractors, Jimmy Demaret, once greeted him with the comment, "Trent, I came across a course you'd love the other day. You take a penalty drop on the first tee."

## Bernhard Langer

Although a thoroughly pleasant and gentlemanly person, Bernhard Langer is not what one would describe as the life and soul of anybody's party. Thus it was hardly surprising that when Des Smyth, the amiable and likeable Laytown and Bettystown pro, was celebrating his victory in the 1993 Madrid Open, Langer would fail to see the point in joining in the festivities. Des was buying drinks for as many of his fellow pros as happened to be in the clubhouse bar of the subsequent tournament venue. He approached Langer and invited the German star to toast his good fortune. Ever polite, Langer declined and, when pressed by Smyth, looked somewhat puzzled and pointed out, "Why, I'm not thirsty."

For all his apparent dourness, Langer can let go occasionally. In 1985, when he won the European Open at Sunningdale, he sauntered down the 18th fairway wearing a police helmet borrowed from a convenient British bobby.

Langer is fastidious to the point of being pedantic. During the 1991 Ryder Cup, he played in one of the four-ball rounds with Colin Montgomerie. The big Scot's caddie was looking at a yardage chart and taking a reading off a sprinkler head (which, for the record, was less than a foot in diameter). Langer wandered over. "How far have you got?" he asked his partner. "124 yards to the green and another 26 on. That's 150 yards into the breeze, a 7-iron," replied the Scot. Langer sized up the situation for the moment and then inquired, in all seriousness, "Where are you taking your yardage from – the front or the back of the sprinkler?"

So accurate are Bernhard Langer's iron shots that he began to question the yardages offered by the R & A in their course planner for St Andrew's in the 1995 Open championship. Either his club selection was faulty (perish the thought), or the yardages were wrong. So the measurements were checked and it was discovered that Langer's hitting was more accurate than the R & A's yardages. Some of the measurements were between five and nine yards out.

## David Leadbetter

Probably the most successful coach in golf, Leadbetter has spawned the use of the word "guru" among the members of the scribbling profession because of the fierce loyalty of his acolytes (men such as Nick Faldo and Nick Price – 9 Majors between them), whose swings and professional careers he has changed. But, like any guru, he does require sacrifices. He helped American pro Brad Bryant with his game, enabling him to win his first Tour event in October 1995. Bryant commented afterwards, "David wanted me to change my takeaway, my backswing, my downswing and my follow-through. He said I could still play right-handed."

## Gavin Levenson

Much is made of the pressure on the players at the top of the golf tree. But if you climb down a few rungs, to the level of the journeyman professional trying to retain the means to make his livelihood, you see pressure in the raw. To illustrate, take one tournament in the life of Gavin Levenson, a player many golf fans may barely have heard of. By 1990, the bespectacled South African had been on the European Tour for eleven years and had total winnings over that period of just over £140,000. But 1990 was a bad year for him. Six missed cuts in a row left him facing the loss of his Tour card. Going into what would be his last tournament of the season, the Portuguese Open at Quinto do Lago in the Algarve, he needed to make the cut in order to stay in the top 120. The alternative was a return to the Tour School at the age of 37. He shot a one-under-par 71 in the first round of the tournament, but conditions were perfect and the score still left him with a tough job to do on the second day. Playing along with the English pro Stephen Bennet, he remarked at the start of the round that this would be the most important 18 holes of his life. He did not want to go back to the Tour School and couldn't face the life of a club professional. He simply had to make the cut. As he approached the 18th hole it was clear to Levenson, now two under par, that he needed a par at the last to make the cut. The 18th at Quinto do Lago is a tough left-dogleg hole, with a large tree at the turn discouraging players from cutting the corner to give themselves a short-iron to the green. Levenson, to the surprise of his playing partners and the consternation of his caddie teed up his ball on the right-hand side of the tee box, a major *faux pas* given that all the trouble was down the left-hand side of the fairway. His caddie took the unusual step of calling his player back after he had begun to address the ball. He pointed out what he took to be a basic error of judgement. But Levenson had not made a mistake. He had made up his mind to go over the tree rather than take the more conservative and cautious route. With the loss of the means of making his living staring him in the face, he calmly told his caddie, "I'll never have a better chance to find out what kind of man I am." Levenson then stood up to the most important golf swing of his life and smashed his ball over the tree, hit his second to the green and two-putted to make the cut. He shot back-to-back 70s on the weekend, to finish in a 6-way tie for 25th and prize money of £2,681. The following year, having retained his card, he went on to win the Balearic Open and more than treble his 1990 prizemoney.

## Sandy Lyle

Lyle, (known on the Tour as "Lily"), described by no less a man than his peer and deadly rival Nick Faldo as "the greatest natural talent in the world", has been having a career verging between the ordinary and the disastrous since his dramatic 1988 US Masters win. Despite his affable and phlegmatic personality, he's been so discouraged at times that he's been tempted to give up the game. His rationale for sticking with it? "I can't quit, I've got too many nice sweaters."

One of Lyle's best friends amongst the European Tour Press corps is David "Dai" Davies of the Guardian. In a career peppered with *faux pas* one of Lyle's classics (and this is not in the apocrypha section, because it was confirmed to me by Dai Davies himself) came when he was asked by Davies to autograph a ball for him. Sandy duly obliged, signing, "To Die, from Sandy."

Once Lyle had a chance encounter with his Ryder Cup captain Tony Jacklin in Kennedy Airport in New York. Jacklin greeted Lyle fulsomely and asked him, "Where are you going?" "To the toilet," replied the Scot.

The Sam Goldwyn of the professional golf circuit was asked at a press conference in 1994 (at a time when the great American prospect wouldn't have been so well-known) what he thought of Tiger Woods. He replied, "I don't know. I've never played it."

Among Lyle's other renowned bricks (one almost literally so) were when he built a new snooker room extension to his house, only to discover that it was too small to take the snooker table. Or when he complimented his hosts in an after-dinner speech in Tokyo on the quality of the Chinese food.

Lyle can be sharp enough when he wants to be. In 1987, he won the Players Championship at Sawgrass in Florida. It's often called "The Fifth Major", and the USPGA Tour (which only has one Major to its name) would dearly like it to become just that. A radio interviewer asked Lyle a question, the answer to which put the event in its proper perspective. "What's the difference between the TPC and the British Open?" he asked. "About 120 years," was the deadpan riposte.

## Colin Montgomerie

*Daily Mail* writer Michael McDonnell tells the story of how the often lugubrious and "difficult" Colin Montgomerie was so annoyed at what *Golf Illustrated Weekly* had written about him that he rang up and instructed them to cancel his subscription. On investigation, the magazine discovered that he was on the free list, so they were happy to comply with his request.

## Jack Nicklaus

Nicklaus is the only player in golfing history to have won twenty major tournament titles. He has taken six Masters, five PGAs, four US Opens, three British Opens and two US Amateur titles. He is also the oldest winner of the Masters, claiming his last title in 1986 at the age of 46, and is one of only four players to have won all four majors.

Even Homer nods and, in the first round of the British Open at Royal St George's in Sandwich, he nodded fit to beat the band. Jack Nicklaus shot the worst round of his professional career, an 83. In fact he was

11 over par for the first 14 holes and managed to scramble pars on the last four. He had four double bogeys in his round and his tee shot on the par-5 14th travelled barely 80 yards. He declined to give press interviews afterwards because he was afraid he would say something he might regret.

Nicklaus became the fourth (and so far the last) player to win all four Major championships when he took the British Open at Muirfield in 1966. But he achieved what the other three (Hogan, Sarazen and Player) did in only four years as a professional.

Never revered for his choice of golfing apparel (some of those check trousers he wore were verging on the felonious), Nicklaus was even less of a shining example of sartorial elegance in his early days on the US Tour. In the 1962 US Open, which he won, Nicklaus dazzled Oakmont by wearing "a pair of twelve-dollar retail pants, iridescent olive-green-blue like the belly colour of a bluebottle." Or so he was told; it transpires that the great man is colour-blind.

Like the famous story of George Washington and the chopping down of the tree ("Father, I cannot tell a lie"), Nicklaus likes to recall how his father stopped him throwing clubs. When he was eleven, the young Jack, playing with his father tossed a club in the general direction of a bunker into which he'd hit his ball. "Jack, you ever act like that again and it'll be the last round of golf you will ever play," said Dad. "And do you know? I have never thrown a golf club since," says Jack. Ahem . . . well, not until the 1995 Open at St Andrew's when he took a 10 at the fourteenth on the first day and threw his club (or did it just slip?) in disgust at his performance.

Nicklaus never needed motivation to win any one of his 18 "Professional" Major championships, he was always "up" for the Majors. But when he came to Augusta in 1986, it was six years since he'd won his last Major. He was highly affronted by an article by Atlanta Constitution journalist Tom McCollister which gratuitously suggested that he was "washed up". He used the article as a spur to win his last Major. When he went to the press tent for the post-presentation interviews the first thing he asked was, "Where's Tom McCollister?" When the guilty party presented himself he grinned and said, "Thanks, Tom!" McCollister, nothing daunted, later threatened to write a piece for his paper on how he had won the Masters for Jack Nicklaus.

Nicklaus spends much of his time nowadays involved in golf course design but golfers would need to beware of one of his creations, at the Old Works, Anaconda in Montana. It's built on a former rubbish tip. The site was a dump for the refuse from an old copper mine. OK so far, but hardly fatal. Except that one of the materials used for extracting the copper was arsenic, and the soil in the area has above-average levels of the toxin. Not a good place to take a divot.

## Greg Norman

Norman holds two records neither he or anyone else would want. He has achieved the "54-Hole Grand Slam". In 1986, he led in all four Major Championships going into the final round. He won only one, the British Open at Turnberry. Jack Nicklaus overtook him at Augusta, Raymond Floyd won the US Open and Bob Tway dramatically holed out from a bunker at Inverness to win the PGA. He also shares with Craig Wood the dubious "Grand Slam of Play-off Defeats". Larry Mize beat him at the second tie hole in the 1987 Masters, He lost a three way play-off in the 1989 Open at Troon (Mark Calcavecchia took the title), Fuzzy Zoeller beat him in the 18-hole play-off for the 1984 US Open and Paul Azinger took the 1993 PGA Championship from him in another sudden death play-off. Of course he also holds the distinction of having blown the biggest 54-hole lead (six shots) in the last round of the US Masters at Augusta, in 1996.

The Australian met his fellow countryman Wayne Grady in the final of the World Matchplay championship in 1990. Neither played very well, but Norman won the title on the second tie hole. Afterwards Grady commented to the press, "I played crap, he played crap, he just out-crapped me."

At the Kemper Open in 1995, Norman was in contention before an unwise shot at the 17th hole in the final round (he hit his ball into the water) knocked him out of the final shakeup. Watching the shot disappear under the ripples, CBS sports announcer Ben Wright commented, "I guess Norman has just found another way to lose a tournament." The Australian, when he heard the remark while watching a replay, didn't take kindly to it and later tackled and upbraided Wright about it very publicly. Wright, upset at this attack on him, reported the incident to his executive producer, Frank Chirkinian, a personal friend of the Australian but a staunch defender of his staff against all comers. In a sometimes heated telephone conversation with Norman, during which certain Anglo-Saxon expletives were exchanged, Chirkinian demanded that Norman apologise to Wright. His parting shot was calculatedly below the belt. "Greg, you could win at Augusta next year by ten clear shots and no one would see you . . . if you never got on camera." Wright and Norman made it up and he and Chirkinian are still friends. Not that the Executive Producer would deliberately have followed other players if Norman was about to win his first Masters . . . !

### Christy O'Connor

During the 1963 Canada Cup (now the World Cup), Christy O'Connor was one of Ireland's representatives. He was teamed up with Jimmy Martin for the event at St Nom La Breteche in Paris. The night before one particular round had been an excessively jolly and festive one for Christy and had resulted in a breakfastless dash to the first tee to be in time for his start. Just before he drove off, he was seen in earnest conversation with a friend, and when he stood up on the tee he blazed his opening drive down the right-hand side of the fairway into some trees. "Everybody thought I had hit a bad shot," he recalled later. "But what they didn't know was that my man was standing in the trees with coffee and a hair of the dog." O'Connor went on to shoot a 68.

Stories abound about Christy, some true, some false. For what it's worth CBS commentator Ben Wright tells a story about a bizarre encounter with O'Connor at Royal Birkdale in 1965 at the Open championship. Wright, who was then a correspondent with the *Financial Times,* checked into work early and wandered into the locker room. There he beheld "Himself" in vest and trousers, shaving. Surprised at this, Wright asked Christy why he hadn't performed his ablutions at his hotel. The Irishman shrugged his shoulders and said, "I couldn't find it". He had been a guest at a party the night before and had taken on board sufficient alcohol to leave him befuddled, as a result of which he couldn't remember the name of the hotel where he was staying. Wandering around Birkdale in the small hours of the morning, he had racked his brain wondering where he might lay his head for a few hours. He ended up sleeping in a sand bunker beside the 9th green. Fortunately, it was a balmy night and he slept like a log. He hadn't lost his caddie's telephone number so he phoned the bagman and instructed him to bring shaving gear and some clothes. The experience, as always, didn't remotely faze the great man, who went on to finish joint second with Brian Hugget, two shots behind Peter Thomson.

### Arnold Palmer

In 1960, an irritating punter unwisely challenged Arnold Palmer to a high stakes game after he'd won the US Open at Cherry Hills. The challenger proposed a $500 Nassau ($500 dollars on each of the nines, and a further $500 on the outcome of the full 18 holes). In 1960, $1,500 dollars was a lot of money. Palmer, who had not encouraged the punter, declined as politely as he could, pointing out that he was flying to Europe the following day. The would-be hustler was scathing, loudly and boorishly informing his companions that Palmer had no bottle. This enraged Palmer sufficiently for him to offer a counter-challenge. He would postpone his European trip by a day and they would meet the following morning. Palmer would give the amateur two shots . . . and the bet would be a $5,000 Nassau. The braggart backed down.

Palmer, on being asked once which players he had admired on television when he had been growing up, pointed out gently that, "When I was growing up they'd just discovered radio."

Playing in the Open at Troon one year, Palmer was searching nostalgically for a plaque which had been erected to celebrate a miraculous shot which had won him the 1961 Open Championship. But he couldn't find it anywhere. He turned to his caddie, Tip Anderson, and asked, "Say, Tip, do you know where that plaque is?" "Sure I do," replied Anderson amusedly. "It's 250 miles away. At Royal Birkdale."

Palmer once overshot the famous 17th green at Pebble Beach and his ball ended up in the sea. CBS commentator and former US Open champion chanced by as Palmer considered his options. "Where do you think I should drop?" Arnie asked the announcer. Venturi looked out to sea. "How about Hawaii?" he ventured.

"Arnie's Army" was a sixties golf phenomenon matched only by teenybopper hysteria over the Beatles. It was said that, when Arnie hitched up his trousers, women in his galleries (and there were hundreds) would swoon. But no fans are more devoted than Howdy Giles, a dentist who did some extraction work on the Great Master and made a ball marker out of the gold taken from Palmer's tooth. (More on Howdy in the "Eccentrics" chapter.) Then there is the other enthusiast, a British journalist who collected Arnie's divots on his British visits for years, brought them all back home and planted them in his own garden. He now has a lawn composed entirely of Arnie's sods.

## Harvey Penick

Fame came late in life to Harvey Penick, author of the best-selling *Little Red Book,* a compilation of his jottings and thoughts from a lifetime devoted to thinking about and teaching the game of golf. Penick, in his days as coach at the University of Texas, helped develop the careers of Tom Kite, Ben Crenshaw and Davis Love, among others. He was already in his nineties when his book, written in collaboration with Texas writer Bud Shrake, brought his name to the attention of a wider public. He died in April 1995 and, as has been recorded elsewhere, his spirit guided Ben Crenshaw to an emotional Masters win that year. Penick was untutored in many of the ways of the world, particularly when it came to business. Shrake did all the negotiating, through his agents, with the publishers of *The Little Red Book,* Simon and Schuster. The publishers, as is customary, agreed an advance on potential royalties and Shrake contacted Penick to give him the good news that his share of the advance would be $85,000. Penick was aghast. "Bud," he croaked. "I'll never be able to raise that kind of money."

## Gary Player

Player was entitled to harbour a grievance against autograph hunters. On one occasion, after he finished a practice round at the Congressional Country Club he was surrounded by a group of them who, in their anxiety to get his signature, pushed him into a lake.

Perhaps it was some animosity related to this incident, or just his enthusiasm for physical fitness, which prompted Player to upbraid a young autograph hunter about his physical condition. The rather corpulent young man proffered his programme to Player during a Seniors event and, instead of getting a signature, got a health tip. "Your parents won't tell you because they love you," Player informed the astonished fan, "but you are fat and you are going to die if you don't stop eating animal fat and start exercising." Subtle!

## Nick Price

While resident in Zimbabwe (or Rhodesia, as it was then), Price was drafted into the Rhodesian Air Force to fight against the forces of black insurgency which eventually took over the government of the country from Ian Smith's regime in the 1980s. Price, much to his relief, never had to fire a shot in anger. In later years he often avoided questions about his military service by claiming that he had tried to get out of the military by telling the authorities that he had a skin disease. "When they asked me what was wrong with my skin, I told them bullets went through it."

## Chi Chi Rodriguez

The teak tough and tiny Rodriguez is noted for his sense of humour and his wisecracks. But he also has a temper and, after a bad sand shot in the 1993 Las Vegas Senior Classic, he threw his sand wedge away in disgust. A spectator picked it up and, to the amusement of the crowd approached Rodriguez and offered to buy it from him for $50. To their surprise, instead of repossessing it, Rodriguez agreed to the sale. Later in the round, an approach shot to the eighteenth finished in a greenside bunker and, as Rodriguez pondered his diminished options he noticed the young man who had bought his wedge amongst the crowd. "Hey, you," he called out. "I wanna rent that wedge for a minute". The new owner obliged, a deal was struck and Rodriguez proceeded to hit a forty-yard sand bunker shot straight into the hole for a closing birdie. Getting out of the bunker, he handed the fan back the wedge and the dollar rental they had agreed on.

## Doug Sanders

Doug Sanders was one of the most colourful players in the professional game. For "colourful" read "downright gaudy". By his own account the two most frequently asked questions on the American Tour when he was in his heyday were, "What did Arnie shoot?" and "What's Doug wearing?" The Imelda Marcos of professional golf admits to owning 400 pairs of golf shoes, most in the sorts of colours and shades which would have him banned from the more exclusive clubhouses. He also owns 200 pairs of trousers to match the shoes and an untold number of shirts and sweaters.

Sanders loved the crowd and was very "giving" in his relationship with fans. On one occasion, however, his availability cost him dearly. Halfway through the 1967 Pensacola Open he led the field by four shots. He'd carded a 67 in the second round and so was in an expansive mood when he came off the 18th. Immediately he started signing autographs. About the only thing he *didn't* sign was his scorecard. He was disqualified and Gay Brewer won the tournament.

Sanders' reputation as a hell-raiser would make Oliver Reed's exploits look like the life of a Trappist monk on assignment in a convent. Brian Barnes, no mean imbiber himself before he abjured the hard stuff for a life devoted to Seniors golf, once told journalist Derek Lawrenson that, "It was Doug who taught me to drink on the course. I remember the first time I played with him and even his golf towel seemed to smell of alcohol. I asked him about it and he told me he soaked it in vodka. My only vice was drink, but he had them all."

One of his other vices was a weakness for women. He was known to chat up attractive females in the gallery as he played. The price he paid for such activities was best summed up by the man himself when he politely asked a young woman to step out of his line as he prepared for a putt, "because I do have an alimony payment to meet every month."

## Gene Sarazen

In 1980, the then Open Champion Seve Ballesteros famously was disqualified from the US Open when he turned up late for his tee time. Rules, he was told, were rules, and no exceptions could be made. But that wasn't the case when Gene Sarazen showed up *two hours late* for the 1922 USPGA championship. He had been playing an exhibition match in Columbus, Ohio and had completely forgotten that he had to get to Pittsburgh for the PGA, being staged in Oakmont. He was reminded by a complete stranger who seemed to be more aware of the golfing calendar than was Sarazen. He managed to catch the last train for Pittsburgh by jumping on to it as it pulled out of the station. The train experienced delays and was an hour and a half late getting into Pittsburgh. The PGA, not wishing to stage their event without Sarazen, the reigning US Open champion, allowed him to play anyway and he duly won the championship.

## Sam Snead

Sam Snead is famous for his silky swing and his record number of USPGA tournament victories. But he was also renowned for his tightness with the large amounts of money that he won during his career. His fellow pro Jimmy Demaret began the rumour that Snead had his money buried in tins in his backyard. Arnold Palmer maintained that the gophers in Snead's yard subscribed to *Fortune* magazine. Snead insists that, after the crack got into the papers, a few times he arrived home one night to find someone in his back garden with a torch and shovel.

Snead's manager, the impresario Fred Corcoran, liked to encourage the impression that the young Snead was a talented hillbilly. He was instrumental in spreading the rumour that Snead had learned to play golf as a barefoot youngster. Once he actually persuaded Snead to play without shoes in an exhibition match. Snead did so for two holes, birdied one and almost birdied the other.

Snead's "love-hate" relationship with the British Open is discussed elsewhere but once, when he was asked why he hadn't defended his 1946 title (which he won at St Andrew's) his response was that "I didn't like the food over there."

The great man never managed to win the US Open but that wouldn't account for the unintentional put-down he experienced at the hands of an unknown spectator who watched him hitting balls alone on the practice ground. After a while, the spectator (he certainly couldn't be described as a "fan") asked Snead, "Hey, when do the pros get here?" Snead's riposte was unusually mild. "I don't know," he replied. "I was just sent out here to break in the course."

## Sam Torrance

The engaging Scot is one of the most popular players on the European Tour. Despite his propensity for suffering bizarre injuries (a broken toe while sleepwalking, for example), his game seems to have got better with age. But in 1993 he passed a remark which quickly rebounded on him. It was at the 1993 Dunhill Cup at St Andrew's. Torrance, playing for Scotland, was approaching the shortest par-4 on the course, the 316-yard 12th. There was a following wind and many of the players were driving the green on this particular day. Torrance was incredulous when he was told by journalist Alan Fraser of the *Daily Mail* that the Swede Joakim Haeggman had just notched up an 8 on this seemingly innocuous hole. Torrance remarked, not unjustly, "How can you make an 8 on a hole like this?" He then hooked his drive into a clump of unplayable gorse. He played a provisional, which ended up in much the same position. He couldn't find the first ball, losing two strokes and then discovered the second in an unplayable lie. Taking another penalty, he got it on to the green in five and then three-putted for . . . an 8. As he walked to the thirteenth tee he passed Fraser and observed, "I suppose that's how you make an 8."

## Lee Trevino

Playing in a pro-am once, Trevino, having already driven, stood and watched his three amateur partners hit off. One by one they sliced their shots, each hitting to precisely the same spot, a distant copse of trees. "What's over there, a nudist colony?" he inquired.

In 1975, Trevino was struck by lightning. As he described it himself, there was a thunderous crack, like cannon fire, and suddenly he was lifted a foot and a half off the ground. "Damn, I thought to myself," he insisted afterwards, "this is a hell of a penalty for slow play." Later, when asked what he would do if he was caught on a course during, a lightning storm again, he suggested that he might hold up a 1-iron for protection. Why? Because "not even God can hit a 1-iron."

Trevino, underneath all the bonhomie and wisecracks is, according to many accounts, a very private man with quite a dark and sombre outlook on life. Hence a statement attributed to him which puts golf in perspective. "If you three-putt today," he observed, "you might be around to three-putt tomorrow. When you stop three-putting, it means you're under the grass looking up."

### Harry Vardon

Vardon, one of the greatest golfers ever, was probably one of the worst putters in the professional game he dominated. He often missed putts from two feet and frequently froze over the shortest of tap-ins. He once observed, "There are many ways of performing the operation successfully. I can claim, however, to be in a position to explain how not to putt. I think I know as well as anybody how not to do it."

Vardon was involved once in a challenge match with a long-hitting opponent. On the day of the match, some of his supporters sympathised with him because of his adversary's length. Vardon inquired, "How long is the first hole?" "350 yards," was the reply. "Can he drive the green?" asked Vardon. "No!" "Well, I can get there in two," Vardon pointed out.

Vardon could be an engaging personality when he wanted to be, but his magnanimity didn't often extend to his opponents. Bobby Jones used to tell the story of playing alongside his idol in the 1920 Open. Vardon was fifty, Jones a boy of eighteen. At one hole on the Inverness course in Toledo, Jones opted to pitch rather than run a ball on to the surface of the green. He bladed the shot and sent it scurrying through the back. Jones was mortified to have played such a juvenile shot in front of the master. Seeking some sort of empathy from the Great Man, he said, "Mr Vardon, have you ever seen a shot worse than that?" The only response he got was a blunt "No"!

## Phillip Walton

Professionally Philip Walton never quite lived up to the promise he had shown as a successful Walker Cup player until the 1995 season, when he won two tournaments and made the Ryder Cup squad. He had had some bad years as a professional so, when he won his second tournament in 1995, the English Open, the affable and highly popular Walton was inundated with very genuine expressions of delight and congratulations by hundreds of fans. It got to the point where, in the days after his victory, he could hardly move without somebody patting/thumping him on the back or shaking him by the hand. In the end he almost wished he hadn't won and was heard to comment to an understanding soul, "I've a pain in my arse being happy all the time."

Walton is a down-to-earth individual who has little time for the "isms" or "ologies" which regularly infest the game. This goes, in particular, for his approach to sports psychologists. On that subject he used to be agnostic but is now a complete atheist. He visited one mind guru, John Allsop, on just one occasion but appears to have had a deleterious effect on the psyche of the psych. "I felt he couldn't wait to get rid of me," Walton told Dermot Gilleece of *The Irish Times*. "And any time he has seen me since then, he always seems to go out of his way to avoid me."

## Tom Watson

The "Huckleberry Finn" of modern golf had his values challenged by the Kansas City Country Club where he had learned his golf. Watson, whose wife Linda is Jewish, had been of the opinion that the club members were anti-Semitic and wouldn't admit Jewish members. When a popular leader of the local Jewish community was turned down for membership, Watson quietly resigned his membership. Local and national media, however, picked up on the story and it became a *cause celebre*, to the great embarrassment of Watson and, even more so, of the Kansas City Country Club.

# CHAPTER TEN

## The Back Page and the Box

*Tales from the Fourth Estate*

### Scribes

It could never happen today, of course (?) but in the 1890s there were still some newspaper subs and editors who knew nothing about golf. In 1899, for example, when Harry Vardon won the Open, Jack White came from behind with a great 75 to take second place. This news was conveyed to one London newspaper by telegraph but lost something in the translation to the printed page. The sub who got hold of the story was clearly more familiar with athletics than golf, because the headline he wrote claimed that White had dashed around the golf course in 7 minutes and 5 seconds.

To illustrate that golf writers can sometimes actually play the game, it is worth mentioning a match between the great writer Bernard Darwin, of *The Times,* who was also an excellent golfer, and the great golfer Horace Hutchinson, who was also an excellent writer. The two men met in the fifth round of the 1910 British Amateur (Hutchinson had already won the event twice). All square after 18 holes, the match went to the nineteenth where Hutchinson drove his ball out of bounds. He tried again and drove his second out of bounds also. He managed to keep his third shot on the course. A lesser player might have conceded but Hutchinson waited to see what would happen to Darwin. The writer teed up and . . . drove out of bounds. He then repeated the error off his second ball before finally driving a *third* OB. Distraught, he then conceded the game to Hutchinson.

Darwin travelled to the USA to cover the first Walker Cup in 1922. But he ended up captaining the side when Robert Harris, the original captain, burned his hand on the sea voyage to the US and was unable to play. Darwin also played in the match, in a tie with William Fownes, winner of the 1910 US Amateur. Three down after the first three holes, Darwin rallied to win the match.

The often obsequious relationship between golf writer and major international golfer is a relatively new phenomenon. There was a time when writers like Leonard Crawley and Bernard Darwin were welcomed in clubhouses as "gentlemen", while the professional golfers were excluded on the grounds that they were "players". (Excuse the cricketing parlance.) On one occasion, Darwin was having a conversation with a club member during a professional tournament when he was approached by Max Faulkner. The golfer attempted to speak to the "hack", only to be rounded on and told, "Don't interrupt, Faulkner. Can't you see I'm talking to a gentleman?"

Darwin certainly followed the rituals of the "gentleman" when covering golf tournaments. One of these was strict observance of the great British tradition of afternoon tea, to be taken precisely at four o'clock. Covering one tournament, he actually informed his readers that "since the hour was four o'clock I had to leave Von Nida still on the course."

Oftentimes journalists must grow into the title "Golf Correspondent", as the reasons for their appointments may leave something to be desired. Consider this story, for example. Darwin had to be replaced by *The Times* management. Peter Ryde was a lowly hack who worked on the letters page of that august and noble publication. He used to play a round of golf some mornings at Royal Wimbledon before he went into work in the afternoon. One day, he happened to be in the line of sight of the sports editor when he and the editor himself were pacing the corridor. The editor was inquiring of his underling who they should choose to replace Darwin. As an earnest of how high the appointment of a new correspondent rated in the mind of the sports editor, he looked up, spotted Ryde and exclaimed triumphantly to the editor, "He plays golf, let's give him a go."

The US President, Warren G Harding, was playing a round one day with the writer and journalist Ring Lardner. Harding was an impatient type and, as President, was used to being deferred to. So on the first hole he claimed the honour, drove off and, without waiting for any of his partners to hit, walked off down the fairway in pursuit of his ball. Lardner, intrigued and annoyed by this behaviour, responded in kind. He didn't wait for the President to get out of range before launching into his drive. It sliced spectacularly before connecting with the branch of a tree which came down on the head of the sheltering President. As he approached his ball and the waiting Harding, who was clearly expecting some sort of apology, Lardner merely observed, "I was doing all I could to make Coolidge President."

The Open Championship at St Andrew's in 1995 was led, at halfway, by a Japanese player, Katsuyoshi Tomori. It was the first time a Japanese had led the tournament after 36 holes. Tomori hadn't a word of English, so his press conference looked like being an interesting affair until an interpreter was rounded up to translate. The problem was that the interpreter had only a slight acquaintance with English himself. One exchange between a member of the press and the interpreter went as follows:

Hack: What do you think of St Andrew's?
Trans: He has no woz!
Hack: Sorry?
Trans: He has no woz!
Hack: Come again?
Trans: He has no woz to express how he feel about St Andlews.

Four British journalists over in the USA for the 1994 US Open at Oakmont decided to play a round in the Latrobe club, which is owned by Arnold Palmer. Stopping at the ninth to wet their parched whistles, they were recognised by Arnie's wife Winnie, a frequent visitor to Britain. "Put those drinks on my tab," she told the attendant, before adding, "and put my tab on Arnie's tab."

During the four-ball/foursomes days at the 1995 Ryder Cup at Oak Hill in Rochester, New York, the Italian player Costantino Rocca arrived in the press tent to be questioned by the *paparazzi*. Rocca's command of the English language is basic, passionate but ungrammatical. One of the first questions he was asked was "Is the language barrier ever a problem in the four-ball or foursomes format?" He clearly couldn't understand the question, which was then translated for him by an interpreter. "No," he replied, flashing his habitual broad grin.

Rocca, one of the most amiable players on the tour, was once approached by a reporter. "Costantino," he said, "Can I ask you a couple of questions?" "OK, two questions," replied the Italian. Susprised at being taken so literally, the scribe responded, "Two questions?" "That's one question. What's the second one?"

The lack of inhibition of Australians is illustrated by an example from CBS broadcaster Ben Wright who, in 1970, travelled Down Under, along with Tony Jacklin and Arnold Palmer, to a Dunlop-sponsored event there. Jacklin and Palmer were contracted to Dunlop, hence their appearance. Wright went along in his role as Golf Correspondent of the *Financial Times*. Palmer and Jacklin were not best pleased to be there, especially as they were expected to make a number of appearances at social events and functions to represent Dunlop. The least attractive of these was one given by the Queen's representative the Governor-General of Australia, Sir John Kerr (who later achieved notoriety by sacking Labour Prime Minister Gough Whitlam). Wright accompanied Jacklin and Palmer to the function (from which they could not escape), and the two men whined all the way to the Governor's Mansion in the limousine sent to collect them.

Both agreed to remain only until a barely decent period had elapsed before pleading early tee times to cover their departure. As it transpired, the function lived down to their worst expectations. The youngest guest appeared to have arrived with Captain Cook himself and the two golfing greats were on the verge of making their feeble excuses and leaving when a spectacularly attractive blonde woman made a grand "entrance" and, suddenly, the evening didn't look so dull after all. The lady in question would go on to great fame in a couple of lucrative marriages but, at the time, was the wife of an

Australian Cabinet minister. Our three heroes, Wright included, fell over themselves in their efforts to make her feel at home (she already was, they weren't). All three managed to surround her when they sat down to dinner, Palmer and Jacklin on either side, Wright banished to the opposite side of the table. The meal progressed convivially as the three men vied to be the most brilliant conversationalist. Then, without warning, the elegantly-clad woman rose about six inches from her seat, impressing Wright with the profundity of her décolletage and, turning to Jacklin and Palmer, said, "Sorry, boys, I've got to let one go." With that, she broke wind loudly and uninhibitedly. According to Wright's account, never was the ardour of three men frozen more rapidly.

When *Daily Mail* golf correspondent Michael McDonnell claimed in an article that the "Vardon" overlapping grip had not, in fact, been developed by Harry Vardon but by a contemporary amateur, John Laidlay (Amateur champion 1889 and 1891), he incurred the wrath not only of the Vardon family but of the descendants of JH Taylor, who had also used the grip as opposed to the then popular "palm" or "baseball" grip. Taylor's son, Jack, insisted that his father had developed the grip, and not Vardon. Then a letter came from a distant relative of Vardon's claiming that McDonnell had "blackened his name". McDonnell learned the lesson of the historian, never to assume that sufficient time has passed for properly marshalled and presented facts to be uncontroversial.

The normally fulsome and quotable David Feherty gave a brief and pithy response to a question from golf correspondent David "Dai" Davies once. The question posed was, "Is there a good reason for European success at the Masters?" The considered response from Feherty was "No!".

How about this for a wonderful piece of advertising copy? A campaign writer for the American equipment manufacturer Founders Club, in attempting to publicise the firm's Dart series of wedges dreamed up the slogan, "If the grooves were any bigger they would be illegal." Shortly afterwards . . . you guessed it . . the clubs were declared illegal.

That most excellent of golf writers the late Peter Dobereiner (who once wrote scripts for *That Was The Week That Was*) came up with the definitive word on Bernhard Langer, a thoroughly pleasant if somewhat intense man who just happens to take too much time to play a round of golf. Dobereiner asked, "Why does Langer linger longer on the golf course than anyone else?"

Post-tournament press conferences must surely take some of the glow of victory from the winner. They can be tedious affairs with a seemingly endless stream of questions. But they are a distinct improvement on the preliminary press conferences which tournament favourites and low scorers must endure after almost every round they complete. On those occasions journalists tend to wander in and out of the room and questions are often repeated. Ben Hogan, never noted for his patience, once snapped at reporters after a round at Augusta, "One day a deaf mute will win this thing and you guys won't be able to write a word."

## Broadcasters

In the days before he became a famous TV voice, the great Henry Longhurst was one of the pioneer radio golf commentators. (He much preferred TV where, he always averred, if your mind went blank you could insert "brilliant flashes of silence" without anybody thinking you'd gone off the air.) In the early days of radio, equipment was heavy, awkward and primitive. Because of its lack of mobility, during one early broadcast of the semifinals of the British Amateur at Hoylake, Longhurst and his party of two sound engineers/pack-horses were deposited on a knoll beside the fifth fairway where they could see the action on two holes. The signal for Longhurst to begin his commentary was the lowering of a handkerchief by another sound engineer on the roof of the clubhouse.

Before the signal came, the first semifinal had already passed. The second was almost through before the white flag was dropped and Longhurst was under starters order's. By the time he began, the players had finished the hole and he had nothing left upon which to commentate. Unable to move from the knoll and required by the exigencies of broadcasting to say something . . . anything, Longhurst merely recreated the play and did a superb commentary on the action which had already concluded, laced with references to the beauty of the surroundings and the very wonder of it all. This went on for the required ten minutes, at which point Longhurst handed over to another commentator elsewhere on the course. He then took himself back to the clubhouse expecting to be patted on the back for his resourcefulness, only to be met by the shamefaced hankie-waving engineer who informed him that, "We had to fade you out after a minute or two, technical hitch, sorry."

Covering one Walker Cup match at St Andrew's for BBC TV, Longhurst was placed in a commentary position by the "Loop", where the holes cross each other, making it difficult to identify which player is playing which hole. Conditions were grim, with the howling wind making players and spectators uncomfortable at ground level and causing untold torment for the BBC crew perched high above the fairway. Slowly Longhurst began to freeze to death. The advancing hypothermia was not abated by any stirring home performances. The British and Irish team was being annihilated. As he grew colder and sorrier for himself, the Great Voice's efficiency and enthusiasm diminished considerably. At one point he found himself shivering in silence and looking at a blurred monitor, wondering why there was no commentary on the play. Slowly it dawned on him. He was supposed to be providing the commentary.

Golf viewers, as the compiler of this modest volume can attest from bitter experience, can be sticklers (dare I say "pedantic"? Probably not!). Once, when Longhurst was doing a commentary on a play-off for the British Open between Peter Thomson and Dave Thomas, a doctor rang in asking the producer to inform the veteran commentator that "There is no "p" in Thomson."

BBC commentator and former pro Clive Clark was the victim of a spectacular misprint when his name was revealed to the crowd on the first tee of the Los Angeles Open by an American announcer unfamiliar with him. He informed the fans that next on the tee was ". . . from London, England, Olive Clark."

Trial by TV is a relatively new phenomenon, but among its victims on the European Tour are Jamie Spence and Mike McLean. Both thought they had done enough to win tournaments, until TV coverage was used to identify rules infractions which caused them to be disqualified. At least, in Spence's case, it was after a third-round score in the 1993 Rome Open. A spectator saw him drop in the wrong place off a path. TV coverage confirmed that the spectator was right. But McLean thought he'd won the Dutch Open before TV pictures showed that he had improved his lie by moving the fronds of a plant near which his ball had lodged. Both should have penalised themselves and were disqualified for signing for the wrong score.

During the 1993 Ryder Cup at the Belfry, BBC cameraman Colin Hazelwood was in his customary position atop a TV tower more than 200 feet up. (In his spare time he's an aerobatic pilot – honest!) Contacted by a puzzled producer as to why he wasn't getting any shots from Hazelwood's camera, the cameraman begged to remind him that it was a misty day and to inform him that it was because he was above the level of the clouds.

The US Masters is one of the few golf tournaments where the TV network (in this case CBS) doesn't call the shots. CBS only pays Augusta National about a third of what the tournament could fetch on the open market. That is because the Masters wants to retain control over the televising of the event. One consequence of that is that CBS only carries four minutes of commercials every hour (half the normal amount), and they tend to be for "solid" commercial institutions like Cadillac and Travellers' Insurance.

For years, CBS commentator Gary McCord sailed close to the wind with some of his comments at the US Masters at Augusta. McCord's well-prepared, "off the cuff" jokiness was considered to be *infra dig* by many Augustans. The end finally came when McCord opined that the grounds staff at Augusta National didn't cut their ultra-fast greens, "they use bikini wax". This was too much for former winner Tom Watson, who wrote a letter of complaint to CBS telling them that the Masters would be all the better for the exclusion of McCord from the CBS team.

Watson was pushing against an open door as pressure came from CBS to dump McCord and although, initially, the network's executive producer Frank Chirkinian was prepared to stand by his man, when push came to shove McCord was launched off the edge of the cliff.

(The text of Watson's letter to Frank Chirkinian was as follows: "Dear Frank, 'They don't cut the greens here at Augusta, they use bikini wax.' Quote by G McCord, April 10th, final round of the 1994 Masters. Directed by Frank Chirkinian. He tried four of his computer-generated similes before he laid this terrible egg. It is sad that he so degraded the last telecast of Pat Summerall. He is the Howard Stern of TV golf and you should be ashamed, rather than champion his 'irreverent' behaviour. Get rid of him, now. Tom")

Another "McCord" (i.e. a well-prepared and professionally delivered piece of spontaneous wit) came at the 1994 Phoenix Open, where he said of one bad shot, "That's what we call a Lorena Bobbitt. A nasty slice".

This was not the first muscle-flexing exercise on the part of the Masters Organising Committee when it came to dictating policy at CBS. After one event the Committee had informed the network that it should withdraw Jack Whittaker as a commentator. His offence? No, he hadn't been selling pornography to past Masters in the Champions locker room or stealing cutlery from the restaurant, he had simply referred to a rather unruly section of the Masters crowd as "a mob". "Mobs" are unheard of at the Masters, so Whittaker had to go.

TV commentator Steve Melnyk was prone, as are the best of us, to the occasional broadcasting gaffe. In 1983, for example, during the Colonial Invitational Tournament he observed that, "Peter Jacobsen is in a position where a birdie will help him more than a bogey." He also said of Phil Mickelson during his highly successful amateur days "His future is ahead of him."

The great BBC Commentator Alex Hay tells this story against himself. He was in the commentary box, along with Peter Allis, for the Walker Cup in 1995 in Royal Porthcawl. The American amateur sensation Tiger Woods was playing an approach shot to the 18th green during one of the matches. The weather was spectacularly filthy in the way that links courses have of throwing everything at you. Woods was not having a great Walker Cup. As he hit his tee shot in the murky rainswept conditions, the BBC cameraman in a position on the fairway did his best to follow the shot but to no avail: he lost it in the driving rain as the droplets covered his lens. In order to shake the worst of the rain off he swung his camera about violently toward the cliffs which skirt the edge of the 18th. The gallery, which had also lost the ball in flight, noticed this emphatic movement and assumed that Woods had pulled the ball out of bounds. Like so many sou-westered lemmings, they dashed towards the cliff. The cameraman, seeing the movement of the crowd, assumed they knew where the ball had gone, so he zoomed in on the crowd staring down on to the rock-strewn beach below the cliff, among whom were official-looking individuals with marshals' armbands. Taking their cue, like the great professionals they are, Hay and Allis began to expostulate eruditely on the pickle into which Woods had plunged himself. "He'll never find it down there," Hay observed. Allis pointed out that finding the ball was not the issue and that the area was out of bounds anyway. The interchange continued in this vein.

Meanwhile Tiger Woods was striding, unnoticed, up the fairway, no doubt bemused by the deep semicircle of spectators and officials perched precariously on the edge of the cliff. As *they* continued to search for his ball on one side of the fairway, he moved to the other side where the ball lay in a ditch unobserved by all but a small number of spectators.

Another cliff story which didn't make it on to the TV screens, but materially affected the coverage of a golf tournament, took place in the 1970s during the Carroll's International Golf Championship at Woodbrook, near Bray. Play was proceeding as normal until the commentators began to run out of golfers to talk about. RTE's Fred Cogley realised that there was a hold-up of some kind around the fourteenth hole, which looks directly down on to the beach. He despatched an emissary to find out what was causing the delay and depriving the TV viewing public of golfers. Shortly after being despatched, the breathless gofer returned to inform Cogley that the delay had been caused by the golfers and caddies pausing to observe and offer vocal encouragement to, a happy couple making passionate love on the sand below in a rerun of the Deborah Kerr/Burt Lancaster scene in *From Here to Eternity*.

Ben Wright, the avuncular British golf writer and broadcaster who has worked for CBS Sports for the better part of a quarter of a century, suffered badly for comments he is alleged to have made about women golfers in 1995. He denied having made the comments, but was crucified by the American press anyway. He is reported as having described the LPGA in the USA as a "butch game" and as having observed that lesbianism hurts their tour. He then allegedly commented that women golfers are handicapped "by having boobs". CBS accepted his denial and kept him in the commentary booth, despite calls that he be sacked or suspended. Subsequently, however, he was forced to admit that he had indeed made the remarks attributed to him and CBS were forced to withdraw him from commentary duties.

In 1975, Wright almost didn't make it to the screen during the Western Open at the Butler National course in Chicago.

In his youth, before he became a golfing scribe and the cultured British voice of American TV golf coverage (he always handled the 15th and 16th at Augusta for CBS), he drove racing cars. Like all those addicted to this pursuit, he occasionally crashed them as well. During one dispute with a stationary wall he lost all his upper teeth, bar the front incisors. Rather than have them capped, for years he wore dentures instead. This is all by way of prologue to his favourite story against himself.

Wright had enjoyed a good night out and returned to his 16th floor room in his Chicago hotel in the early hours of Saturday morning. He was in jovial humour despite an annoying summer cough. Prior to turning in he paid a final visit to the bathroom but as he was flushing the toilet he was caught unawares by a volcanic cough which dislodged his dentures and sent them swirling down sixteen floors to the sump of the hotel's detritus. Thinking quickly he shoved his hand into the bowl after the disappearing dentures and instantly regretted it. He was almost sucked into urinary perdition himself and was relieved to disengage his arm before it was tugged from its socket.

Reflecting on his situation, he remained calm. Obviously he couldn't appear on camera or in the commentary booth with part of his face missing. He would simply ring his wife in North Carolina and ask her to get a spare set to him ASAP. He dialled and a sleepy, grumpy voice answered. Wright was unprepared for the sound of his own voice when he heard it. The pithy and pointed conversation went something like this:

"Dharlingh, I'b gop a pobbem wip by teep."

"Who is this?"

"Ip me. Ben. I'b lawped by teep."

"Are you drunk? Why are you ringing me at . . . five o'clock in the morning?"

"By teep. I flupped deb down de john."

"Go to bed, you drunk." End of conversation. She hung up.

Wright remained calm. If he couldn't get a spare set in time for the afternoon broadcast, then he would simply get back the set which had been eaten alive by the hotel plumbing. He rang the number for the hotel maintenance engineer. As best he could, through gums clenched tighter than the buttocks of a downhill skier, he explained his predicament.

When he'd finished there was a long silence at the other end of the line.

"Hello, hello, are you shtill dere?" he inquired anxiously.

"Yes, Mr Wright. I'm still here. I'm just not sure I'm hearing you right. Do you seriously expect me to go looking for a set of false teeth in the middle of two thousand tons of shit? And even if I did, and even if I found them, are you telling me you'd actually wear them again?" Then he too hung up.

The normally unflappable Wright was now becoming just a little bothered. It was 6.00 am. He hadn't had a wink of sleep and he was in a gummy situation. He waited for an hour and then did the only thing he could think of. He phoned the room of his executive producer, the small but monumentally imposing Frank Chirkinian.

"Frank, I'b losht by denshures."

"Christ, is that you, you stupid Limey bastard? What goddam bar are you in?" the gravel-voiced Chirkinian barked.

"Frank, Frank, bon't ham up. I'b ib by roob, jut along the corridor."

"Just get a goddamn taxi and be at the course for the rehearsal. OK? "

Wright's increasingly frantic and pleading tone finally convinced Chirkinian that his announcer was in difficulty.

"OK, meet me in the lobby in twenty minutes."

Wright did as bid. As he waited for Chirkinian to arrive, he watched his colleague Jack Whittaker at the reception desk, racked with embarrassment, trying to explain to the porter that he had (for the second time that week) left his car rental keys in the pocket of the trousers he'd sent out to be cleaned. As Chirkinian approached, Whittaker attempted to explain his predicament to the executive producer.

"Sorry, Jack. Ben's got first call this morning. Show him, Ben, smile!"

Wright obliged. Whittaker briefly forgot his own problems and whistled. "Can I get you a carrot?" he asked, in a reference to Wright's unfortunate resemblance to Bugs Bunny.

Chirkinian then took matters in hand. Miraculously, one of his associate producers, Chuck Will, had been bound for a Saturday dental appointment. Chirkinian arranged that Wright take his place. The dentist was the eloquently-named Dr Russell Fu. That orthodontic magician and his staff took an impression of the announcer's upper jaw and within three hours had produced a perfect set of dentures. The day had been saved. Wright would make it to the 3.00 pm rehearsal.

But Chirkinian wasn't finished. He decided that the camera rehearsal was payback time for the hassle which Wright had given him. As the CBS commentary team went through the holes they were covering on the back nine, it came to the Englishman's turn to do his piece to camera. Confidently displaying his brand-new teeth, he went through his routine. "I'm Ben Wright and I'll be covering the 15th hole. It's a 456-yard par five . . ."

At the end of everyone's spiel, the rehearsal was played back to give the announcers an opportunity to correct any fault or unnecessary foible. One by one they popped up in vision, but when it came to the 15th, instead of the handsome rounded features of Ben Wright making their appearance, a huge set of clacking teeth moved castanet-style in synch with the voiceover.

"I'm Ben Wright . . ." said the teeth. ". . . I'll be covering the 15th hole. It's a 456-yard par five . . ."

Not long afterwards, Wright acquired a brand-new set of capped teeth.

Frank Chirkinian's lack of political correctness is best illustrated by this tale. At a dinner function once, he was placed beside a Chinese woman with whom he was not acquainted. His opening conversational gambit was, "Pardon me, do you do laundry?" Unfortunately for Chirkinian, the woman's command of English was excellent. Fortunately for him she had a sense of humour.

Channel Four's 1994 *Cutting Edge* programme on Northwood Golf Club caused well-merited pandemonium when it was broadcast. The "fly on the wall" programme showed up all the bigotry, small-mindedness, snobbery and chauvinism which is part and parcel of far too many golf clubs. The board of the club allowed the cameras in and, according to Kate Woods, the programme producer, permitted it to be transmitted in its original version. "All agreed it showed Northwood as it was that autumn," she commented, when the reaction to the members of the club (not the programme – which was excellent) proved to be so overwhelmingly negative. "The club is open. There is no bar as to who should join the club. We've got Dr Shah, we've got a couple of coloured members. There's no bar, so long as you've got a reasonable income," was just one of the mind-numbing comments heard during the broadcast. That one was down to the vice-captain. Another choice remark of one of the male members was the thoroughly modern . . . "I fail to understand how women can turn up at nine o'clock in the morning and play golf. I know my wife couldn't. She's got to get the breakfast."

John Feinstein, in his excellent book *A Good Walk Spoiled* (one of two equally excellent tomes of that particular title), records how Curtis Strange was affected by the expanded coverage of golf on TV. Normally, broadcasts were limited to play on Saturday and Sunday in all but the most important tournaments. This meant frequent fines for Strange, whose temper and bad language were notorious. Cameras picked up the former while highly sensitive parabolic mikes brought TV viewers the latter. Then, with the growth of 24 sport cable and satellite TV stations, coverage was expanded to all four days and the mikes were live on the first two days as well. After his first fine under the new regime, Strange phoned a PGA official and enquired irately, "You mean to tell me I can't get away with 'goddammit' on *Thursdays* any more?"

Peter Alliss has been getting away with some outrageous idiosyncrasies in his BBC broadcasts because of the injection of that rare and elusive commodity, "personality". He has that wonderful quality of the elder statesman of not seeming to care what he says. For example, at the 1994 British Open, as Nick Price made his way down the 18th rather than talk about the Zimbabwean's performance, Alliss was thanking BBC viewers who had written to him. He took the gold medal for trivia when he conjured up one Reg Sparks, "who wonders if a Sister Woodburn, who nursed him in the war when the Turnberry Hotel was a hospital, was still alive and, if so, he sends her his love." Only Alliss would not have had his TV director screaming at him to shut up and get on with it, or would have blissfully ignored him anyway even if he had.

Tom Weiskopf managed a total of four second-place finishes in the US Masters but never contrived to win a green jacket. In 1986, in his new job as golf broadcasting analyst for CBS, he watched Jack Nicklaus, at the age of 46, win his sixth Masters. As he got ready to putt on the par-3 16th, another commentator asked Weiskopf what he reckoned Nicklaus might be thinking of at that time. Weiskopf snapped back, "If I knew what was going through Jack Nicklaus's head, I would have won this golf tournament."

The large and uninhibited Australian Wayne Riley was being interviewed after a round of the 1991 PGA Championship when, for some extraordinary reason, he was asked, "What do you do in your spare time?" Treating the question with all the deference it deserved, he shot back with, "Sex . . ." Then, as the interviewer's face went puce, realisation dawned and he inquired, "This isn't live . . . is it?" Too late!

The great golfer Byron Nelson appeared as an announcer in one of ABC's earliest golf broadcasts, where he was working as an expert analyst with one of the network's leading commentators, Chris Schenkel. During one of the early tournaments of the year, Schenkel referred to the extreme length of the player's drives and inquired of Nelson what was the reason for it. Nelson responded nervously, "Chris, the boys are hitting the ball longer now because they're getting more distance."

One of the BBC's Radio 5 commentators allowed his natural exuberance to get him into hot water with his beloved after the 1995 European Ryder Cup victory. When Phillip Walton sank the putt which won the Cup for Europe after they had trailed 9–7 going into the singles, Allan Green got a mite overexcited and carried away with the sheer joy of the occasion. Later that night he phoned his wife and began the conversation with, "What a day! Didn't think we had any chance, but we did it." His wife didn't want to know, she had only one thing on her mind. "Who was the woman you were kissing on the 18th green?" she asked, with, no doubt, a certain amount of asperity. Green was unabashed and asked that a total of four similar offences be taken into consideration. "It could have been Suzanne Torrance, Jane James, Trish Johnson or Helen Alfredsson." Later, when he discovered it had been Suzanne Torrance (the actress Suzanne Danielle), he made sterling efforts to get hold of a copy of the video.

To put the acquisition of rights to the Ryder Cup by Sky Sports into perspective, independent ratings experts estimate the audience for the final day of the 1995 Oak Hill event at 1 million viewers. The estimated audience for Radio Five Live's coverage was six million. (Sour grapes? Never!)

# CHAPTER ELEVEN

## *Potpourri*

*All the stuff that wouldn't fit anywhere else*

### *The Origins, History and Traditions of Goff, Gowff, Kolven and even Golf*

The Scots have the more compelling claim to having devised the game of golf, though there is a Dutch game which was played along frozen waterways in the Middle Ages which is occasionally proposed as an alternative precursor. (This is usually done to grig the Scots!) Should an Englishman wish to establish ownership, he might point to a golfer-like figure in a stained-glass window in Gloucester Cathedral dating from 1350, though this might be an anchorite with a staff flailing demons. The earliest documentary reference to the game comes from a law passed in March 1457 by the Scottish Parliament in which it is ordered that "goff be utterly cryit doune and not usit." Five hundred years later, the game of golf still exists, but where's the Scottish Parliament?

Other claimants to be "ye onlie begetter" of modern golf also exist. The Romans played a game called "paganica", featuring a leather ball stuffed with feathers. A similar French and Belgian game called "chole" can be traced back to the 12th Century. By the 14th century, the Dutch were playing the game of "kolven" which they still claim is golf's clearest antecedent, while at the same time the Chinese had invented "suigan". The French game of "jeu de mail" which became popular in England as "pall mall" may also have been a forerunner, but, as mallets were used and the object was to hit small targets over short distances, it is more similar to croquet.

159

The original rules of golf, "Articles and Laws in Playing Golf" (The Rules of the Gentlemen Golfers, 1744), numbered only 13 in total and basically insisted that, once the ball was put in play off the tee, it couldn't be changed and must be played wherever it lay, except in water and certain other hazards.

In 1593, John Henrie and Pat Rogie paid a stiff price for playing the sport they loved. No two-shot penalties or loss of stroke and distance here; they were imprisoned for playing golf when they should have been in Church. The charge sheet accused them of "Playing of the gowff on the links of Leith every Sabbath the time of the sermonses."

Prince Andrew is just the latest in a long line of British "royals" to have taken to the game of golf. The earliest was King James IV of Scotland, ignoring the law passed by his own parliament the previous century. His granddaughter Mary, Queen of Scots, was also an enthusiast before her handicap and head were chopped by her cousin Queen Elizabeth 1.

Though the Royal Burgess Golfing Society of Edinburgh claims to have been founded in 1735, the Honourable Company of Edinburgh Golfers (1744) is commonly acknowledged as having been the first club established. It was founded ten years before the more illustrious Saint Andrews Society of Golfers (1754), which in 1834 took its present name, the Royal and Ancient Golf Club of St Andrew's. The oldest English club was Royal Blackheath (1766), near London. According to tradition, golf was introduced to England in 1608. The first clubs established outside Britain were the Calcutta Golf Club of East India (1829) and the Royal Bombay Club (1842). The first golf club established in the western hemisphere was Canada's Royal Montreal Golf Club, founded in 1873. Although it is believed that golf was played in America during the colonial period, (introduced no doubt by independently-minded emigrant Scots to tweak the noses of the Redcoats), there is no documented proof of this. In 1888, the St Andrew's Golf Club of Yonkers, New York, was established. Some authorities say this is the oldest golf club in the US with a continuous existence.

Old Tom Morris and Willie Park, over a thirty-year period, played dozens of challenge matches for considerable sums of money. The matches also attracted a lot of gamblers anxious for a flutter on the outcome. The final match took place in Musselburgh in 1882. Park was two up with six to play when the referee suspended the game until the huge crowd settled itself. Some of the more fanatical supporters had been interfering with the balls of the players. As it happened, the game stopped outside a well-known local pub, Foremen's Ale House, so Morris and the referee decided to wait it out inside the premises. Park remained on the course, getting hotter and hotter under the collar as there was no sign of opponent or referee emerging. Finally, his patience snapped and he sent in an ultimatum that he would play out the remaining holes on his own and claim the match if Morris didn't resume. Old Tom just ignored him and ordered another drink. Park did as he had threatened and the two never played one another again.

Old Tom's son, Young Tom, was probably the best golfer of his own generation and a few on either side but his life was marked with tragedy. He won four Open championships in a row but, in September 1875, in the middle of a challenge match at North Berwick (he and his father were playing Willie and Mungo Park), a message came that his wife had given birth to their first child but was seriously ill. Before Young Tom could leave for St Andrew's a second message came to say that his wife had died. He only played two more rounds of golf, to honour commitments already made, and he died three months after his wife on Christmas Day 1875, the copious consumption of alcohol having played a major part in his demise.

The man credited with responsibility for bringing the game of golf to the USA is expatriate Scot John Reid. He asked a friend of his, Robert Lockhart, who was visiting Scotland, to bring back to the USA a set of clubs. He then laid out three golf holes at his home in Yonkers, New York and, along with some friends, formed the St Andrew's Golf Club in 1888.

The oldest golf club (the implement, not the society) in existence is believed to be one for which a record $1.25 million was paid in 1994. The club, an iron reputedly used by King James IV of Scotland in the early 1500s, was discovered at Hatton Castle. It is thought to have been purchased by the king from a bowmaker in Perth in 1502.

The first known reference to the making of a golf ball comes in a poem written in 1743 called "The Goff" by Thomas Mathison. It reads:

> *. . . the work of Bobson; who with matchless art*
> *Shapes the firm hide, connecting every part,*
> *Then in a socket sets the well-stitched void*
> *And thro' the eyelet drives the downy tide;*
> *Crowds urging crowds the forceful brogue impels*
> *The feathers harden and the leather swells.*

The expensive "featherie" ball, basically a leather pouch stuffed with goose feathers, tended to confine the game to a well-to-do elite or to those prepared to spend hours on the links looking for featheries despatched to oblivion by their unskilful owners. Even Allan Robertson, one of the earliest professionals and one of the most adept ball makers, could only manage to manufacture six balls a day. But in the middle of the 1840s, the Paterson family of St Andrew's made the game more accessible by patenting the "gutta-percha" or "guttie" ball. The material for the ball arrived wrapped around a statue from the East of the Hindu god Vishnu. Robert Paterson decided to experiment with this tacky, pliable material and ended up testing the result on the links. After a few false starts he got the formula right and the rest . . .

The great Scottish golfer Allan Robertson, regarded as the first professional golfer, was also the first golfing Luddite. When the gutta-percha ball made its first appearance, he stood to lose out in the making of the much more expensive featheries, so he waged a one-man war against the new invention. He bought up existing stocks of the balls and paid caddies to bring in any they found on the St Andrew's links. He then burned the lot! He also had a row with his apprentice, Old Tom Morris, about gutties and they parted company as a result.

The guttie itself was rendered obsolete in the late 19th century when the Haskell ball was devised by the Goodrich Tyre company of Akron, Ohio. It consisted of wound elastic thread covered by gutta percha. It was known as the "bounding Billy" in Britain because it was hard to control around the greens.

The idea of putting dimples in golf balls to improve and increase their flight was introduced by William Taylor in 1905. Many players, having discovered that their gutties went farther after they'd been used for a while, would hack up their balls before teeing off.

One technological development which went nowhere was also introduced in 1905. That consisted of filling balls with liquid. At different times experiments were tried with water, glycerine and even treacle.

The wooden golf tee was "invented" by Dr William Lowell, a New Jersey dentist. He originally made them from gutta-percha, but that proved unsatisfactory, so he switched to wood (white birch). The first tees were painted green but later changed to red and became known as "Reddy tees". Lowell made a considerable sum from his invention but, unfortunately, the patent he took out was inadequate to withstand the many slight variations which came on the market in the years after the use of tees became popular.

The trade in antique golfing artefacts is on an ever-rising graph. In 1995, an old "feathery" golf ball made by David Marshall of Leith between 1815 and 1830, and stamped with the initials of Dr RH Blaikie, a founder member of Luffness Golf Club, was sold at an auction in Edinburgh for £19,995. A lot of money for a golf ball, especially one that's guaranteed to take about 100 yards off your drives.

### Strictly Legal

In October, 1995, two Dublin-based golfers, both members of the Royal Tara GC in County Meath, fought out a legal case which could have had serious implications for all lovers of the sport. Michael McIlkenny, who plays off a handicap of 14, sued Peter Henshaw (8) for £30,000.

McIlkenny claimed that he had just replaced the flag on the fourth green at Royal Tara and had walked about twelve paces when he was struck by a ball hit by Henshaw from the fourth fairway and knocked unconscious. He further claimed that there had been no warning shout of "Fore" from Henshaw. McIlkenny, three years after the incident, was still suffering from tinitus (a ringing in his ears).

Henshaw disputed McIlkenny's version of events, alleging that McIlkenny had been well off the green and that, when he had pulled his shot left, he and his partners had all shouted "Fore". Therefore he disputed that he had been in any way negligent.

The Circuit Court Judge, Judge Spain, ruled that the preponderance of evidence suggested that Mr McIlkenny had, in fact, been further away from the green and closer to the fifth teebox than he imagined. Mr Henshaw had suffered a mishit and "he could not be held responsible for that" (which will be a great relief to all professionals and bad news for their caddies). While sympathising with the plaintiff for the injuries he had suffered, he dismissed the case as Mr Henshaw had, "behaved as a reasonable person would have done. In other words, he had taken all necessary precautions."

In 1994, 57-year-old John Buckingham of Sherwood Forest Golf Club was accused by two of his partners of cheating. Graham Rusk and Reginald Dove claimed that Buckingham had twice moved his ball with his foot and twice illegally replaced lost balls. He was playing in the Sherwood Open at the time, top prize £15. He took a case against the two men for defamation and lost. The exercise cost him £250,000 and also attracted far more publicity than the original allegations ever did. For example, if he hadn't taken the case he wouldn't even have been mentioned in this book.

A judgement by a Canadian Court in November 1993 has some interesting implications for golf courses with lots of water who are in the habit of retrieving balls from the depths, cleaning them off and selling them back to members through the pro shop. A court in British Columbia acquitted a teenager who had been caught redhanded late at night wearing a wet suit and carrying a bucket of balls recovered from one of their water hazards. The boy's lawyer argued that the boy was only doing what the course itself did in its contract with a local scuba diving club. The owners of the course, Mayfair Lakes Management Corporation, made a profit of almost $20,000 per annum on the arrangement. In his judgement, Judge Brian Davis acquitted the boy and then went even further. He ruled that the recovered balls were still the property of their original owners and that only one ball, a range ball with giveaway red stripes, actually belonged to the course. The defence lawyer in the case, David Tarnow, pointed out afterwards that "Golfers should realise that, even if they have the unfortunate experience of shanking one into a lake, they still have the right to reclaim it later."

In 1922, a taxi driver who had survived the first world war unharmed (mind you, he was chauffeur to a general and they were not renowned for putting themselves in harm's way) lost an eye when a ball was sliced from St Augustine's Links on to a road and through the window of his car. In the case of *Castle* V. *St Augustine's Links,* he was awarded damages against the club on the grounds that the hole was too near the road and therefore constituted a public nuisance.

A dispute over money between the operators of the Manor House Hotel in Moretonhampstead in Devon, and a local man, David Flitt, led to a bizarre car chase and a day in court.

Flitt, who seems to have intensely disliked people he described as, "fat bastards who play golf" decided to settle the argument with the hotel course by driving his Austin Montego over and back across the 13th and 14th greens (causing £9,000 worth of damage). He then nearly mowed down a four-ball before doing a spectacular handbrake turn on the 4th fairway. By the time he got back to the main road, he was being pursued by seven police cars and a helicopter. For his impromptu design renovations he was sentenced to eight months in jail, fined £500 and handed a two-year driving ban. (He has also been turned down for membership of Manor House Hotel GC.)

The 1995 Film Turkey of the Year was probably *To Wong Foo, Thanks for Everything, Julie Newmar,* a movie about drag queens which dragged, and then dived. But it had at least one interesting repercussion in that one of the characters, played by John Leguizamo, was a TV (transvestite, mother!) named Chi Chi Rodriguez. A certain member of the USPGA Senior Tour with a vaguely similar name (OK, so it's exactly the same, it's just that I instinctively act for the defendant in these cases) took grave exception and sued the makers of the film. The action was settled out of court for an undisclosed sum.

## Hustlers

In a recent poll of 362 readers in *Golf Digest* magazine in the USA 84% of those surveyed said that they bet on the outcome of their golf matches. The average wager they admitted to was $12.

Titanic Thompson was one of the great con men of golf. One of his favourite scams was to arm himself with a talented but unknown golfer as a "caddie". His particular favourite for a while was Ky Laffoon, who went on to become an excellent professional. Thompson would then antagonise potential opponents by deriding their game before delivering the punch line, "Hey, even my caddie could beat you." The irate opponent would accept the challenge, which would include a large side bet, and Laffoon would proceed to skin him alive with Thompson carrying the bag.

Lionel Platts and Hedley Muscroft, two English pros who had their best years in the 1960s and early 1970s, have always believed they were hustled by Christy O'Connor in Royal Dublin many years ago. That may well be the case, because it takes one to know one and Platts, in particular, was renowned for making and taking on all sorts of weird challenges. But on one occasion, O'Connor was due to play them at his home course and sought a fourth player in the locker room. He invited a very good local member, Noel O'Neill, to join them. O'Neill, because of a limp, did not look to be much a challenge to Platts and Muscroft, even accompanied by "Himself". However the two Irishmen boiled and peeled the English pros and gratefully took the money on offer. As O'Neill hobbled away, well content with the day's work, Platts, who figured he'd been hoist with his own petard, shouted after him, "You can drop the limp now."

Bobby Riggs, who died in October 1995 at the age of 77, was a championship tennis player who challenged Billy Jean King to a match in the 1970s when she was at the height of her powers. But he was scammed by a Las Vegas gambler by the name of Ted Lacey. Riggs played Lacey in a golf match for a large sum of money and was beaten. He knew he'd been hustled by an expert and afterwards, in the locker room loudly, proclaimed that, although he intended to pay up, he was aware that he had been "taken" by an expert. Lacey denied the allegation and, to establish his bona fides, offered to play Riggs the very next day at his own game for double or quits.

Riggs duly set up the tennis match, confident that he was going to get his money back. But Lacey had him on the tennis court as well, he was much younger and fitter than Riggs and made up in mobility what he lacked in comparative skill. It wasn't until the match had been won by Lacey, and Riggs had had time to think, that he realised the golf game had only been a tee-up for the real kicker . . . the tennis match.

Bing Crosby, a scratch golfer and a qualifier for the US Amateur Championship in 1940, had just lost a round with a friend, John Montague, in the Lakeside Country Club when Montague challenged him to an unusual game. "I can beat you with a shovel, a bat and a rake," he claimed. Crosby took up the challenge. Montague creased a drive down the fairway with his bat but his second shot finished in a bunker. Crosby was on in two, thirty feet from the hole, when Montague used the shovel to escape from the bunker. Crosby got down in two and watched as his opponent used the rake like a snooker cue and potted the ball for a four. Crosby had seen enough and headed back for the clubhouse.

The name Masashi Yamada is well known around Pebble Beach. In February 1995 Mr Yamada, surprisingly from Japan, was one of the privileged amateurs admitted into the AT&T Pro-Am (formerly the Bing Crosby). The format of the AT&T involves a professional and amateur better-ball score over four rounds. Good high handicappers are favoured. The expression "good high handicapper" should be an oxymoron but, in this day and age of well-protected handicaps, it often is not. Mr Yamada, a fifteen handicapper was playing with Bruce Vaughan, a professional unheralded even amongst the entries under "Vaughan" in any golfing *Who's Who*. On the basis of Vaughan's form, they shouldn't even have made the cut (he shot a 71 and 75 on the first two days – and added a 79 on the fourth. Thanks to some inspired play, for a "fifteen", from Mr Yamada the team, however, went 63, 65, 64. Then, on the last day of the Pro-Am section of the event, they shot a 59 and ran out winners by the entire Seventeen Mile

Drive. Naturally, there were those begrudging and suspicious individuals who questioned the honour of the Japanese. Indignantly he produced a handicap certificate, not from the Japanese Golf Association, but from the Mangijo Country Club near Tokyo. At first officials had no option but to accept his bona fides, despite the fact that he played more like a scratch golfer than a scrubber. Then someone probed a little more deeply and discovered that the Mangijo Country Club was owned by one Masashi Yamada, whose JGA handicap just happens to be a highly competitive *six*. Mr Yamada had, effectively, lopped nine shots a round off his team's better-ball score and got away with it.

Well, almost got away with it! He was immediately disqualified and asked to return the trophy. This he stoutly refused to do. Furthermore, rather than falling on his sword as other dishonoured Japanese were wont to do, he tried to gain entry into the pro-am run before the highly prestigious Visa Taihiyeo Masters in November, 1995. Now, there's a brass neck for you!

Rather illadvisedly, someone once tried to hustle the Chairman of Augusta, Jackson Stephens. Stephens has a personal fortune of $700 million and, like many of the super-rich, couldn't be bothered playing golf for high stakes because money doesn't mean very much to him any more. This annoyed a high roller with a mere $10 million of his own money who wanted to take on Stephens at cards for a worthwhile pile of cash. He antagonised the Augusta chairman so much that Stephens offered to cut cards for the high roller's entire fortune. The offer was declined!

In the interests of good neighbourliness, in the 1950s, the US State Department organised a tour by a number of professional golfers to sixteen South and Central American countries. The games played in Argentina were the occasion of some egregious gambling coups. At the San Andreas Country Club, for example, Sam Snead stood up to a fifteen-foot putt for a birdie in a match against a South American opponent on whom the local gamblers had clearly got very generous odds. The putt was one of fifteen feet, straight downhill and Snead hit it perfectly. To his consternation, just before it rolled into the hole the ball bounced backwards. On examining the area, the American noticed a circle of green coloured toothpicks guarding the approach to the hole, placed there by the local gamblers.

### Celebrities

The great American writer and humorist Mark Twain was the man who coined the much-used phrase "Golf is a good walk spoiled." (Good name for a book, that!) He may have formed this opinion of the game while accompanying a friend around a golf course. The friend was an exceptionally bad player, given to gouging large lumps of turf from the fairways whenever he managed to get his ball on the fairway. Afterwards, he asked Twain what he had thought of the course. "Best I've ever tasted," was the tart response.

Tim Brooke-Taylor, star of *The Goodies* and many other British TV and Radio comedy hits, once took no less than twelve shots to get himself out of a bunker at Effingham in Surrey while partnering Tommy Horton in the Harry Secombe Golf Classic. The comedian, who required all his sense of humour on that occasion, had actually managed to block it out of his mind and forget how many strokes he had taken in the sand until he was reminded of it years later by a spectator who had witnessed the earth-moving operation. Brooke-Taylor reckons that he was the inspiration for the famous *Hamlet* cigar ad which depicts the similar travails of a cigar-smoking hacker.

WC Fields was as enthusiastic a golfer as he was a drinker. His two hobbies were related. He once said, "It was golf that drove me to drink and, you know, I don't know how to thank it." He was asked whether he thought golf clubs for women were a good idea. "Yes," he responded, "If there's nothing else to hand."

Fields was once playing a round with Errol Flynn when he dislocated his knee. Flynn managed to help the bulky comedian back to the pro shop where the professional offered to pop the knee back in. Fields agreed without turning a hair. The pro warned him that it would be extremely painful.

"Don't concern yourself on that score, kind sir, pain means nothing to me," said Fields, though he was observed to take a long draught from the inevitable hip flask he carried with him at all times. The pro, seizing his chance, pushed the knee back into place abruptly. Fields howled with the pain of it all. The pro wasn't impressed. "You know," he offered, "my wife had a baby last week and she didn't make as much noise as you."

"Yes," retorted Fields, "but they weren't trying to push it back in, were they?"

Fields used to enjoy a tipple, indeed a number of tipples, while out on the course; especially when he was playing with his friend Oliver Hardy. But some of the more exclusive clubs around Los Angeles didn't approve. One of these was the Lakeside GC. So whenever Fields played with Hardy over that track he "played the course sideways". This meant hacking the ball *into* the trees and using the five minutes for ball-searching to wet his whistle.

The elitist Los Angeles Country Club was notorious for its snobbish attitude towards applications for memberships from Hollywood actors. One actor, lusting to join, is said to have sent the membership committee reviews of some of his performances to demonstrate that, whatever else he might be, he clearly wasn't an actor. Randolph Scott, one of the best golfing actors of his day, tried on many occasions to join but was always blackballed. Eventually he retired from acting and went into the oil business. He also moved from his Hollywood haunts to a house adjacent to the club. Then, in a masterstroke, he reapplied under his real name, George Randolph Crane and was accepted before the bulk of the members realised who he was. True to form, however, once his membership was an unhappy *fait accompli,* he was approached at a function by one of the club's board of governors who informed him that, "The board would really appreciate you doing your best to keep your old movies off TV."

The great romantic lead Douglas Fairbanks was a keen golfer and a good one, too. His work on the greens, however, did not match his work on screen. After one competition he was asked how he had performed. His response was a laconic "Like a motorboat; you know, putt . . . putt . . . putt."

The pint-sized actor Mickey Rooney enjoyed his game of golf. That is to say, he enjoyed *the* game of golf. More often than not, he failed to appreciate his version of it. When he was playing badly he tended towards displays of temper. He is reputed to have started one round with a brand new set of clubs and fared badly with them. Throwing a tantrum, Rooney tossed away the clubs after nine holes, bought a completely new set and played the back nine with *them*.

Bob Hope became the comical chronicler of the golfing misdeeds of two famous American politicians: Spiro Agnew, the man who would have succeeded Richard Nixon if he hadn't been forced out of office himself and Gerald Ford, the man who did succeed him. Hope emphasised the waywardness of both men, especially off the tee. Of Gerald Ford he said that the President had made golf a contact sport. Even the President himself played up the joke, noting in 1984 that he was improving at the game, "because I'm hitting fewer spectators." Hope maintained that in the case of Agnew he couldn't cheat on his score, "because all you have to do is look back down the fairway and count the wounded."

Jack Lemmon is one of the great unspoilt regions of modern pro-am golf. In all his years he has experienced not a whit of success. He has failed dismally, year after year, to make the cut for the Bing Crosby (now AT&T) pro-am. So bad is his golf that, in 1983, he was lying ten on one of the holes at Pebble Beach and still had a 35-foot putt. As he studied the line he turned to his caddie and asked, "How does this one break?" "Who cares?" was the bored response.

Lemmon, according to his frequent partner, Peter Jacobsen, would trade one of his Oscars just to make the cut at the AT&T. In his hilarious book about the US Tour, *Buried Lies,* Jacobsen describes what he describes as the Infamous Hanging Ice Plant Wedge Shot at the 16th at Cypress Point. This is one of the scariest holes in golf. It measures 215 yards to a peninsular green, the tee shot usually heading into a strong wind. Sixty feet below the precipitous cliffs are grey seals who merchandise "experienced golf balls". Often the pros will take a driver on the hole. Jacobsen and Lemmon were playing with Clint Eastwood and Greg Norman. Lemmon's drive was one of his worst of the day. Watched by two other groups on the tee (it's a notorious bottleneck), by a gallery of three to four thousand people, and by millions on TV he tickled it off the tee towards the right-hand cliff. It stayed aloft because of the presence of an ice plant, but it was perilously close to the edge of the drop. Undaunted, Lemmon, who is accustomed to being in positions the professionals only have nightmares about, climbed out to play the shot, egged on by Eastwood and watched with mounting concern by his partner, Jacobsen. As Lemmon addressed the ball, standing at an acutely dangerous angle, Eastwood grabbed him by the belt. Jacobsen grabbed Eastwood by the arm. Norman laid hold of Jacobsen and Norman's caddie Pete Bender manhandled his boss. Like the Breughel masterpiece depicting a group of blind men clinging in a line to each other this human golfing chain waited for Lemmon to swing his wedge, breaking most of the 90-odd rules of golf in the process. Lemmon somehow managed to get the ball on to the fairway to a huge ovation from the crowd. Pumping the air triumphantly, he now approached his third shot. He was seventy yards from the green, wedge still in hand. A few waggles later and he directed his third shot, a full shank, right into the Pacific ocean.

American rock band Hootie and the Blowfish are all madly keen golfers – which just shows how unhip they are. They have become regulars at Tour Pro-Am events. But they are not altogether hooked on the dignity of the game. They are unlikely ever to be invited to Augusta, after a stunt they pulled at one Tour event in 1995. They brought along bunches of condoms in packages which were disguised to look like tee packets.

Tennis player Ivan Lendl hasn't quite been able to translate his obvious athleticism into success on the golf course. In a 1995 pro-am, he hit five balls in a row into a water hazard. This prompted the dual-purpose observation from TV commentator Roger Maltbie that "Grass isn't his best surface."

Comedian Bill Murray is another US Pro-Am regular and his antics are much enjoyed and appreciated by many, but not, it would appear, by the former PGA Tour Commissioner Deane Beman who took issue with some of Murray's more juvenile pranks. This prompted the riposte from Murray, "It's a Nazi state out here . . . he's just another screwhead too big for his britches." So tell us how you feel, then, Bill!

Actor Christopher Lee, as well as being an excellent Dracula, is a pretty fiendish golfer. He's played to scratch and now plays off about eight. Once, playing in a pro-am with the scatological Wayne Riley, he caught the Aussie on a bad day. Riley had been hitting the ball all over the golf course, was intensely displeased with himself and was letting everyone know. However, he had managed to take his mind off his own game (a difficult feat for most pros) for long enough to admire the ability of his film star partner. While they waited for the course to clear in front of them at one hole, Riley asked Lee what age he was. Lee was somewhat taken aback but ventured the information that he was sixty-eight. To the delight of the crowd around the tee, (and to the secret satisfaction of Lee himself), Riley observed, "You know, for an old geezer you don't half give it a fucking whack."

US President Bill Clinton is a keen golfer (when he gets the time to play), and a member of the Chenal Club in Little Rock, Arkansas. But he is not allowed, choose his own golf clubs or even a favourite brand of ball. Instead, he must carry fourteen different branded clubs with him each time he plays and use a different type of ball at every hole, in case manufacturers might cash in on his particular choice.

## Golf and the movies

Gene Sarazen once flirted with the notion of a movie career. In the early 1920s (with three Major wins already under his belt), he rolled into Hollywood on an exhibition tour. There he was feted by the studios and told he had the potential to be a movie star. He stuck around for a while, having his picture taken showing stars how to swing a golf club, until he was cast in a Buster Keaton movie. Sarazen didn't much take to the pratfalls of the slapstick Keaton comedy and, after making a few screen tests, got bored waiting for the big breakthrough and headed back to the golf circuit.

Ben Hogan has had a film made about him *(Follow the Sun)* but not Bobby Jones. That situation is to be rectified by *Stroke of Genius,* to be made by American producer Kim Dawson. However, his pedigree doesn't augur well, he also produced *Teenage Mutant Ninja Turtles,* and he's attracted to the project because of the example set by *Chariots of Fire* which, according to Mr Dawson has "proven that period films about sports figures can and do garner critical and box-office success." Dawson's preferred option to play Jones is heart-throb Brad Pitt.

Golf afficionados might find it difficult to recognise the real life persons depicted but for the fact that their names are mentioned, but here is the publicity blurb from the poster for the Ben Hogan biopic *Follow the Sun,* starring Glenn Ford.

"The real-life love story of two kids from Texas, Ben and Valerie Hogan – the guy who never gave up, and the girl who never let him down." "They made the great American dream come true – TWICE."

LPGA player Muffin Spencer-Devlin is an enthusiastic *Star Trek* fan, (aka a "Trekkie"). But she hasn't just watched and enjoyed the series, she's actually played in it. She had a walk-on role in the *Star Trek Voyager* series and played a cameo role as a member of the *Star Trek* medical team in the film *Star Trek Generations.*

Peter Jacobsen, one of the most amusing and likeable characters in golf, finally gets to win a Major in the Kevin Costner movie *The Tin Cup.* He was cast in the film as a pro and his part calls for him to take the US Open championship. Tough role, that! Don Johnson and Gary McCord also feature in the movie, as do the products of the Taylor Made company, which reportedly paid Warner Brothers a $50,000 fee to ensure screen exposure for their clubs.

## Rules

One of the least successful rulings by an official at a Major was the decision by a USGA official at the US Open in 1919. During a play-off

Walter Hagen sliced his tee shot at the 17th into the rough. His ball finished on a patch of muddy ground and was trampled by spectators. The official ruled that Hagen could not lift and drop. Hagen disputed the ruling but the official was unbending. Showing some of the native cunning which made him one of the world's greatest golfers, Hagen insisted that the ball be positively identified as his. The official had no choice but to disturb the ball by turning it over. By the time Hagen finally accepted that the ball was his, it had been effectively dislodged from its plug-hole and most of the mud had been removed. Hagen won the play-off to become 1919 US Open champion! If you've got yourself in a hole, stop digging.

The 1937 British Amateur Championship was staged at Royal St George's, Sandwich. One man, a Brigadier-General Critchley, was so determined to play that he not only crossed the Atlantic on the *Queen Mary* but also hired a plane to take him to the course from Southampton. As luck would have it, the liner was delayed by fog and docked late. Scampering on to the plane, Critchley knew the timing was tight so he ordered the pilot to buzz the clubhouse so that the officials would know he had arrived. It was all to no avail. The Brigadier was *six minutes* late for his start time and was disqualified. Ironically, another competitor had been on board the *Queen Mary* as well. He'd come all the way from Burma and travelled right across America but he hadn't hired a plane to get from Southampton. He arrived four hours late and had to turn around and head home without having hit a ball.

The great British golf journalist Leonard Crawley once played a round of golf with a man who infuriated him by quietly breaking almost every rule in the game. In the rough he never had a bad lie, and on the green he did everything short of moving the hole closer to the ball. Crawley let everything pass but, when both men got into the locker room, the journalist hauled off and punched his opponent on the jaw. "That was for cheating," he explained. "Now let's go and have a drink."

Craig Stadler, the engaging "Walrus", who gives himself a harder time than he does anybody else, was once disqualified from a tournament for using a towel. On the 14th at the Torrey Pines GC in La Jolla, California in the 1987 Andy Williams Open, Stadler's ball nestled under the branches of one of the eponymous trees. Rather than take a penalty drop, Stadler decided to hack the ball out as best he could. But the ground under the tree was wet and muddy and, being a fastidious type, (well, OK, so he's a bit of a slob, but he's a very pleasant slob!) Craig decided to kneel on his towel. When tournament officials checked his card (already signed), they discovered that he had not assessed himself a penalty of two strokes for improving his lie. Having signed for a wrong card, Stadler was duly disqualified.

Some golfers never seem to learn that in an argument with a Rules Official they will, almost inevitably, come second. It's like arguing with a referee in soccer or, as that great poet Pam Ayres once put it, "It's statistically proven in chapter and in verse/That in a car and hedgehog fight, the hedgehog comes off worse." In one such dispute, Jose Maria Olazabal was the hedgehog, European Tour Tournament Director John Paramor was the automobile. Olazabal was plugged in a bunker in wet conditions and decided he'd look for a ruling. He insisted that the ball was unplayable, Paramor refused to give him relief. After a prolonged and occasionally heated discussion, Olazabal handed Paramor a club and said, "Here, you try and play it!" He didn't get his free drop but he did get a £250 fine.

American Tom Weiskopf, winner of the 1973 British Open, was known as a man who liked to party. He reckons his best ever round of golf came when he barely made the first tee after an all-night party. He bogeyed the first two holes and then drove into trees on the third. He called for a ruling but, when the PGA rules official Clyde Mangum got to Weiskopf's ball, he realised that Weiskopf's lie wasn't the problem (it was fine) but the player himself. He inquired of Weiskopf what particular rule needed clarification to be asked, "Clyde, can you get me an egg sandwich and a carton of milk?"

Playing in a Seniors Tour event in Charlotte in 1993, Arnold Palmer hit his ball into a water hazard but his ball wasn't actually in the water. He noticed that a TV tower lay between his ball and the green and appealed to the referee for line of sight relief. This was granted, so Arnold was entitled to a free drop. The question, however, was where to drop the ball. He was, in effect, on a island surrounded by water. The referee duly informed him that his nearest point of relief was in eight feet of water. Although Palmer's swing is still fast he would never have been able to drop, address and swing without drowning so he declined the relief and hacked out from where he was.

The most infamous recent dispute over the rules of golf was the spat between Greg Norman and Mark McCumber at the World Series of Golf in 1995. Norman observed what he alleged was McCumber removing a spiked-up blade of grass from his putting line. He drew McCumber's attention to the breach of the rules but the American insisted that he had merely been removing an insect. Norman demurred, informed a PGA official and refused to sign McCumber's card. When the Tour declined to take any action against McCumber, he threatened to withdraw. Instead, he stayed and won the tournament.

(As a postcript it is worth noting that one of Norman's fellow pros approached him on the practice area the following day rubbing his eye and asked, "Greg, can you help me, a spike mark has just flown into my eye.")

During the 1994 Volvo Masters, Seve Ballesteros, playing on his beloved Valderamma Course (joke!), got stuck behind a tree on the 18th. His ball landed near a hole and Ballesteros, looking for that great bolthole of the professional, the free drop, insisted that it had been made by a burrowing animal (Rule 25 1a – I know because I just looked it up!). PGA European Tour official John Paramor assessed the scene and decided that there wasn't enough evidence that the hole had been created by such a creature. Seve, presumably wanting to summon witnesses from the trees or the subsoil who would testify that they had indeed dug the hole, took issue with Paramor. "What more evidence do you need?" he berated the PGA official. "That is a hole, isn't it? You have made your decision, and I disagree with it, so now who do we ask?"

"Me!" Paramor pointed out. He's the Chief Referee, you see!

A recent Committee meeting at Ashridge Golf Club in Hertfordshire in England was discussing the possibility of allowing relief from footmarks left by the many deer which inhabit the environs of the course, when a member who had played golf in Australia pointed out that, in his antipodean golf club, relief was allowed to players whose balls strayed into kangaroo tracks. The club chairman said he saw no reason why Ashridge should not allow similar relief . . . why members should not be allowed lift and drop should their ball become lodged in a kangaroo footmark!

In addition to match formats covered by the revered and stodgy Rules of Golf, there are many enterprising variations and wrinkles which are practised. Many of these seem to have originated in the evil imagination of some frustrated American contract killer during a lull in gang warfare. Here are a few examples. First, the fairly familiar:

The Scramble – a four-ball team event in which everyone tees off and the best-positioned ball is chosen. All four members of the team then hit from that position and the same situation repeats. Once on the green all balls are placed within six inches of the chosen player's marker. Each player's drive must be chosen at least twice.

The Nassau – If you win the front nine you win one Nassau, if you win the back nine you win a second, and by winning both you have clearly taken the overall eighteen holes as well, so you win a third Nassau. Congratulations! Hopefully there was a lot of money riding on each Nassau.

Skins – Three or four players try to win a hole outright. Each hole is worth one skin. If no one manages a win the Skin is carried forward to the next hole, and so on until someone wins a hole. They thus win all the Skins accumulated up to that point.

Then there are the interesting variations . . .

Gruesomes – a foursomes match/scramble with a difference. Instead of playing alternate balls, your opponents choose the *lesser* of the two shots played by your team (preferably the one which ended up out of bounds or in the rough).

And the other wrinkles . . . ?

How about Hustons? This requires a male player who has not reached the ladies' tee with his drive to play the rest of the hole with his trousers down. There is a refinement of this torture called the Texas Dangler. I will leave it up to your imagination to work out the sanction involved in that one!

Or a Gilligan? This is a Mulligan in reverse. Mulligan is that beneficent golfing angel who allows you to replay any one truly awful shot per round. Gilligan is his malignant, twisted, perverted cousin, a diabolical figure who entitles your opponent to force you to replay any one of the best shots you might hit during your round.

Or a Whoosh? This is a loud shout which your opponents are entitled to unleash at any stage during a round in order to put you off your stroke.

Nice people who devised those, huh?

For many years (since their Junior days) there has been little love lost between Sandy Lyle and Nick Faldo. Their rivalry was accentuated for Faldo when Lyle was first to win a British Open and then become the first Briton to win the US Masters. The rivalry between the two men is amply illustrated by an incident in a Kenyan Open many years ago. Lyle was being blinded by the sunlight reflecting from the head of his putter and got the bright idea of fixing a strip of tape to it. In doing so, he contravened the rules of golf which prevent a player from changing the characteristics of a club during a round. Faldo spotted the sticky tape after a few holes and inquired about it. Lyle told him what it was for and Faldo made no further comment. However, at the ninth, Faldo informed a rules official about the transgression and Lyle was disqualified. Subsequently, the rule was modified to allow players to cut down on glare from clubs.

PROBABLY APOCRYPHAL

*All the anecdotes in this section come with a built-in credibility gap and a health warning.*

Those two great golfers Arnold Palmer and Jack Nicklaus both happened to be designing golf courses in Ireland at the same time. Nicklaus was responsible for realising the dream of Tim Mahony at Mount Juliet in Thomastown, Co. Kilkenny, while Palmer's company was selected to create a championship course for Dr Michael Smurfit at the Kildare Hotel and Country Club in Straffan, Co. Kildare. It has often been unfairly alleged that Arnold Palmer plays only a minimal role in the development of many of his company's projects, the bulk of the work being done by his partner Ed Seay. The story is told that, on one of his many visits to Thomastown to oversee the progress of Mount Juliet, Nicklaus was returning to Dublin airport by helicopter. He was asked by the pilot would he like to fly over the K Club and have a look. Nicklaus, under no tremendous time pressure, agreed. The pilot approached the magnificent Straffan estate and hovered low over the Liffey to give Nicklaus a close look. The great man was impressed with his old rival's handiwork. "Very nice," he's reputed to have said, "Has Arnold seen it yet?"

A well-known Dublin businessman (no names, no pack drill!) who is notorious for his outrageously large bets on his golfing prowess was quickly running out of opponents at his club who were willing to play him even for sums which he would consider to be petty cash. One day he found himself playing an older member who, although not long off the tee or the fairway, always seemed to manage to poke his ball down the middle, chip immaculately, sink one or two longish putts and save par or bogey. His steadiness was in marked contrast to the powerful but erratic play of the businessman who, within a few holes, had lost a considerable amount of money and who was becoming frustrated at being ouplayed by someone he had clearly viewed as easy pickings. One of the par-threes at the club is fronted by a bunker as deep and wide as Omaha Beach. The older member's tee shot finished in its jaws embedded in the sand in a classic "fried egg" lie. The businessman saw his chance. He offered his opponent a doubles-or-quits bet. "Doubles or quits says you don't get out of the bunker in one." The older member looked at his lie and jumped up and down a few times to study the green which began about a foot above his head. "You're on!" he declared. He then turned his back on the green and hacked his ball back out onto the fairway behind the bunker!

Rumour has it that an extremely cocksure golfer stood on an elevated green inspecting a short par-four with his unimpressed caddie.

"That's only a decent drive and a putt," he observed confidently to the sceptical bagman. He then overswung wildly, topped his ball and watched it roll down the hill stopping short of the women's tee.

When they got to the ball, the caddie solemnly handed him his putter for the second shot!

Given the level of misogyny evident in many golf clubs, this item is actually quite believable. According to legend, the Royal St George's Golf Club in Sandwich once housed a notice which read "Ladies wearing trousers are requested to remove them before entering the clubhouse." The sign is all the more credible when one recalls that for a long time the club displayed another one which read "No dogs; no women."

Responsibility for this story lies with Dermot Gilleece of *The Irish Times*. According to unverifiable reports, a company managing director, as a reward (and a bonding exercise?), brought three of his executives to his golf club for a round. Somewhere on the front nine a mobile phone began to ring, incensing the boss and causing the executives to look nervously at each other. The boss insisted on the culprit who had brought the infernal phone out on the course to own up immediately. His underlings eyed each other nervously but no one admitted the offence. Finally, still ringing, the phone was located in a bunker. The managing director answered the call. "Hello," prattled an obviously relieved voice at the other end of the line, "would you do me a great favour and bring the phone into the clubhouse with you? I've forgotten where I left it."

Lionel Platts, who had his heyday as a professional in the 1960s, was a long hitter and, like many a gunfighter in the old west, drew a lot of irritating challenges from amateurs who fancied their chances of outdriving him. Mostly he managed to avoid any macho nuisance contests but on one occasion he took on two especially insistent individuals. Standing on the tee, he offered an apparently irresistible challenge. He bet the two buckos that they couldn't get their drives *and* their second shots past his *seven-iron*. Convinced that large sums of money were about to come their way the two challengers teed off and blasted their drives miles down the middle of the fairway. Whereupon Platts gripped his seven-iron, turned his back on the fairway and slammed his shot in the opposite direction. "OK, guys," he grinned, turning to the dumbfounded pair. "Now get your second shot outside of that."

An edition of the *Irish Golfer* from August 1899 carries the unlikely story of the young boy who found himself in court. He was about to be sworn in to give evidence by a judge whom he instantly recognised. The judge inquired of him, "Do you know the nature of an oath, lad?" The boy is supposed to have replied, "Yes, sir. I used to be your caddie."

There are many variations of this story, but legend has it that an elderly member dropped dead of a heart attack while walking between the twelfth green and the thirteenth tee at Hazeltine in the USA. As he lay on the path surrounded by his playing partners, the group behind caught up and found themselves faced with a dilemma. There followed a rapid consultation and all four agreed on a course of action; as one, they removed their hats, paused briefly and then played through.

A Scottish caddie was escorting another visiting hacker around the hallowed ground of St Andrew's. The golfer, an American, was on a gardening expedition, gouging divots from the Scottish earth which had supported entire colonies of earthworms. His scoring was modest but he seemed quite excited by it all. With two holes to go he announced to the caddie that he had negotiated the first sixteen in ninety-one strokes. In the unlikely event of his playing the Road Hole and the eighteenth in par figures, he would post a 99.

"You know," he informed his dour and unimpressed bagman, "I'd move heaven and earth to break 100 on this great course."

"Try heaven," was the caustic response. "You've already moved most of the earth."

Golf in Japan, for those fortunate enough to be members of a club, is an unbelievably expensive hobby. The story is related of how four

Japanese golfers travelled to the west of Ireland and went to the local club for a round. They ran into the Secretary Manager and, in halting English, inquired about green fees.

"Ninety quid, lads," he advised them. "A bit steep, maybe, but it's a great course."

The four paid up happily and played their round. They enjoyed it so much that they returned the following day. Again they encountered the Secretary Manager and handed him an envelope.

"What's this?" he inquired.

"Green fees," he was told. He opened the envelope and found it contained £360. He ran after them and handed it back.

"Here you are, boys. Your money back. You're members. That was the annual subscription you paid yesterday."

This story has been associated with so many people it has to be apocryphal, but Chi Chi Rodriguez insists that he once played with an amateur in a pro-am who started off with eight straight 8s. At the ninth, he three-putted from seven feet for a nine. According to Rodriguez his caddie pointed out to him, purely as a matter of interest, that if he'd two-putted he'd have had nine consecutive eights on his card. To which the hacker replied, "What do you think I am, a machine?" (Sound familiar?)

The following conversation, reportedly, was overheard at Royal Dublin between an American visitor and his caddie in the days when a three-wood was known as a "brassie". The player was in heavy rough a long way from the hole and, while the caddie waited for him to make his club selection, the American was dutifully patting down the grass behind the ball in glorious contravention of the rules of the game. When he'd quite finished he turned to the caddie and asked, "Is that a brassie lie?" The caddie studied the situation for a moment and responded, "No! Not yet!"

Archie Compton, as a playing pro, could have dented the course of golf history. He led the 1930 Open Championship at Hoylake after shooting a 68. Sadly, he added an 82 to his opening round. Bobby Jones won and captured the other three "Majors" that year as well. As a teaching pro Compton was a legend. He bullied and browbeat his pupils rather than cajoling and flattering them. Once he is said to have driven a woman to take up an eight-iron and whack him across the shins. Ever the consummate professional, as he hopped around on one leg, in between yelps he shouted, "That's it. Now you've got it!"

Slow play is supposed to be the bane of the golfer's life, though one has to inquire why, if that is the case, there are so many slow golfers. One of Harry Vardon's famous stories concerned a four-ball stuck behind an old codger who was crawling along, advancing the ball a few yards at a time and positively refusing to let them through. Having passed through the land of frustration, in sheer desperation they began to pepper the area around him with their shots. Within minutes his caddie arrived back with a note which read "Mr _____ presents his compliments and begs to point out that, though he may be playing slowly, he can play a damn sight more slowly if he sees fit."

Glenna Collett Vare was one of the great amateurs in the women's game. She won six US Amateur Championships. She was not the kind of golfer to play in the Ladies' Medal but she once entered the Philadelphia Country Club Ladies Club Championship. In honour of her entry and assuming she would win easily, the committee belatedly ordered up a new trophy from a Philadelphia jewellery store. They were assured by the hard-pressed jewellers that, despite the short notice, the cup would be ready for presentation after the final. Unfortunately for both club and jewellers, Mrs Vare really hit form in the final and, as she approached the turn in a commanding lead, the tournament committee began to panic and make urgent calls to the jewellers for the trophy. Mrs Vare won on the fourteenth but there was still no trophy to present to her. According to legend, an enterprising committee member volunteered to go home and grab one of his Dog Show trophies just to have something to present to the winner.

When it came to the presentation, Mrs Vare accepted the trophy graciously before examining it closely and walking off in high dudgeon. The committee gathered around the temporary trophy which had clearly given offence. On closer inspection, its terrible secret was revealed. The inscription read "Best Bitch in Show".

This little incident is supposed to have happened at the Vista Valencia club in Santa Clarita, California. A woman, apparently, teed up her ball at the first tee and topped it into the water seventy yards away. She then proceeded to repeat the shot four more times before she managed to put one on the fairway. When she got to the 6th, which overlooked the same stretch of water, she had not yet managed to tee up when a scuba diver emerged from the water and placed half a dozen balls at her feet. "Here," he said, "looks like you might need these," before turning around and waddling back into the hazard.

# CHAPTER TWELVE

## Four Majors and a Biennial Brawl

### The Majors

Top Ten Major Winners (Figures include USA and British Amateur Championships)

| | |
|---|---|
| Jack Nicklaus | 20 |
| Bobby Jones | 13 |
| Walter Hagen | 11 |
| Ben Hogan | 10 |
| Gary Player | 9 |
| Arnold Palmer | 8 |
| Tom Watson | 8 |
| Gene Sarazen | 7 |
| Sam Snead | 7 |
| Harry Vardon | 7 |

(The above tale excludes the nineteenth century amateur, John Ball, who won the Open in 1890 and a total of eight British amateur championships. Nicklaus also has 19 second-place finishes, and Palmer 10.)

Over a quarter of a century, from 1971 to 1995, 100 Majors (excluding Amateur championships) have been played. In that time 69 have gone to Americans, 16 to Europeans, 8 to Australians and 7 to South Africans.

Jack Nicklaus was the dominant winner with 10 victories, Tom Watson won all of his 8 during the same period, while Nick Faldo and Seve Ballesteros have both claimed 5 each. (Faldo has since added a sixth.)

According to statistics compiled since 1980 by Sal Johnson of *Golf Digest,* the typical Major winner of the last 15 years is 33 years old, 5' 11" tall and weighs 12 stone 2 lbs. He went to college in the USA, lives in Florida (even if he's not American), is married and has 1.5 children. His average rounds were 69.55, 68.63, 69.38 and 69.31 for a winning total of 276.87.

The first man to achieve a reverse Grand Slam (Grand Slump?) was Craig Wood, who in the 1930s lost play-offs for all four Majors. Like his modern equivalent Greg Norman, Wood only won two Majors, in his case the Masters and US Open in 1941.

In 1933, he lost a play-off for the British Open to Denny Shute. The following year, Paul Runyan beat him out for the USPGA. One year later, Gene Sarazen's famous Albatross forced a play-off in the Masters which Wood lost. He then had a four-year respite before losing the 1939 US Open to Byron Nelson in another play-off.

Billy Casper has won three majors the day after the tournaments were scheduled to finish. His 1970 Masters victory came in a play-off. When he won the US Open at Winged Foot in 1959, a thunderstorm eliminated a day's play and an extra day had to be added. Then, in the 1966 US Open at the Olympic Club, he won an 18-hole play-off.

Majors tend to have an emetic effect even on golfers who are accustomed to the rigours of weekly competition. As Jeff Sluman, the 1988 US PGA Champion once put it, "You can always tell the first day of a Major the minute you walk into the locker room. The line for the bathroom is always a lot longer."

## The Open

The Open had its origins in the presentation by the members of Prestwick Golf Club of a red Morocco-leather belt to the winner of a professional tournament. The following invitation was sent out to clubs in 1859.

"It is proposed by the Prestwick Golf Club to give a Challenge Belt to be played for by Professional Golfers; and the various clubs in Scotland and England are requested to name and send the best players on their Links not exceeding three to compete for it. The game to be 36 holes or three rounds of Prestwick Links, the player who succeeds in holing his ball in the fewest number of strokes to be the winner."

Only eight men entered the competition which was won by Willie Park who only had to play for a single day in order to win the trophy. The competition took place on 17 October, 1860.

In 1979, Prestwick decided to re-enact the first Open played over twelve holes at the course. The competition drew 120 entries, but there were immediate problems because of the nature of the course. Holes criss-crossed, some greens were shared and several players were hit by the balls of unsuspecting opponents. No one was badly hurt but the following year, when the re-enactment itself was to be revived, several caddies refused to take part because they felt it was too dangerous, so the tournament never took place.

Young Tom Morris won four successive Opens, the first in 1868, succeeding his father as champion. He beat the previous scoring record by 5 shots with a 157. When he won in 1870, he'd reduced the record to 149 strokes.

The oldest winner of the Open is Old Tom Morris (so called, not because he was old, but because he was the father of Young Tom Morris). Old Tom won his fourth Open in 1867, when he was 46 years old. Ironically, he outlived Young Tom, who died at the age of 24 after winning four Opens himself.

The youngest winner of the Open was the aforementioned Young Tom Morris. He won his first title the year after his father won his last, in 1868, also at Prestwick. He was only seventeen years old at the time. He then went on to win the next four Opens.

The 1876 Open turned into something of a fiasco. It was staged at St Andrew's, sort of . . . What happened was that somebody forgot to book the course for the event and the professionals had to compete for the course with R&A members and artisans. (Can you imagine it today? "Eh, 'scuse me, Nick, you're goin' a bit slow, would ye mind if we played thru?") The two leaders of the tournament, as it reached its closing stages, were Bob Martin and David Strath, the only players to break 90 over the first eighteen holes. Martin posted a 90 in the afternoon making Strath the clear favourite. But at the fourteenth, Strath's drive hit a spectator on the forehead and knocked him cold. *He* recovered from the impact and the shock remarkably quickly but Strath didn't. The incident cost him a six at the hole, he dropped another stroke at the next and, as he played the last three holes, it was getting darker. Hoping to save time and not expecting to get up with his approach, Strath played his second at the famous road hole before the match in front had finished. He connected all too well with the ball, and it was only prevented from dribbling on to the cursed road by the leg of one of the players on the green. Strath only managed to tie Martin's 176 and, as soon as he finished his round, Martin's people insisted that Strath should be disqualified for hitting into the match in front. Unable to make a ruling, the organising committee ordained a play-off for the following day, but Strath refused to play on the grounds that a decision should first be reached on the Martin protest. He had no intention of winning a play-off and then being stripped of the title on a disqualification. Martin merely walked the course the following day and won the Open.

Harry Vardon still has more Open victories to his credit than any other player. He won six altogether, in 1896, 1898, 1899, 1903, 1911 and 1914. He was 44 when he won his last title at Prestwick.

In the modern era, two players have won five Opens each. Peter Thomson, the Australian, claimed his five in 1954, 1955, 1956, 1958 and 1965. In, arguably, a more competitive era (when the world's best competed), Tom Watson won in 1975, 1977, 1980, 1982 and 1983. Watson also won his five Opens on different courses, Carnoustie, Turnberry, Muirfield, Troon and Birkdale.

The highest score for a single hole at the Open Championship was recorded by one thankfully anonymous player at the first staging of the tournament in 1860. He carded a 21 on one of the holes at Prestwick.

In 1883, Willie Fernie recorded a ten at one hole when the Open was staged at Musselburgh. He still won the championship and remains the only player to have had a double-digit score at one hole and win the Open.

Everyone remembers the two-and-a-half-foot putt Doug Sanders missed to lose the 1970 Open at St Andrew's but there were no TV cameras around in 1889 when Andrew Kirkaldy missed a putt of one inch to lose out to Willie Park Jr at Musselburgh. Kirkaldy fresh-aired the putt on the 14th and, like Sanders with Jack Nicklaus, finished in a tie with Park. He lost the 36-hole play-off by five shots.

When Harry Vardon and JH Taylor tied for the Open in 1896, the play-off had to be postponed by a day because both men were scheduled to appear at a tournament in North Berwick.

After winning two Open titles at Muirfield, the great James Braid christened his son Harry Muirfield Braid.

The first prize for the first eleven Opens (all staged at Prestwick) was a special leather belt. When Tom Morris won it three times in a row he kept it. In 1871 there was no Open, partly because Morris had the trophy which had been presented at all the previous Opens. So, in 1871, the organisers offered as a prize the famous silver claret jug with the proviso that it could never be won outright.

In 1902, Sandy Herd became the first player to win the Open using the new Haskell ball, which consisted of wound elastic thread covered by gutta-percha. Herd used the same ball during all four of his rounds.

Only one French golfer has ever won the British Open. The 1906 French Open Champion, Arnaud Massy, won the Open championship the following year. He was also the first player from overseas to win, and the first from the continent of Europe. Not until Seve's victory in 1979, was there a repeat performance from a continental European.

Only three amateur golfers have ever won the Open championship.

They were John Ball in 1890, Harold Hilton in 1892 and 1897 and Bobby Jones in 1926, 1927 and 1930.

Two Open milestones occurred on one of the fourteen occasions when the event was staged at Muirfield. The 1892 Open there was the first occasion on which the tournament was staged over 72 holes. Previously it had finished after 36. Wind forward seventy-four years to 1966, and the Championship was extended to four days instead of playing 36 holes on the Saturday.

In 1890, John Ball became the first Englishman and the first amateur to win the Open. He also won a total of eight British Amateur championships and his record of nine major championships as an amateur is second only to the thirteen won by Bobby Jones. In 1878, Ball had finished fifth in the Open at the tender age of 14.

Scottish golfer John Panton wasn't made to feel very much at home during the 1946 Open at St Andrew's. After he finished his round, Panton went back out on to the course to practise his putting. When they discovered what he had done, officials disqualified him.

The 1949 "Ball in the Bottle" incident at Sandwich has often been cited by golfers, especially Irish ones, as the reason why Harry Bradshaw lost the Open to Bobby Locke that year. Bradshaw's ball wound up in a bottle at the fifth hole and, instead of awaiting a ruling, he attempted to play it as it lay. He only succeeded in moving the ball about 30 yards and took a double bogey six on the hole. He went on to tie with Locke and lose the Open in a 36-hole play-off. What many people fail to take into consideration is that Bradshaw's unfortunate stroke of luck came during the *second* round of the Open. It wasn't as if it slowed his momentum during the crucial final round. He still had 49 holes to go. Without being overly revisionist, it is fair to credit him with the fortitude he showed in overcoming this bad break but not to simplistically subtract two strokes from his final total and say that it cost him the Open.

In that same Open Championship at Royal St George's, the American, Charles Rotar, became the only person to be disqualified from the

Open for using an illegal club. He was eliminated for using a Schenectady putter which had been completely legal when it was used by Walter Travis to win the 1904 British Amateur Championship at the same venue.

The shortest hole on the rota for the Open is the famous "Postage Stamp", the 126-yard 8th hole at Troon. Despite its lack of yardage, a German amateur competitor, Herman Tissies, took 15 shots to complete it in 1950.

In 1952, when Bobby Locke won the Open at Royal Lytham, he became the last player to do so while wearing a tie on the course. He also used a hickory-shafted putter.

Possibly true, possibly journalistic invention, but the story goes that, in 1951 at the Open championship at Royal Portrush, the eventual winner Max Faulkner tempted fate by signing autographs "Max Faulkner – Open champion" after the second round.

Ben Hogan played in a solitary Open, which he won, in 1953. It was his "year of years". Asked in 1954 why he hadn't gone back to defend the title he won at Carnoustie, he observed in his normally informative manner, "I guess I had something else to do."

Arnold Palmer's visits to the Open in the 1950s and 1960s were what made it something other than a tournament in which Peter Thomson would beat the local talent almost every year. He gave it renewed respectability. But the major-domos of British golf had been partly instrumental in overseeing the decline of the Open in the 1930s and 1940s when few of the big-name Americans bothered travelling. For example, Byron Nelson played in 1937 at Carnoustie. By then, he acknowledges, the pros were allowed into the clubhouse but not their wives. Only on the last day were the wives allowed admission to that "Holy of Holies", and only then because it rained. Mary O'Connor, wife of Christy, remembers the same thing happening many years later at a Scottish Open venue which she declines to name. On that occasion, when it rained the players' wives sheltered in an outside toilet.

Sam Snead wasn't the most enthusiastic supporter of the Open. His reluctance to travel was probably related to his notorious closeness with money. "What do I want with prestige?" he once mused. "The British Open pays the winner $600 in American money. A man would have to be 200 years old at that rate to retire from golf." Neither was Snead the most reverential of players. On his winning trip in 1946 to the first Open in seven years, he travelled to the hallowed St Andrew's and scandalised all and sundry as the train passed by the Old Course by commenting, in all innocence, "Hey, that looks like an old abandoned golf course. What do they call it?"

He did develop a genuine appreciation for the charms and the pitfalls of the Old Course and was duly proud of his victory and trophy, if not of the financial awards which accrued. In fact, he reckoned his caddie made more money from his triumph than he did himself. On the 18th he gave the ball he used during the final round to his caddie, "Scotty". The bag man told him tearfully, "I'll treasure it all my days," but within an hour his pragmatism and greed had got the better of his sentimentality. "That ball was worth some cash and Scotty proved it," recalled Snead. ". . . he sold it for fifty quid. so he made more off the Open than I did."

One of Jack Nicklaus's most embarrassing golfing moments came in the 1966 Open at his beloved Muirfield when, by his own admission, he "whiffed" a shot. It was the only time he was ever guilty of an "air shot" in a Major. What happened was that his ball was sitting high in the rough on the par-5 17th hole after his second shot had gone through the green. He took his wedge to it and slid it neatly under the ball without even moving it. However, he chipped the next one close, made par and won the Open.

In 1973 Tom Weiskopf, never a great fan of the Open, the crowds, the weather, Scotland or anything else to do with the event, won at Troon and became an instant convert to the mystique of the Open and of the wonderful Scottish courses on which it is usually played. So enamoured did he become of the course on which he won his one and only Major championship that he adopted "TROON" as his personalised car licence plate.

The classic Turnberry Open of 1977 where Tom Watson went head to head with Jack Nicklaus for two rounds and won (the rest of the field was nowhere) is probably the best in the history of the event. But one of the most intriguing and consequential took place a few years earlier at Muirfield, in 1972, between Tony Jacklin and Lee Trevino. Jacklin had made his big breakthrough in Lytham in 1969 and had gone on to win the US Open the following year. The garrulous Trevino was the holder. Because of Trevino's non-stop flow of conversation, a lot of pros didn't like playing with him. He upset their rhythm and concentration (maybe that was the intention, because Trevino could be a very different person off the course). Standing on the first tee before the final round, Jacklin admonished his opponent, "Lee, we don't need any conversation today." To which the gabby Trevino retorted, "Tony, you don't have to talk. You just have to listen."

The turning point in the round, the championship and, arguably, in Jacklin's career, came at the 17th hole of a tense "match". After driving into a bunker Trevino was off the green in four, Jacklin was off in two. As he approached his shot Trevino had, in effect, given up any hopes of winning. He muttered to Jacklin, "It's all yours, Tony." Miraculously, he then sank the chip to make an impossible 5. Jacklin, completely unnerved and already probably celebrating in advance, took four more shots to get down. The loss of that Open shattered his confidence and, after three years at the top, he never again challenged for a Major championship. "God is a Mexican," Trevino quipped afterwards. Jacklin, reflecting morosely in later years on Trevino's Houdini act, commented, "When things have gone against me I have always tried harder because I felt I would always come out better at the other end. But this situation broke my faith in that. I can't explain it any other way."

As the second round of the Open was due to begin at Muirfield in 1980 a car was found in a greenside bunker on the 9th hole. The previous evening a motorist had, apparently, taken a wrong turning coming out of the tented village. (One wonders why!) He drove across the 9th green and ended up in the sand.

Approaching the climax of the 1981 Open at Royal St George's, Sandwich a policeman, having difficulty controlling the crowds on the

18th fairway, resolutely refused to allow a blond American in a red sweater past him. The American kept insisting he had to get to the green, the policeman was having none of it – until it was pointed out that this particular American, one Bill Rodgers, really needed to get to the green in order to hole out and win the Open championship. The policeman relented and allowed the golfer to pass.

At the 1985 Open at Sandwich, American Peter Jacobsen, like Othello, "did the State some service" when he crashtackled a streaker who pranced across the 18th green as the American's round was drawing to a close. Afterwards he insisted that, as a result, a new statistical category should be created for professional golfers, that of Leading Tackler.

Christy O'Connor Jr is the only golfer to have shot seven consecutive birdies at the Open. He did it en route to a spectacular 64 in 1985 at Royal St George's, Sandwich. His run began on the 4th and helped him to finish third that year behind Sandy Lyle.

## The US Masters

The Masters came about partly because the Augusta National course could never hope to host the US Open. In June, the traditional Open month, temperatures in Georgia can exceed 100 degrees. The month of April was chosen for the tournament because that was when the leading national sportswriters were returning to their northern bases after covering baseball's spring training camps in Florida. Jones himself objected to the title "The Masters", considering it gauche and presumptuous. He favoured "The Augusta National Invitation Tournament", but the gentlemen of the press wanted "The Masters", so that is what it became. Total prize money for the first Masters was $5,000. The first prize was $1,500. Ticket prices for the first tournament were $5 for a season ticket, $2 for a daily ticket and $1 for the practice round.

The "shot that rang around the world" (typical golfing hyperbole) and which established the Masters as an important tournament was, of course, Gene Sarazen's second shot to the par-5 fifteenth during the final round of the second staging of the event, in 1935. As Sarazen was about to tee off there was a huge roar from the 18th green and he was told that the tournament leader, Craig Wood, had just birdied the hole to take a three-shot lead over him. The newspapermen were already preparing their stories about Wood's triumph. Sarazen drove off and hit his ball about 250 yards. He knew that to stand any chance at all of catching Wood he needed to eagle the 15th so, although his ball was in a tight lie, he decided to go for the flag, risking disaster in the lake in front of the green. Because he didn't think he'd get the ball in the air with his three wood on such a tight lie Sarazen asked his caddie for the 4-wood. "Mister Gene, you got to hit a 3-wood if you want to clear that water," the caddie observed. "Hey, hurry up, Gene, I got a date tonight," tossed in Sarazen's playing partner, Walter Hagen.

Sarazen hit that 4-wood as hard as he could. Afterwards he wrote about watching the flight of the ball, "I saw it hop straight for the cup, and then, while I was straining to see how close it had finished, the small gallery behind the green let out a terrific shout and began to jump wildly in the air. I knew then that the ball had gone into the hole."

With one shot, a rare albatross (or double-eagle in American parlance), Sarazen had shattered Wood's lead. Within minutes 5,000 spectators had abandoned the 18th and charged out to the 16th to follow Sarazen home.

When Sarazen got to the green the young boy reporting the scores to the master scoreboard, via a telephone link, was vainly trying to convince the master scoreboard operator that Sarazen had got a two at the fifteenth. The operator kept telling the young boy that he meant a 2 at the short 16th. The boy kept repeating that Mr Sarazen had put the ball into the hole with his second shot at the 15th.

Sarazen had an uneventful final three holes and beat Wood in the play-off for one of the most famous and dramatic golfing victories ever.

The 12th hole at Augusta, set amidst the beguiling pines and drained by Rae's Creek, used to be an old Indian burial ground and has been the graveyard of many hopes of success in the final stretch on Masters Sunday. But few players view it with such venomous hatred as Tom Weiskopf, who took thirteen strokes to hole out in the first round in 1980. He hit five balls into Rae's Creek which guards the front of the green. The following day he improved by six strokes, taking a seven. Afterwards, he described the 12th as "a hell-hole"!

Jack Nicklaus has had his problems on the 12th as well. In 1995, he shanked his tee shot and then admitted afterwards that it was not the first occasion on which he had suffered the dreaded "S-word" at the hole. In 1963, still only a Baby Bear in stature, he had done likewise and watched as the ball whizzed just over the heads of Bobby Jones and Clifford Roberts sitting in a nearby buggy. When Nicklaus recalled the story in 1995 he was asked by a journalist, "Is that what Bobby Jones meant when he said you played a game with which he was not familiar?"

After the Tortuous Twelfth comes the Terrible Thirteenth and Tommy Nakajima probably still has hot and cold flushes when he thinks about it. His troubles began, as do those of most Masters competitors, when his second shot found Rae's Creek in front of the green. He incurred five penalty shots for various offences, including grounding his club in the hazard and having the ball strike his foot. Eventually he carded a 13.

Obviously not the most practical of golfers, Johnny de Forest (aka Count de Bendem) came across his ball stuck in the bank of the brook in front of the 13th. De Forest decided that, although the brook was swollen, he was still going to play the ball. Accordingly, he took off his left shoe and sock and rolled his trousers up to his knee. Then, ingeniously, he placed his bare foot on the bank and stepped into the deep water with his still-shod right foot!

The Masters is played on one of the world's great courses but US pro and golf commentator Johnny Miller clearly believes it to be far better than any European course. His theory on why so many European players win the tournament goes as follows. "They have nothing like this back in Europe. For them, Augusta National must be like going on a blind date, opening the door and being greeted by Sharon Stone." Which might account for the contoured greens.

The Champions Dinner is one of the annual rituals of Masters week at Augusta. At this meal, the menu is decided by the reigning champion. It used to be a largely "beans and taters" type of occasion until European players began to win the Green Jacket with almost metronomic regularity. The 1989 dinner rose to new heights of weirdness, as far as the traditionalist palates of the American champions were concerned. 1988 winner, Scotland's Sandy Lyle, had asked that the main course should be that stomach-churning Scottish dish, haggis. When it was piped in and served, Lyle records that the assembled champions were suspicious. "They were all like a bunch of schoolkids peering at it, moving it around with their forks and glancing round the table. Finally, they looked at me and asked, 'What is it?' I told them it was just spicy beef."

Perhaps they figured it was the realisation of a dream of Ireland's David Feherty who, setting out his "fantasy" menu, once said that he would "insist on cooking it myself and then poison every past champion, so making it easier to win the tournament."

One of the features of the Masters had always been the absence of regular Tour caddies, a major bone of contention with some pros. The invited guests of the Masters Committee were expected to use local caddies. It worked well for Fuzzy Zoeller on his first trip in 1979. He claimed afterwards that he just held out his hand as he stood over his ball and played whatever club his caddie put into it. Famously, he won on his debut. In 1983, that policy changed and players were allowed to bring their own caddies, though not everybody did. In another break with tradition, yardage books and range balls were provided by the club for the first time.

The hazard in front of the 13th and the 15th has been the watery grave for many a golfer (most notably Seve Ballesteros, who had a winning chance in 1986), but, during the first round of the 1947 tournament, Jimmy Demaret showed what could be done when he played a shot out of deep water at the 15th. The ball came to rest within four feet of the pin and Demaret sank the putt for the most unlikely of birdies.

You might wonder why anyone would actually want to hurry around the Augusta golf course but, in 1947, Gene Sarazen and George Fazio were first off the tee in the final round. They finished one hour and fifty-seven minutes later, Sarazen scoring a 70. In 1960, George Bayer and Jack Fleck went around in one hour and fifty-two minutes Bayer shot a 72, Fleck a 74.

Sam Snead nearly threw away the 1952 Masters by putting his tee shot at the 12th into Rae's Creek. He then managed to drop his ball into a depression and from there hit it on to the long grassed embankment below the green. A six looked on the cards from that position but then the Snead luck returned and his fourth shot went into the hole. He went on to win the tournament.

In 1954, Billy Joe Patton caused a minor sensation by almost becoming the first amateur to win the Masters. He endeared himself to the Southern crowd with his "aw-shucks" approach to life and golf and appalled stylists with the blurry speed of his backswing. But he was undone by his own adventurousness and by the water on the par-5 13th and 15th. He went for both greens, took a seven on thirteen after going underwater and a six on fifteen. Had he laid up (isn't hindsight wonderful), he could have parred both. As it was, he missed tying Hogan and Snead by a single stroke.

Patton had two other top ten finishes in the Masters, the only other amateur to emulate him being Charlie Coe. Coe also survived eight cuts, the most of any amateur competitor. In addition, Coe was the low amateur six times (1949, 1951, 1959, 1961, 1962, 1970) The youngest amateur to compete was Tommy Jacobs, who was just seventeen years old during the 1952 Masters. Chick Evans, at 69, was the oldest amateur competitor when he was invited to Augusta in 1960. Jodie Mudd set the standard for debutant amateurs in 1982 with a 67.

In the 1960s, Retief Waltman emerged as a fine young South African golfer. By the age of 25 he had won the South African Open twice and had represented his country in the Canada Cup (now the World Cup). He was invited to play at the Masters and opened well, with a 72. Unfortunately, he added a 77 on the second day and didn't make the cut. Most golfers would shrug their shoulders and chalk it up to experience; not Waltman, he handed his clubs to fellow pro Dave Thomas, gave away everything else associated with the game, and quit golf completely.

Tragically and famously, Roberto de Vicenzo lost the 1968 Masters because he signed an incorrect scorecard. He actually tied for first with Bob Goalby but failed to notice that his playing partner, Tommy Aaron, had added a stroke to his card. He signed for the higher card and had to accept the score, thus finishing a shot behind Goalby. The popular Argentinean was philosophical about it afterwards, an attitude in marked contrast to his modern-day successors. He shrugged off his error, saying, "I think maybe I make a few friends. That means more than money. What is money, anyway?"

Just to be relentlessly trivial, you might like to know how a potential champion prepares for the final round of the US Masters. In 1980, at the age 23 (just – he turned 23 the day before the tournament), Seve Ballesteros watched *Saturday Night Fever* at his rented house and for breakfast had *four* fried eggs, bacon, toast, raisin bran, grapes and coffee. (The Breakfast of Champions?) Despite this feast, and despite holding a ten-shot lead after the first nine holes on Sunday he played like a complete plonker over the final stretch bogeying the 10th, 13th and double-bogeying the 12th. As he stood on the 15th, he heard that Gibby Gilbert had cut his lead to two, but a birdie on fifteen and three pars on the way home made him the youngest ever winner of the Masters.

Ben Crenshaw, a great student of the game and the lore of golf, found himself in a winning position coming to the 13th in 1984. Just as his famous 1995 victory had a touch of the spiritual about it (coming in the week of the death of his mentor Harvey Penick), Crenshaw made a crucial decision in 1984 based on another quasi-ghostly episode. He was dithering over his second shot, wondering whether or not to go for the green or lay up. He looked into the crowd around the 13th fairway to see if he could spot his father, hoping for some direction from that source. Instead, highlighted by a shaft of sunlight, he saw Billy Joe Patton. Recalling how Patton had come to grief by being overly adventurous on the par-fives in 1954, Crenshaw opted for safety and laid up. He won the Masters that year. On being told this story some time later, Patton was greatly surprised. "He must have had visions," the great amateur said. "I wasn't there."

Sandy Lyle's 1988 victory was characterised by almost as much press interest in his Dutch girlfriend, Jolande Huurman (now his wife), as in the Scot's achievement in winning with the aid of a near-miraculous fairway bunker shot on the 18th. At some point during the week, Lyle complained of a cold but announced that it was getting better due to the attentions of his girlfriend. Fascinated by this revelation, the press delved more deeply and discovered that Jolande was tickling Sandy's toes at night, which therapy he believed was curing his cold. Go on, try it and see!

Lyle's subsequent dive in form was painfully illustrated during the 1990 Masters but the pain was not confined to the golfer himself. His shots were so errant that he hit spectators with his ball on three separate occasions. But his slump was not as meteoric as that of Mike Donald between the first and second rounds that year. Donald led with a 64 after the first round, but shot an 82 in the second to miss the cut.

Even though the Masters is the only Major which sends players out in the second and subsequent rounds on the basis of their scores, John Daly and Ian Woosnam actually partnered each other for all four rounds of the 1994 tournament. Afterwards, Woosnam's wife asked her husband concernedly whether Daly would be joining them on holiday.

The Augusta National Masters Organising Committee has often been accused of being behind the times but that proved, literally, to be the case in 1995 when, a full year after democracy came to South Africa, the old South African flag was seen to be flying over the clubhouse as the tournament began. The mistake was rectified within 24 hours.

*The Good, the Bad and the Ugly at the Masters – (Best and worst scores at each hole)*

| HOLE | PAR | BEST SCORE | WORST SCORE |
|------|-----|-----------|-------------|
| 1. | 4 | 2 (By four players) | 7 (By ten players) |
| 2. | 5 | 3 (By many players) | 10 (Sam Byrd, 1948) |
| 3. | 4 | 2 (By six players) | 8 (Douglas Clarke, 1980) |

| | | | |
|---|---|---|---|
| 4. | 3 | 1 (Jeff Sluman, 1992) | 7 (Nathaniel Crosby, 1982) |
| 5. | 4 | 2 (By four players) | 8 (By three players) |
| 6. | 3 | 1 (By three players) | 7 (Jose Maria Olazabal, 1991) |
| 7. | 4 | 2 (By four players) | 8 (By two players) |
| 8. | 5 | 2 (Bruce Devlin, 1967) | 12 (Frank Walsh, 1935) |
| 9. | 4 | 2 (By three players) | 8 (By two players) |
| 10. | 4 | 2 (By three players) | 8 (By two players) |
| 11. | 4 | 2 (Jerry Barber, 1962) | 9 (By three players) |
| 12. | 3 | 1 (By three players) | 13 (Tom Weiskopf, 1980) |
| 13. | 5 | 2 (Jeff Maggert, 1994) | 13 (Tommy Nakajima, 1978) |
| 14. | 4 | 2 (Brett Ogle, 1993) | 8 (Nick Price, 1993) |
| 15. | 5 | 2 (Gene Sarazen, 1935) | 11 (Jumbo Ozaki, 1987) |
| 16. | 3 | 1 (By six players) | 11 (Herman Barron, 1950) |
| 17. | 4 | 2 (Tommy Nakajima, 1989) | 7 (By seven players) |
| 18. | 4 | 2 (By three players) | 8 (Jumbo Ozaki, 1994) |

Eclectic Score **33**    Eclectic score **163**

| UPS AND DOWNS | 1st | 2nd | 3rd | 4th | Total |
|---|---|---|---|---|---|
| Best Ever Rounds | 63 | 64 | 63 | 64 | 254 |
| Worst Ever Rounds | 92 | 89 | 89 | 95 | 365 |

In winning the 1989 Masters, Nick Faldo claimed the record for holing the longest putt in the event when he sank one which measured 100 feet for a birdie on the 2nd green in the third round. In 1955, Cary Middlecoff knocked in a putt for an eagle of 75 feet on the 13th green.

Between the first Masters in 1934 and the 1963 event only four championships were won with scores in the 270s. But, since 1963, 17 players have finished at least nine under par (279) with Jack Nicklaus (1965) and Ramond Floyd (1976) sharing the record for low score on 271.

Some other Masters milestones include the best "come from behind" performance of Jackie Burke who won in 1956, having made up nine strokes in the final round. Jack Nicklaus won by a record nine shots when he shot his 271 in 1965.

Individual scoring achievements include those of Dan Pohl who, in his first Masters in 1982, scored back-to-back eagles on the 13th and 14th followed by birdies on the 15th and 16th to leave him six-under for the four holes. In 1988, Curtis Strange shot a 1, 2, 3, 4 on the 12th, though not in sequence. Raymond Floyd was 14-under for the par-fives when he shot his 271 to win in 1976. Meanwhile, in 1956, William Booe and Johnny Revolta each shot 10 consecutive bogeys.

In the 1936 Masters, Craig Wood shot an 88 in the first round and then scored a 67 in the second, an astonishing difference of 21 strokes.

The worst scoring in a single round at the Masters was in 1956, when 28 players recorded scores of 80 or more on Saturday and 29 did likewise on Sunday.

From 1937 onwards, Sam Snead played in 44 consecutive Masters tournaments, in the course of which he played a total of 10,702 strokes

## US Open

Pebble Beach is the only public golf course to be on the rota for the US Open. Unlike other US Open courses, it also stages an annual USPGA Tour event, the AT&T.

The best closing round in a US Open was the amazing 63 of Johnny Miller at Oakmont in 1973. The round gave him a spectacular "come from behind" win.

So appalling was the reputation of golf professionals in the 1890s that, when the 1898 Open was won by pro Fred Herd, the USGA refused to give him the trophy unless he put up money as security for it. The Committee members were afraid that Herd would pawn the trophy and drink the proceeds.

The great Englishman, Harry Vardon, won the 1900 US Open on a promotional visit to the USA when most of the competitors would have been fellow British professionals. He famously lost the 1920 US Open when he dropped a stroke to par on each of the last seven holes (he was fifty years old, ill and had played 99 holes of golf in three days) and was beaten, along with Ted Ray, in a play-off with Francis Ouimet in 1913, but his non-involvement in the 1912 Open is perhaps as interesting as any of the other excursions. He had planned to travel to the USA in an attempt to repeat his triumph of 1900, but his visit had to be cancelled because of a bout of ill-health. He must have felt hard done by at the time, but his chagrin would not have lasted long. His passage had been booked on the maiden voyage of an impressive new liner named the *Titanic*.

The second US Open, staged at Shinnecock Hills in 1896, included a black player in the field. He was John Shippen, the 16-year-old son of a Baptist missionary to the Shinnecock Indian reservation. When the professionals in the field, mainly Scottish and English immigrants, were told about Shippen, they threatened to withdraw. They were told by Theodore Havemeyer, who was bankrolling the event, that Shippen was playing no matter who withdrew. The youngster was actually tied for the lead after the first round but an 81 on the second and final day pushed him down to fifth.

Johnny McDermott is the youngest player to have won the US Open. He was only 19 when he won, in 1911, at the Chicago Golf Club. Just for good measure, he won it again the following year. He was also the first native-born American to capture the title.

When former caddie Francis Ouimet shocked the golfing world by beating the great Vardon and Ray to take the 1913 US Open at Brookline, one of the most interesting things about his win had nothing to do with Ouimet himself; his caddie, Eddie Lowery, who carried Ouimet's bag, was only 10 years old.

The USGA has a habit of tricking up its Open courses, already difficult enough, for the week of the Championship. The rough intrudes well into the traditional preserve of the fairway and is allowed grow so tall that players can find themselves stuck in the sort of grass familiar to veterans of the Vietnam jungles. The tradition may have begun at the Scioto Country Club in 1926, at an Open won by Bobby Jones. One of the competitors, Jock Hutchison, is said to have remarked to a USGA official, "I lost a ball in your rough today. I dropped another ball over my shoulder and lost it, too; and while I was looking for that one, I lost my caddie!"

In 1929, Walter Hagen was out on the town, prior to the final round of the US Open, when someone told him that the tournament leader, Leo Diegel, was already tucked up in bed. To which Hagen's famous riposte was "Yes, but is he sleeping?" Hagen won, Diegel finished third.

The 1930 US Open at Interlachen is best remembered as one leg of Bobby Jones's never-to-be-repeated Grand Slam, but he had his fair share of luck in winning it. During the second round, Jones showed himself to be human when (as detailed elsewhere) he topped his attempt to reach the green on the par-5 9th in two. The ball headed straight for a lake but skipped across like a flat stone, allowing Jones to pitch on to the green and sink his putt for an unlikely birdie. Then, on the 71st hole, just a shot clear of Macdonald Smith, he pushed his drive and couldn't find his ball. As it happened, the USGA referee following his game (who just happened to be President George Bush's father) ruled that the ball had gone into a water hazard, so he was not penalised stroke and distance. He escaped the hole with a five.

We're all familiar with the unique play-off mechanism of the USGA in the US Open: if two or more players are tied after 72 holes, they come back the following day and play 18 more holes. But in 1931, Billy Burke and George Von Elm managed a 72-hole play-off. In those days ties were broken by players competing over 36 holes, and after the first 36 the two men were still inseparable, so both had to come back the following day and play 36 more holes, after which Burke had won, *by one stroke,* 148 to 149. It must rank as the tightest US Open ever.

The US Open is the only Major championship never won by Sam Snead. Had he done so, he would have joined Gene Sarazen, Ben Hogan, Gary Player and Jack Nicklaus as the only players to have won all four Majors. At the Philadelphia Country Club in 1939, Sam Snead had probably the best chance he would ever have of winning his first

US Open but a snowman (an 8) at the 72nd hole ruined his chances. Snead needed only a par-five at the last to beat Byron Nelson but he was under the impression he needed a birdie. (Ernie Els nearly came to grief in similar fashion more than half a century later.) Off the tee he ended up in the rough; risking everything unnecessarily, he tried to play out of the long grass with a 2-wood. He plugged the shot into a fairway bunker 100 yards shy of the green. He tried to hit an 8-iron out but barely shifted the ball. Second time around, he managed to get the ball to the green but it was 30 feet away and he three-putted. The eight put him into a tie for fifth place and Byron Nelson won his only Open after a three-way playoff. Afterwards Snead commented, "If I'd murdered someone I'd have lived it down sooner than the '39 Open."

In a departure from ritual, Nelson and Craig Wood were asked after they both shot rounds of 68 in the first play-off in 1939 (Denny Shute had shot a 76), whether they wanted to opt for a sudden death shoot-out to decide the destination of the championship. Both men seemed rather surprised at the suggestion, and preferred to come back and do it all over again the following day in traditional US Open style. When they did, Nelson won with a 70 to Wood's 73.

The eagerness of Porky Oliver to get his final round over with in the 1940 US Open at the Canterbury GC in Cleveland, Ohio may have cost him the championship. Oliver had tied with Lawson Little and Byron Nelson but it was discovered that he had teed off half an hour early so he was disqualified. Little won the play-off.

Lloyd Mangrum benefited from a stroke of good fortune in the 1946 US Open at the Canterbury GC in Cleveland, Ohio. At one hole Byron Nelson's caddie, Eddie Martin, accidentally kicked Nelson's ball. This resulted in a one-stroke penalty which cost Nelson an outright win. He tied with Mangrum and lost the play-off by one shot.

That was where Mangrum's luck ran out. He was the club pro at the Tam O'Shanter Club in Chicago. As a gesture, Mangrum allowed the owner of the club, George May, to put the Open trophy on display. In retrospect, it was not a good idea. During the winter of 1946/47, the

Tam O'Shanter clubhouse was burnt to the ground and the US Open trophy melted.

In 1950, Mangrum lost the US Open at the Merion Club in Ardmore, Pennsylvania, not to Ben Hogan but to a bug. It came to rest on his ball when he was about to putt. He picked up the ball to remove it and was told that he had just incurred a two-shot penalty. The penalty put him into a tie with Hogan, who won the play-off.

In 1955, to the surprise of everybody, Ben Hogan was caught by a virtually unknown professional, Jack Fleck, in the last round of the US Open at the Olympic Country Club. With a birdie at the eighteenth, he forced a play-off with the four-time champion. The following day he shot a 69 to Hogan's 72. Ironically, Fleck accomplished the feat with Hogan's own clubs – well, sort of. Hogan had just established his own manufacturing company and Fleck had ordered a set. Hogan had actually delivered the new clubs to Fleck personally before the tournament began.

One of the most controversial US Open play-offs was in 1962, when Arnold Palmer played Jack Nicklaus over 18 holes at Oakmont, 40 miles away from his birthplace. Palmer was at the height of his popularity, Nicklaus was the young, out-of-state, pretender. Arnie's Army was augmented for the occasion by a battalion of steel workers from Pittsburgh, more used to insulting the opponents of the Pittsburgh Steelers than in observing some of the finer points of golf etiquette. Nicklaus, then quite overweight, had to endure catcalls and jibes of "Hey fatty, hit the ball in here." "Step on his ball, Arnie," and worse, from the gallery. The stewards struggled, unsuccessfully at times, to keep order on the fans. Beer cans were thrown and reporters were, allegedly, tossed into sand bunkers. None of it seemed to bother Nicklaus, who shot a 71. Palmer, visibly upset by the behaviour of some of his fans, shot a 74.

Arnold Palmer is just as famous for his collapse over the closing holes of the 1966 US Open at the Olympic Club in San Francisco as he is for any of his famous Major victories. Palmer led by seven shots with nine holes to play but was pegged back by Billy Casper who forced a play-off. Shattered by having given up such an invulnerable lead, Palmer duly lost the play-off.

Byron Nelson, after retiring at the age of 34 to the Texas ranch purchased from the winnings made during his amazing 1945 "streak", was persuaded to become a golf broadcaster in the 1960s. At the 1967 US Open at Baltusrol he walked around the course, studied it and predicted in a pre-tournament interview that the winning total would be 275. This didn't please the Baltusrol members or grounds staff. The previous Open winner at Baltusrol, Ed Furgol, had shot a 284. But Nelson was proven absolutely right when Jack Nicklaus sank a 30-footer on the 18th to win with a score of 275. Lucky guess, really!

Lee Trevino's career as golfer and joker was launched by his surprise win in the 1968 US Open at Oak Hill near New York. He was so little-known that, when he first showed as a contender, hundreds of Italians and Italian-Americans came out to the course from the Big Apple, thinking he was one of theirs. Asked afterwards by one imaginative reporter what he intended to do with his winnings, he firmly established his ethnic credentials by insisting, "I may buy the Alamo and give it back to Mexico." Afterwards, when he actually visited the historical site for the first time he changed his mind, observing of the ruined building that "Well, I'm not going to buy this place. It doesn't have indoor plumbing." The following year, when the almost equally obscure Orville Moody took the title Dave Marr, jokingly, hailed the winner as having brought the Open title back to America.

The most ludicrous (or challenging) tricking-up of a course by the USGA probably took place at Winged Foot in 1974. Hale Irwin won that year, largely because somebody has to, but did so in a score of 7 *over* par. Afterwards, Jack Nicklaus was scathing about the men in the blazers from the USGA whose annual contact with the professional players of golf takes place at the US Open. "They tried to preserve their almighty power – or almighty par," he commented. "They really made a joke out of it." Jim Colbert hit one ball into the rough and watched it sit down in the pasture like an obedient dog. "When I was walking down the fairway, I saw a bunch of USGA guys down on their hands and knees, parting the rough, trying to find my ball. I knew I was in trouble."

The US Open that year became known as "The Massacre of Winged Foot".

One of the great shots (flukes) of recent Open championships (Corey Pavin's 4-wood to the 18th at Shinnecock Hills notwithstanding) was undoubtedly that of Tom Watson at the short 17th in Pebble Beach in the final round of 1982. Although the two men were not playing together like they did at Turnberry, it was effectively a head-to-head between Watson and Jack Nicklaus. Nicklaus looked to be in control over the closing stretch. As always at Pebble Beach (where Nicklaus had won in 1972), the rough around the 17th was penal and that was where Tom Watson's ball rested as he approached the green. An up and down looked unlikely, just keeping the ball on the green would be an achievement. Instead Watson stunned the gallery, and himself, by holing the shot from ankle-deep grass. His celebratory dance was a victory shuffle because the shot which, he said, "had more meaning for me than any other shot in my career," won him his first and only US Open championship.

In 1984, Fuzzy Zoeller and Greg Norman were fighting it out for the US Open. Zoeller was playing just behind Norman, who holed out a putt from off the green for a par. Watching from down the fairway Zoeller assumed Norman had just birdied the hole and probably won the Open. He took out his white towel and waved it over his head in a gesture of surrender. In fact, he tied for the championship and won the play-off the following day.

In 1991, a rare Irish appearance at the US Open became an extraordinary Irish disappearance, when Ronan Rafferty decided he'd had enough of Hazeltine midway through his second round. He was already eleven over par and had no earthly chance of making the cut. He turned to his playing partner Craig Parry and told him he was going to the toilet. He may well have done so but he never reappeared to continue his round. As journalist Joe Howard put it, "the toilet he had in mind was several thousand miles away."

*USPGA*

Up to 1958, the USPGA Championship was the only major based on matchplay rather than strokeplay. The arrival of TV hastened the end of the format as producers didn't much like matches which might conceivably finish out of range of their cameras.

Walter Hagen is the only player to have won four consecutive USPGA titles. He won from 1924–27, inclusive. It has often been claimed that the reason Hagen won four consecutive PGA championships (aside from the difficulty of beating him as a matchplay opponent) was out of fear of discovery. After his 1924 victory he had, unwisely, despatched the PGA trophy back to his hotel in a taxi while he went out searching for some interesting tiles to spend the night on. But the trophy never turned up at the hotel. Nobody knew any better as long as Hagen kept winning but in 1928 he was eliminated in the semi-final and had to, shamefacedly, own up. The PGA stumped up for a replacement trophy. The original was to reappear in the 1930s in the warehouse of a company which had just taken over Hagen's golf equipment plant. Ironically, with the original trophy restored, the PGA itself managed to lose the replacement.

The 1929 final of the PGA was played in the days of the stymie. Players did not lift their balls on the green and would often have to chip over an opponent's ball to hole out. The loser, Johnny Farrell, had a bad day. Twice he knocked Leo Diegel's ball into the hole in attempting to overcome a stymie (not unlike a snooker)

In 1932, Al Watrous only had to stay awake to win the PGA Championship. He was nine up on Bobby Cruickshank with 12 to play at the Keller GC in St Paul, Minnesota. He was probably composing his victory speech, because Cruickshank caught him. He shot a 30 on the back nine to tie the contest and beat Watrous in a play-off.

The biggest winning margin in the PGA during its matchplay years was in 1938, when Paul Runyan beat Sam Snead 8 and 7 to take his second PGA title.

In 1953, the great Ben Hogan did not win the USPGA, for the simple reason that he did not play in it. The case can be made that in that year Hogan actually won a professional Grand Slam. He'd already won the Masters and the US Open (at Oakmont) and then he travelled to Carnoustie and won his sole British Open championship. But he failed to win the Grand Slam proper, because the USPGA and the British Open were staged almost simultaneously. The PGA was won by Walter Burekmo.

There has been some debate about the validity of the USPGA Championship being described as a "Major". The argument runs that its quality is reduced by the inclusion of twenty American club pros and by the fact that it is usually played in intense heat in August. When the subject was brought up with the 1988 winner Jeff Sluman, his response was "Fine, I'll accept the fact that I can't count mine as a major when you go and tell Nicklaus that his five don't count." (Interestingly no one has ever argued about the validity of the description "Major" when applied to the three other tournaments because they admit amateurs, or that the British Open is often played in freezing conditions and gale-force winds which can change within minutes to bright sunshine and placid conditions, thereby putting some players at a competitive advantage. So there! Hah!)

In a row which was to have consequences for Augusta the following year, the founder of Shoal Creek GC, Hall Thompson, due to stage the 1990 USPGA Championship, caused consternation in an interview about the exclusive Alabama Club. Proving that political correctness hadn't permeated American country clubs, he observed of membership of Shoal Creek that . . . "we don't discriminate in any other area except blacks." He let loose the dogs of war, and the USPGA threatened to pull the event from Shoal Creek unless it changed its policy. It did but then had to prove its *bona fides* by finding an African-American who would stump up the $35,000 initiation fee and put up with the kind of people who were members of the club. They were fortunate a 66-year-old black, Louis Willie, joined nine days before the championship.

Ironically, the USPGA itself was not without unclean hands in the same regard. The 1962 USPGA Championship was to have been played in Los Angeles (it was played instead at Aronmink, Pennsylvania), but the Californian Attorney-General's office prohibited the tournament because the PGA's laws violated the Golden State's constitution. At the time, membership of the PGA was restricted to "professional golfers of the Caucasian race, residing in North or South America". Even more ironically, the PGA was won that year by Gary Player, representing a country which actively discriminated in its laws against blacks.

The victory of the unknown and unheralded John Daly at Crooked Stick in 1991 owed so much to happenstance as to be a virtual impossibility. Daly began as the *ninth* alternate, with no hope whatever of getting into the competition proper. Even after a number of players declined invitations for various reasons (among them Mark James, Lee Trevino and Ronan Rafferty), he was not much closer to getting the nod. Then an incredible series of coincidences propelled him towards the biggest win of his short career. The last legitimate entrant to withdraw, as is well-documented, was Nick Price, whose wife was about to have a baby. That allowed in the sixth alternate, Bill Sander. Because it was Wednesday afternoon and there was no possibility of a practice round over the almost unbelievably long course, Sander declined the place. It went to Mark Lye, who turned it down for similar reasons. The PGA were now down to the eighth alternate Brad Bryant. Bryant wasn't playing very well and his mother-in-law had been taken ill. Assuming he wasn't going to be playing, Bryant had made plans to visit her with his wife during the week of the PGA. He wasn't about to change his plans. The final place was offered to Daly, who had driven all the way from his Memphis home on the off-chance of getting in. He played Crooked Stick the following day (with Price's caddie "Squeaky" Medlin) without the benefit of a practice round and went on to a famous victory.

## Ryder Cup

The great Walter Hagen captained each of the first US Ryder Cup teams from the initiation of the tournament in 1927. Ten years later, he became the first captain to win in the opposition's home venue when the USA defeated GB and Ireland, 8–4, at Southport and Ainsdale. Hagen had prepared a victory speech suitable for the occasion on small cards but, as he waited while his friend the Prince of Wales introduced him to the crowd, the cards blew away. When he stood up to speak, fazed by the disappearance of his carefully scripted remarks, he blurted out the solecism, "I'm proud and happy to be the captain of the first American team to win on home soil." There was a pause, as the crowd waited for him to correct himself. The vacuum was suddenly filled by a native voice which pointed out to him that he meant, "foreign soil." Recovering his composure admirably, Hagen replied, "Yes! But you'll forgive me for feeling so much at home over here."

Both the players and the spectators were surprised and somewhat dismayed at the length of the grass on the greens at the Lindrick club in Yorkshire, where the 1957 Ryder Cup was staged. But there was a perfectly simple, if not very satisfactory, explanation. The greenkeeper was under the impression that the event was beginning the following day and was unpleasantly surprised to see the two teams arriving a day earlier than expected.

The participation of the old "Britain and Ireland" team in the Ryder Cup was an unmatched catalogue of utter failure. Only since the inclusion of European players, and the arrival on the scene of the likes of Ballesteros, Olazabal and Langer, have the contests been more even. One former captain of the British and Irish side, Brian Huggett of Wales, candidly admitted that, "We had six players in our team worth their salt, but the other six were only putting the blazer on." The great Christy O'Connor, veteran of ten consecutive Ryder Cups, between 1955–1973 (B & I snatched one win and one halved match in all that time), once observed that the B & I captains seemed not even to countenance the possibility of victory. Rather than telling their players to "Go out and win," the catch phrase was "Let's go out and put up a good show." Tony Jacklin, the non-playing captain identified with the change in fortunes in the 1980s, knew what it meant to "have your brains beaten out. I know what it feels like to sit at the back of the aeroplane and wear plastic shoes. It just makes you feel embarrassed."

There was little love lost between Ben Hogan and Arnold Palmer – King and Young Pretender in the late 1950s – and it spilled over into the 1967 Ryder Cup at Houston in Hogan's native state. Hogan was probably looking for an opportunity to assert his authority over the charismatic Palmer and took the seemingly extraordinary step of leaving him out of some of the series of games. The decision was prefaced by a discussion the day before the match started about the choice of ball the Americans would use (their own 1.68" or the European 1.62"). Palmer breezed into the locker room a day later than any of the other members of the American team, having been participating in the World Matchplay Championships. He greeted Hogan cheerily with a "Good morning, captain." This drew the response "Good morning, Arnold, you're a day late." Palmer's riposte was designed to establish his credentials rather than his excuse; Hogan would have been familiar with his schedule. "I've been in England winning the World Matchplay Championship." He paused and then inquired, "What ball are we playing?"

"Who said you're playing?" was Hogan's acid response.

(1967 was where Hogan introduced his players at the opening ceremony as "The finest golfers in the world." The ploy worked, they won by a 15-point margin.)

Palmer had a lucky break once in a four-ball match alongside Gardiner Dickinson against Peter Oosterhuis and Bernard Gallacher. The match was in St Louis, Missouri and the USA won, 18 and a half to 13 and a half. At one hole, Palmer hit a cracker of a shot and was congratulated by Oosterhuis's caddie. "Great shot, Mr Palmer," he exclaimed. Unfortunately, with his next breath he broke one of the cardinal rules of golf. "What club did you use?" he inquired. Oosterhuis and Gallacher lost the hole and Palmer and Dickinson won the match 5 & 4.

England's Mark James made his Ryder Cup debut in 1977 and remembers it vividly. He was paired with Tommy Horton against a lethal combination of the two greatest golfers in the world at the time Jack Nicklaus and Tom Watson. "We held them to 5 & 4," James recalled. "We weren't intimidated but we had an inkling they might be slightly better than us."

Quite the best-remembered shot in a losing cause for Europe was that of Bernhard Langer against Hale Irwin at the 18th at Kiawah Island. It was the infamous six-footer for victory which would have meant a halved match for Europe and retention of the cup previously retained with a tie at the Belfry in 1989. It is worth remembering a couple of things about that final match, though. Firstly, Irwin was extremely fortunate to have been in a position to win the hole. He hooked his drive off the tee and it was destined for one of the distinctive Kiawah Island sand beaches which adjoined many of the fairways. "Miraculously", after the American TV coverage returned from a commercial break, the ball was actually on the *fairway*. It is also worth remembering that, contrary to what many believed, the putt was not a simple two-foot tap-in and it did not result in Langer losing the match, he was already one up with one to play.

The hype over the missed putt might have blighted the career of a lesser player, but Langer brushed off the disappointment and won the German Masters the following week, thanks to a successful putt on the 18th hole from six feet. Afterwards the committed Christian put down the miss to God wanting to test his faith. "I look at it this way," he said, "There has only been one perfect man in the world and we crucified him. All I did was miss a putt."

The towering figure on the European side in Ryder Cups since his breakthrough in the early 1980s has, of course, been the great Spaniard Seve Ballesteros. He has an enviable record of success, especially in foursomes and four-balls (more often than not in partnership with one of his fellow countrymen – usually Jose Maria Olazabal). Even with his powers failing him due to injury in the 1990s, he still managed to find inspiration for the Ryder Cup and dominated the team to such an extent that, when he arrived for a photocall in 1993 with the rest of the team and it was discovered that he was wearing the wrong sweater for the shoot, Sam Torrance jokingly inquired "Should the rest of us change?"

Torrance had a notoriously embarrassing moment before the 1993 Ryder Cup thanks to an admitted *faux pas* of the American team captain, Tom Watson. The pre-tournament gala dinner (attended by up to 800 people) almost inevitably turned into a marathon autograph hunt. Watson decided that he was not going to have his team's very essence drained by the act of signing hundreds of autographs, so an instruction was issued to players to request people to hand in their dinner menus to team officials and they would be signed during the week. Which was all very fine in theory, until Sam Torrance trotted across to Watson, unaware of the edict, and asked the Great Man to sign his menu. Watson declined. Torrance returned to his table in high dudgeon and all Watson's subsequent attempts to explain his policy to the Scotsman fell on deaf ears. Just as at Kiawah Island two years before (but for far more innocuous reasons), the atmosphere between the two sides had been soured before a ball was struck.

The most successful European player at the 1995 Ryder Cup was the self-effacing David Gilford. He played in two four-balls with an out-of-form Seve Ballesteros but the great Spaniard acted as a highly effective cheerleader for the Englishman as they beat Brad Faxon and Peter Jacobsen 4 & 3. Seve was very upfront about his advice to Gilford. "I talk to him at the beginning," he told the press afterwards, "and tell him he is the best player out there. I know I cannot speak to him later because I won't be in the fairway." And so it proved, with Gilford making most of the shots which won the match. He finished two under par to Seve's three over, but don't underestimate the effect of Ballesteros on Gilford's game.

It hasn't escaped the notice of Irish golf fans that three Irish professionals have been instrumental in sealing the result of three European Ryder Cup triumphs (well, all right, two wins and a draw). All have done so with the assistance of out-of-the-ordinary shots. For the record, the nasty downhill putt of Eamon Darcy's at the 18th at Muirfield Village in 1987, in his match with Ben Crenshaw, virtually guaranteed victory for Tony Jacklin's side. Christy O'Connor Jr's great 2-iron shot at the 18th at the Belfry in 1989 did likewise, and Philip Walton needed to beat Jay Haas in the penultimate match of 1995 at Oak Hill to give Bernard Gallacher his one and only win as European captain. One can argue about the style of Walton's victory (a nervous bogey at the 18th being enough to settle a match where he had been dormie three), but none can dispute the quality of his teeshot at the par-3 15th which put him in his winning position.

216

# CHAPTER THIRTEEN

## *Would You Believe It?*

*Strange tales from golf's Twilight Zone*

### Speed and Endurance

On 18 June, 1987 James Carvill played Warrenpoint Golf Course in Northern Ireland (which measures 6154 yds – almost exactly three-and-a-half miles) in 27 mins 9 secs. He allowed the ball to come to rest, as per the rules of golf, before undertaking each shot. His average speed per mile was well under eight minutes (7.77 minutes per mile), a speed which few golfers could sustain even without the distraction of playing golf shots. Six years earlier, the American 1500-metre Olympian, Steve Scott, had taken 92 shots to get around a course in 29 minutes 33.05 seconds.

A 22-year-old, four-handicap golfer, Sue Ledger, a member of the East Berkshire club, set a new women's world record by playing 18 holes in 37 minutes 24 seconds, at Wokingham, in September 1995.

The Irish professional Jimmy Kinsella sacrificed a certain amount of speed in the interests of scoring when he shot a 73 in 1972. Riding a bicycle around the Skerries course in North County Dublin, he completed his round in 42 minutes 13 seconds.

On 21 July, 1964, sixty-one year old Dick Hardison took forty-nine minutes to shoot a 68 at the Sea Mountain GC in Punaluu, Hawaii. He shot a 30 on the back nine in twenty-four minutes.

Using one ball and completing the round in a one-over-par 73, a group of 48 golfers played the 7108-yard Kyalami course near Johannesburg in South Africa in 9 min 51 sec.

Over a twenty-four hour period between 27-28 November, 1971, Australian Ian Colston played 401 holes at Bendigo Golf Club in Victoria. He completed 22 full rounds and even managed four sudden-death tie holes without the aid of oxygen or a golf buggy.

Using a golf buggy Charles Stock managed to sneak in 783 holes at the Arcadia Country Club in Lyndhurst, Ohio on July 20, 1987. The buggy must have been turbo-charged, and he must have been allowed to play through rather a lot, but he averaged 1.8 rounds every hour. Driving a buggy around the Arrowhead Country Club in North Canton, Ohio in the USA, David Cavalier played 846 holes of golf over 24 hours on 6-7 August 1990.

Colin Young of Pattingham in England managed 70 rounds in a single week in July 1989. He played them all on the Patshull Park Golf Club in his native town. He averaged 180 holes a day or 7.5 holes an hour.

Alain Reisco managed to play three rounds of golf on three different continents in the same day. Reisco is an airline executive and he was joined on the day by three colleagues, Sherl Folger, Marvin Fritz and Art Sues. The four-ball teed off at 5.00 am at the Royal Mohammedia GC in Casablanca in Morocco. By 1.30 pm, they were playing the Torrequebrada GC at Malaga in Spain. Finally, after jetting to the USA, they played the North Hills Country Club in Manhasset, New York, starting their round at 6.30 pm.

On 12 June, 1939 Ernest Smith played five rounds of golf in the same day. His fatigue level was accentuated by virtue of the fact that he played the five rounds in five different countries. He played in Scotland, Ireland, the Isle of Man (well, it does have its own parliament!), England and Wales. For the record, Smith shot rounds of 70, 76, 76, 72 and 68. Two over "fours" for 90 holes of golf on the same day.

Peter Bown of Blandford in Dorset is a collector of golf courses. Obviously, he doesn't keep them locked away in his drawer, he plays them. So far, he has fitted in 434. The first course he ever played was Ashton-under-Lyne in Lancashire, where his very first teeshot was an unfortunate air shot. The best course he has played during his global and domestic peregrinations was (in his opinion, anyway) Pine Valley and he is a charter member of the Golf Collectors Society. (Name self-explanatory.)

Merle Ball from Florida didn't take up the game of golf until he was 64. In the ten years since then, he has played on an ever-growing number of courses. In 1988, he played 130 courses in all 50 states of the USA, playing right-handed. In 1989, he played in 50 states in 51 days, but this time he did so left-handed (his trip incuded a hole in one in Hawaii on the third day). In 1990, he played 220 holes in one day at his home course, the Sun 'n Lake Country Club in Sebring, Florida. (110 holes right-handed and 110 holes left-handed). In 1991, he played a total of 1,290 rounds of golf (that's an average of 3.53 a day!) in addition to hitting 65,800 balls in practice, far more than the average professional. In 1992, he was named Golf Nut of the Year by the American Golf Nut Society. He reckons he's played 870 courses since he signed his first scorecard ten years ago.

Want longer arms? Try Albert Rayner's approach. He set a world club swinging record of 17,512 revolutions (nearly five swings per second) over a 60-minute period in Wakefield, Yorksire on 27 July, 1981.

### Swingers

An Australian meteorologist named Nils Lied drove a golf ball 2640 yards, or one-and-a-half miles, across ice at Mawson Base in Antarctica in 1962.

On April Fool's day, 1991 Canadian Ian Evans played a golf shot from a height of 20,341 ft on Mt Aconcagua in Argentina. Aside from astronaut Alan Shepard duffing a 6-iron shot on the surface of the moon it is the "highest" golf shot known.

Arthur Lynskey climbed the 14,110 foot Pike's Peak in Colorado on June 28, 1968 and drove a ball off the top of the montain. He later claimed that he'd driven the ball more than 2 miles. 200 yards out and 2 miles down!

The USA itself became the world's biggest golf course in 1963 when Floyd Satterlee Rood played "through the green" from the Pacific to the Atlantic Coast between 14 September, 1963 and 3 October, 1964. He completed his round (without a fine or other penalty for slow play) in 114,737 strokes. He lost 3511 balls on a course measuring 5468 *kilometres*.

Were the surface of the moon not pockmarked with craters even bigger than a John Daly divot, the energy expended on earth to drive a golf ball three hundred yards would send it scurrying along for a mile along the fairways of our nearest and dearest satellite.

In the space of a single hour, Cheshire golfer and showman Noel Hunt drove 1536 golf balls! Only balls driven over one hundred yards into a target area were counted in this shoulder-numbing exercise.

The longest recorded drive by a sexagenarian was one of 515 yards by 64-year-old Michael Hoke Austin in the US National Seniors Championship at Las Vegas, Nevada on 25 September 1974. With the aid of a 35 mph tailwind Austin, a strapping 6' 2" and an ample fourteen-and-a-half stone in weight (203 lbs), drove more than 60 yards past the flag on the par-four, 450-yard, fifth hole at the Winterwood course.

Let's say you're unhappy with your swing but you still enjoy the fresh air and camaraderie of a good game of golf. Why not ditch the clubs and simply *throw* the ball around the course? An American, Joe Flynn, holds the record for this enigmatic variation on pitching. He went round Port Royal in Bermuda (6228 yds) in 82 shots on 27 March, 1975 and saved on caddies' fees in the process.

Variations on the game of golf with which we are familiar include an obsession with driving golf balls over tall objects, a sort of golfing equivalent of steeplechasing. The build-up of urban centres and the relative absence of church spires adjacent to golf courses has dampened down this interesting practice, but in the 18th and 19th centuries it was not an uncommon pursuit of golfers in search of an interesting side bet. In 1798, for example, two Edinburgh golfers named Sceales and Smellie (sic) were given an allowance of six balls each to clear the spire of St Giles Cathedral in Edinburgh. Both managed to put their balls over the weathercock of the tower, a height of 160 ft. The achievement has been emulated since, and then, in the 1840s, a Scottish writer Donald McLean put down his pen, picked up an extremely lofted club and drove his ball over the Melville Monument in St Andrew's Square in Edinburgh, which measures 154 ft. in height.

English golf pro and writer Laddie Lucas once blindfolded himself and shot an 87 round the Sandy Lodge course.

Charles Boswell of Birmingham, Alabama went six better. Blinded by shellfire in World War II, he took up golf after the war and once shot an 81.

If you're still congratulating yourself on having broken 100 for the first time, don't be too depressed by the achievement of Thomas M'Auliffe in shooting 108 at the Buffalo Country Links in upstate New York. Now 108 is not such a great score, except when you reflect that M'Auliffe has no arms. He posted his score by holding the club between his right shoulder and his cheek.

At Abergele GC in Clwyd in Wales, David Morris hit 1,290 practice drives in an hour on 21 May 1988. That's an average of a drive every three seconds. One wonders does he play as quickly when he takes his game to the course.

## Age

Sam Snead became the first player on the USPGA Tour to shoot his age in an official event. The following day he went out and beat it. In the Quad Cities Open in Illinois, in July 1979, Snead, aged 67, shot a 67. The next day he shaved a further stroke off his unique record.

Players like the great Christy O'Connor regularly shoot their age. But then, he's only a mere colt of 70 or so. Arthur Thompson had to wait until he was 103 years old before he shot his age at the Uplands course in Victoria in British Columbia in 1973.

The youngest player to shoot his age (so far) is one Robert Leroy Klingaman, who shot a 58 at Caledonia Golf club in Pennsylvania in August 1973.

Charlie Law probably beat his age by more shots than any other player ever has. On May 20, 1984, at the age of 84, Law shot a round of 75 over the Hayston Course near Glasgow.

American Joe Jiminez came close in 1995 in the Ameritech Classic to emulating that margin, but his achievement must rank as one of the all-time great "shoot your age" stories. He shot a 62 (that's not a misprint if it reads 62!) Jiminez is 69 years old.

The oldest known professional golfer at the time of writing is probably Joseph Thomas, a member of the USPGA in Columbus, Ohio. He is ninety-five years of age. (Here's hoping he hasn't passed away by the time this gets to print.) In 1991, Britain's oldest professional, Ray Gray of the Evesham Golf Club, died at the age of 87. He'd been the club's first and only pro for 62 years.

## The Natural World

They may have 29 Major wins between them but Jack Nicklaus and Gary Player were no match for a swarm of South African killer bees. The two men were playing an exhibition match in Zwartkop in 1966. On one hole they were attacked by the bees and fled. Rather than return to their balls, they agreed to halve the hole and move on. Game, set and match to the bees, really!

The well-timed surreptitious cough has often been the difference between watching your opponent slide the ball confidently into the hole to win the match or jerk it three inches to the left and five feet past. However, it was not one of Dr Sherman A Thomas's playing partners who caused him to miss to the left on the 17th green at the Congressional Country Club near Washington DC, it was the honking of a goose (or whatever it is geese do – this is a book on golf, not ornithology). Dr Thomas, being a passionate man, was not about to let matters rest, shrug his shoulders and stride placidly to the 18th tee. No, instead he set about the goose with his putter and killed it stone dead with nicely balanced follow-through to the head. For this act of callous revenge on a defenceless creature he was fined $500 . . . for killing a goose out of season! The judge who heard the case refused to accept Dr Thomas's excuse that the goose had been badly wounded by his approach shot and he had merely been putting it out of its misery.

This is one for those who oppose golf courses because they are an environmental blot on the landscape. Somehow a huge beech tree, five feet in diameter, at Killermont Golf Club in Glasgow, collapsed when it was struck with the full force of a ball hit by a member.

In the 1995 Murphy's Irish Open at Mount Juliet, the eventual winner Sam Torrance shot a birdie on the tricky par-three third. He then proceeded to hit another off his drive at the fourth. This one, however, was of the feathered variety. He knocked a magpie out of the sky with his tee-shot.

In 1921, one PM Gregor of Kirkfield, Ontario badly needed a long putt to win a match but he left his putt just a roll short of the cup. However, as he walked forward to tap the ball in and move to the next hole, a grasshopper landed on it and knocked it into the cup, giving Gregor the hole and the match.

On May 4th, 1934 Lawson Little (US Open Champion in 1940) hit his approach shot on to the green on the 17th at St Andrew's only to see a Persian cat, clearly in serious training to be a dog, pick it up and run away with it. After checking for more cats in the vicinity, he was allowed to respot the ball.

Corkman Michael McEvoy left a donkey with little choice but to disappear with his ball when playing the third hole at Midleton Golf club in 1922. One of his drives struck the unfortunate donkey, who was unwisely grazing on the fairway. The ball lodged in the donkey's ear and he hightailed it for the woods in terror. McEvoy found his ball (but not the donkey) among the trees and took a double bogey on the hole.

During the 1968 British Open at Carnoustie, one of the competitors, John Morgan, was about to hit a shot on the tenth fairway when a rat took a leap at him and bit him. After getting treatment for the wound, Morgan was able to continue his round.

Playing in the PGA Championship at Wentworth in 1991, Irishman David Feherty bent down to examine what he took to be a dummy rubber snake one of his many practical joker friends had left for him, when the snake, an adder, bit him. Feherty suffered both from snakebite and from shock and commented afterwards that "I considered beating the living daylights out of it but it's probably got a wife and snakelets."

During the 1972 Singapore Open, Jimmy Stewart (om, no om relation to the actor) was about to hit a shot when he was attacked by a 10-foot cobra which rather fancied that his ball was a juicy egg. Stewart managed to teach the cobra a lesson it forgot rather quickly, because he killed it with his golf club. As if that wasn't enough for one poor golfer to have to contend with, a second snake slithered from the cobra's mouth and Stewart was forced to take similar action with the cobra's last dinner.

In a tournament in Zambia, Sandy Lyle asked for a ruling from a referee as his ball had come to rest in the middle of a swarm of black ants. The referee studied the situation for a while and then advised the Scot that he was only entitled to relief from a swarm of red ants!

Jerry Towns stood on the tee of the 136-yard 7th hole at The Woods Golf Course in Cochran, Georgia and watched in dismay as his ball hit the putting surface and spun back into the water guarding the green. He then looked on in astonishment as a 14-inch bass swallowed his ball and spat it back out on to the green, close to the hole. Completely floored by what he had just witnessed Towns missed his birdie putt.

In the worst competitive tradition, during a match in Arkansas a woman hit a ball into a bunker. Climbing in to play it, she realised that she was not alone: a sleeping rattlesnake was sunning itself. Out she jumped and resolutely refused to go back in. She threw herself on the mercy of her opponent, who was about as sympathetic a character as the Roman Emperor Nero. It was pointed out that relief of any kind had to be refused as the snake constituted a loose impediment which could not be removed from a hazard. The ball would have to be played where it lay. Trembling, the woman actually climbed back into the bunker. Her opponent, in an attack of generosity of spirit, agreed to stand by with a rake in case the rattler might happen to wake up.

## Stranger Than Fiction

The City Golf Club in London might be accused by Puritanical *dirigistes* of having its priorities somewhat askew. Despite its name, it doesn't actually possess a golf course on which its members can play. Neither does it have a locker room, a putting green, a professional or indeed any of the accoutrements that contribute so much to the essential "golfiness" of golf courses. In fact, its well-appointed premises in Fleet Street in London don't even have a single golfing photograph, club, ball, tee or artefact of any kind. The club did have a driving range at one stage, but dropped it as a pointless exercise. Its members, like those of other London gentlemen's clubs, simply eat and drink there before falling asleep behind their newspapers.

In 1904 CH Allison, a member of the Woking Golf Club in England, was involved in a titanic matchplay tussle when he hit his approach shot to the 18th on to the clubhouse roof. Determined not to concede he acquired a ladder from somewhere, climbed out on to the roof and played the ball where it lay. He managed to get the ball on to the green and sink the putt to halve the hole.

Oscar Grimes qualifed to play in the Western Open in 1939 but he didn't fare very well in the tournament itself. One of his drives went berserk, hit a hamburger stand, cannoned into the cash register and came to rest in an open drawer.

In 1951 in Wichita in Texas, a Mr Moody Weaver was practising his game. He was either a very aggressive golfer or he had managed to become well loosened up, because he took a particularly violent swing and succeeded in breaking both his legs in two places.

Why he would want to is beyond me but on 9 February, 1980 Lang Martin of Charlotte, North Carolina succeeded in balancing seven golf balls vertically. And no, I don't know whether they were balata or surlyn.

In 1895 one James Cheape (after whom Cheape's bunker is named) held the Royal and Ancient to ransom. He possessed the rights to gather shells from the St Andrew's links. This gave him the right to dig for the shells if he chose to do so. With the Open coming to the course that year, Cheape threatened to dig up the sixteenth fairway, which adjoined his property, unless he was given viewing rights there. The R & A, wisely, gave him what he wanted.

The man from the "Soft Ice" ice cream company thought he'd found the ideal spot to park his van and do business on the opening day of the 1995 Open championship at St Andrew's. He obviously didn't know much about golf (or maybe he shared Sam Snead's first impression of the course), because he'd opened for business on the first fairway.

The performance of the Japanese golfer Katsuyoshi Tomori in the first two rounds of the 1995 Open championship at St Andrew's (he led at halfway) attracted a Japanese following even larger than usual to the third round. Tomori prepared for his third round by getting in some practice on the putting green. When he turned to make his way to the first tee, about fifty yards away, he found his way blocked by dozens of Japanese who had been watching him practice. As he looked up and caught their eyes, the entire crowd bowed in unison.

One day you're up . . . Tommy Armour, the great professional of the teens and twenties, won the US Open in 1927. The following week, he was playing in the Shawnee Open where, at the 17th hole, he took 23 strokes after hitting one ball after another out of bounds.

It's everyone's dream to see their ball disappear into the hole off the tee. But in the case of a player at Blackmoor Golf Club in England, it was not such a boost. After he teed off he watched as his ball sailed out of bounds and into a chimney-pot 120 yards away. Naturally, as luck would have it, the owner of the house and his wife were sitting in front of the fire as the ball descended.

The emergency services were called posthaste to the Point Grey Golf and Country Club in Vancouver, Canada when it was feared a 95-year-old member, Justice JM Coody, had suffered a heart attack. It proved, however, to have been a false alarm. A member passing by the judge sitting in his golf buggy had inquired whether there was anything wrong and thought he received the reply "Heart failure." The judge was actually having problems with his buggy and had muttered "Cart failure."

Playing in the 1980 Corfu International Championship, one Sharon Peachey drove off and then watched as her ball collided with that of a competitor playing a different hole. To illustrate that there is little justice in this cruel world and none at all in golf, Sharon's ball plummeted to the ground, losing distance, and came to rest in a pond.

How often can a player claim to have parred a hole without touching grass? According to Dermot Gilleece of *The Irish Times,* it happened to Tom Malone during a society outing in Dundalk in 1994. At the 18th hole, he drove into a fairway bunker. His second shot ended up in a greenside trap. He fluffed his first effort, but his second attempt from the trap bounced straight into the hole.

In one of the most bizarre golf matches ever played (presumably for a bet), in 1912, one Harry Dearth, a well-known singer at the time, donned a suit of armour and played a match at Bushey Hall GC against an unnamed opponent. He lost 2 and 1. Clearly his iron play wasn't up to scratch!

American pro Rick Hartmann, while he played on the European circuit, was noted for his innate ability to incur bizarre penalties. His most outrageous self-inflicted wound came when his ball lay in the semi-rough underneath an oak tree. He was standing waiting to play his shot when he idly picked up an acorn and hefted it at the trunk of the tree. The projectile smacked off the bark with great force, bounced back and hit his ball. Hartmann incurred a two-shot penalty.

Since the famous TPC course at Sawgrass in Florida opened in 1982, an average of 269,000 balls a year have been reclaimed from its various water hazards. This means that more than 3.75 million balls have disappeared in 14 years.

A Swedish amateur of no visible golfing prowess was playing in a pro-am at Woburn with Ireland's David Feherty. Conditions were wet and miserable and the Swede, despite being out of contention on almost every hole, insisted on getting his money's worth by playing out for a sequence of triumphant sevens and eights. On one hole he was, yet again, in the rough. After his partners had helped search for his ball with increasing frustration, the Scandinavian abandoned his efforts once the statutory five minutes had elapsed. He then insisted on dropping another ball over his left shoulder and playing that. But when he turned to address his second ball, he couldn't find that either. Another search began, which proved fruitless. The doughty Viking was persuaded that his assistance was no longer necessary in compiling a score for the hole. He walked on to the next tee. When his partners arrived he announced that he had found the missing ball . . . in the hood of his rain-jacket!

The great Bobby Locke managed to wrap his ball in material as well. Playing the 12th at Royal Dublin in the 1936 Irish Open, Locke lost sight of the ball as it approached the pin. When he got to the green there was no sign of the ball so, just in case, he lifted the pin out of the hole to see if the ball was there. It fell at his feet, having been caught up in the flag. He then made the short putt for a birdie.

While Mary Brown waited to putt out on the 18th during a playing of the Southern California Women's Open, a sudden cloudburst stopped play. When it restarted, the green was completely waterlogged and the cup full of water. Ms Brown putted and watched in considerable chagrin as the ball simply floated over the hole. She was allowed to putt again after the hole was drained as tournament officials ruled that she had been unfairly victimised.

Not many professional golfers withdraw from tournaments because they are dissatisfied with their sartorial standards, but Mark Calcavecchia did. He was playing in the 1986 Kemper Open at the TPC-Avenel Course in Potomac, Maryland when he drove a ball into a ravine. Climbing down to get to it, he slipped into a mud puddle and covered himself in slime. A few holes later, he withdrew from the tournament.

Harry Vardon once watched a truly awful golfer miss his ball completely and then lose it. The incident happened at a course in Totteridge in England. The player had, using a wedge, hit the ball with his eyes closed. He only succeeded in hitting the ground about a foot behind the ball, dislodging an enormous divot. When the player opened his eyes he looked around in extreme puzzlement, unable to locate the ball. It was resting under the divot.

Sam Snead once got help from an opponent. Playing in the 1938 PGA Championship in Shawnee-on-Delaware, Pennsylvania, Snead was on the green when his opponent Jimmy Hines chipped for the hole. Hines's ball hit Snead's and both rolled into the hole for birdies.

During World War II, when certain materials were in short supply, a tournament was held in Pochefstroom, South Africa in which wooden balls only were used. The Wooden Ball Championship was won by AA Horne who shot a 90.

John Humm from Long Island, New York, once shot a 34 for nine holes using only one golf club, a 3-iron. He should have stuck with what he was good at, because the very next day he went out and shot 40 over nine holes, using a full set of clubs.

Kent Kluba and Raphael Alarcon, two professionals, may need to include compasses among the paraphenalia they bring out on the golf course with them. In 1985, during the French Open, they finished the second hole and went off in search of the third tee. Unfortunately, they missed it and found themselves on the thirteenth fairway before they realised their mistake.

At the age of 68, Harriett O'Brien Lee chipped into the hole no less than five times in a single round at the Meadows Golf Club in Greyeagle, California.

An English golfer named John Beck once putted into his own hat. He had just sent a putt on its way when a gust of wind blew his hat off and it landed right on the line of the ball, which duly popped into it.

Please don't try this sort of thing on your home course, but in 1980 a woman won her local club championship by breaking her opponent's arm. Margaret McNeill faced Earlena Adams in the Boone Golf Club Championship in North Carolina. The match was about to go into a sudden death play-off when McNeill took a practice swing and struck Adams on the arm, breaking it in the process. Because Adams couldn't continue the match, McNeill was adjudged the winner.

By his own account, the American golfer and commentator Bob Rosburg once mishit a shot into a clubhouse drainpipe. The ball scurried up the pipe and popped out on to the carpet of the men's locker room.

"Don't put your daughter on the stage, Mrs Worthington," advised Noel Coward. "Don't become golfers," was a piece of advice which Mike Turnesa clearly didn't offer his sons. He had seven of them and six became pros. The best known were Jim, who won the 1952 PGA Championship, and Joe. Informed that Joe was leading the 1926 US Open, his irascible father responded "Well, why wouldn't he be, he spends enough time on the golf course." The only failure of the family was Willie. He remained an amateur all his life. Mind you, he did managed to squeeze in a couple of victories in the US Amateur Championship (1938, 1948).

A local rule in a British golf club during the Second World War generously allowed players to take cover while bombs were falling "without penalty for ceasing to play."

Welshman Phillip Parkin injured his leg during the 1985 Open championship at Royal St George's, Sandwich and looked like he would be unable to finish his round because he was unable to walk. To the rescue came a gallant playing partner, none other than Nick Faldo. He carried Parkin piggyback and enabled him to complete the round.

US pro Curtis Sifford has seen his shots land in some unusual places in his time, but none more bizarre than when his ball landed in a hot dog during the Quad Cities Open in Iowa. Sifford was permitted to remove the ball from the hot dog, and the mustard from the ball, before resuming his round. Not fazed by the experience, he managed to hit his next shot on to the green.

One of David J Russell's better efforts disappeared altogether. Which was strange, because it had landed close to the edge of the fairway. This was during the 1991 Cannes Open. Later, it emerged that a woman had taken the ball as a souvenir of her visit to the event. She excused her behaviour by saying "But I thought they had plenty of them in their bags."

Payne Stewart once lost his knickers in a golf bet. At least, the Americans call them knickers. We call them plus-fours. (But "knickers" makes for a far better opening, don't you think?) Unwisely, he bet three LPGA women pros that he would beat their better ball. The bet was that, if he lost, he would remove his plus-fours on the 18th. If he won, they would remove their shorts. Well, he lost and, to a cacophany of catcalls he duly doffed his "knickers" on the 18th.

A member of a golf club in Kent, the Wildernesse, managed such a wild shot off the first tee that it went straight through the window of the pro shop and ended up in the cup of tea that the pro had just brewed for himself. (The cup of tea was fine, but the professional was injured by the flying glass from the window.)

*Golf Digest*'s idea of the worst "avid" golfer in the world is Angelo Spagnola. He took part in a competition organised by the magazine to find the biggest duffer who regularly haunts a golf course. Mr Spagnola, from Fayette City, Pennsylvania put all other hackers into true perspective with an excruciating 18-hole total of 257. (Pros have won 72-hole tournaments with less.) This included a record-setting 66 on the 17th hole. Mr Spagnola's per hole average (excluding the apocalyptic 17th) was 11.23.

Ian Baker Finch, the 1991 Open Champion, who has been having a disastrous streak of missed cuts in recent years, is an extremely handsome man. Women, not unnaturally, appear to find him very sexy indeed. On one occasion in a USPGA tournament, he hit his ball into a water hazard and, rather than take a drop, he went in after it, after first removing his trousers, shoes and socks. Below the waist, he was down to his boxer shorts, taking the shot. When he got to the next tee, as he lined up for his drive, a number of women fans took up the chant "Hit it in the water! Hit it in the water!"

Arnold Palmer used to have a particular female fan in Palm Springs who would come out in force to greet him whenever he played in tournaments in the area. She would get so carried away with her proximity to the great man that she used to whisper endearments to him, such as "darling," "lover," and "sweetie;" except she didn't always whisper them. On more than one occasion Palmer would be lining up to take a shot when the woman would scream "Go, lover," from somewhere in the gallery. "It's not the best thing for your concentration," Arnie once told the writer George Plimpton.

Talk about an appropriate name! Three members of the Togood family proved . . . forget it . . . finished first, second and third in the same tournament. The 1956 Tasmanian Open was won by Peter, his father Alfred finished second and his brother John finished third. Nothing like keeping it in . . . forget it.

If you were under the illusion that golf pros are sensitive, caring types then go back to the planet Mars. The following were the responses of Nick Faldo, Seve Ballesteros, Colin Montgomerie and Nick Price to a question from *Golf World* magazine. The question was, "You have a one-stroke lead going up the 72nd hole of the Open. You hook your drive and it will definitely go out of bounds unless it hits a lone spectator in the head. While the ball is in the air, do you say to yourself: (a) Please miss him/her, there's always next year. (b) Hit that sucker and bounce back into the fairway?"

Faldo's response was "Please let it hit that sucker, but don't hurt him. Don't draw blood. I hate the sight of blood." Seve was even more pragmatic. "Hit him right in the middle of the head." Clearly he wasn't going to take any chances with an unfortunate ricochet. Montgomerie tried to cloak his cold-bloodedness by insisting. "I've got to say (a), haven't I?" while Price got it just about right (for a golf pro) with "Hit him – and I'll give him the ball afterwards." Not the prize money mind you, or even a share of it; just the ball.

Mike Warfield, a romantic type at heart, and a devoted golf nut, found an unusual way (the big chicken!) to propose to Carmen Minning. While they were playing together, he wrote the words "Marry Me" on her golf ball. She was flummoxed at first but accepted his unusual proposal. Afterwards, he told her that, had she said nothing and hit the ball out of bounds, he would have taken that as a "No!"

Cyril Walker, the 1924 US Open Champion, was a slow player. One of the slowest. So slow he actually got arrested for it back in 1930. It happened at the Riviera Club during the Los Angeles Open. He was being his normal deliberate self. But the tournament organisers simply got sick of interminable delays and disqualified him. Walker, an Englishman, stoutly refused to leave the course and had to be physically dragged away by the Los Angeles police.

John Laupheimer, once an executive with the US Golf Association, used to throw dinner parties in men-only clubs for the press. Nothing wrong with that, you might think. Except that at the time he was Commissioner of the Ladies' Professional Golf Association.

Richard Boxall, the English professional, managed to break his leg when he swung at a ball on the 9th tee of the 1991 Open Championship at Birkdale. So bad was the break that people standing 150 yards away heard the bone fracture and assumed it was a gunshot. One wag observed that, had the accident happened on the 10th, Boxall would have been the only man in Open history to have gone out in 34 and back in an ambulance.

In 1953, a Scottish golfer hit an approach to the 5th hole at St Andrew's, which shares a huge double green with the 13th. He hooked his shot viciously but the ball still ended up in the hole. Unfortunately it was the 13th hole! Later in his round, he sliced a shot on the 18th and watched it hit the roof of a passing lorry. It then sailed through the door of the clubhouse, finally coming to rest in the bar!

Ken Gordon, a member of the USGA executive, was once called upon to give a ruling in his underwear. It happened while he was having a nap in his hotel room adjoining the National Golf Links in Southampton, Long Island, NY. There was a knock on the door and outside stood a golfer and caddy. The man informed Gordon that he had pulled his approach shot to the eighteenth on to the hotel roof and the only way to get to it was through Gordon's bedroom window. Never one to stand idly by while a fellow golfer was in difficulty (other than a matchplay opponent), Gordon allowed the man through. Unfortunately, his ball was in the gutter and three attempts to drop it on to the roof for a penalty only resulted in it rolling back in. Leaning out the bedroom window, semi-naked, Gordon instructed the golfer to place the ball where it had landed when he dropped it. The competitor obliged and pitched from the roof back on to the course. He then climbed back through the window and headed for the green while Gordon resumed his disturbed nap.

What's in a name? Not much if the recent experience of the San Diego Open is anything to go by. It's gone through marginally more name changes than Elizabeth Taylor (not that anyone ever actually called her Mrs Burton, or Mrs Fortensky). A continuing boon for the signpainting industry, in 1981 it was known as the Wickes/Andy Williams Open. In 1983, a change of sponsor meant it became the Isuzu/Andy Williams Open. In 1988, Andy was still hanging on but Isuzu had given way to the Searson Lehman/Hutton/Andy Williams Open. The following year Andy Williams finally gave up the ghost and it was "simply" the Searson Lehman/Hutton Open. In 1991, it became the Searson Lehman Brothers Open and the following year it was the Buick Invitational of California. What identity crisis, for God's sake?

In 1994 (the year before he captained his first winning Ryder Cup team), Bernard Gallacher had a street named after him in the Scottish town of Livingston. What's so odd about that? Nothing, it's just that Gallacher was born in the town of Bathgate.

When it comes to making and, more importantly, marketing golf clubs, no company has been more successful in recent years than the Callaway Corporation of California, makers of the range of "Big Bertha" metal woods. The New York Stock Exchange launch of the company, when it went public on 28 February 1992, will give an indication of just how successful it is. The opening offer for the three million shares was $20 per share. Within less than half an hour, they were being traded at $36 a share. In that opening day's trading, the company's book value increased from $160 million to $288 million. Chi Chi Rodriguez, who had been given shares in the company when he signed on and endorsed their products, earned more during the first twenty minutes of trading than he had in his entire career as a golf pro. Since 1992, Callaway stock has increased in value by 600%. Many of the executives with the company, who were given shares and share options in lieu of large salaries in the early days of the company, are now multi-millionaires. All on the back of "Bertha", a brand name many of them opposed at the time of its launch, believing that women would not play with a club so named. Company CEO Ely Callaway pushed through the "Bertha" label name.

The man who probably makes more money from the game of golf on an annual basis than anyone else is Karsten Solheim, the manufacturer of Ping golf clubs. His wealth is estimated at between $400 and $500 million.

If an extraordinarily fit and enthusiastic US PGA Tour player was to participate in every professional tournament on the American circuit, and make every single cut, he would end up walking a total of 691 miles from tee to green in the course of a very long, and physically and mentally exhausting year's work. The average length of US tour courses is 6988 yards, or 3.97 miles – that's almost 16 miles per tournament.

We've seen a lot of different putting methods and putters. The broomhandle putter and the Langer grip are just two of the more recent products/methods devised to get the pill into the green's mouth. But few can have been as desperate as US Tour pro Mike Hulbert. He was so distraught over his putting that in the first round of the AT&T at Pebble Beach in 1995 he actually putted *one-handed*. What's more, it worked. Using his right hand only, he shot a 68.

Contrary to popular belief the USA is not entirely and utterly obsessed with golf (the national pastime is, of course, making money). A recent survey showed (shock, swoon) that only 6.5% of all Americans have ever played, watched or read about golf.

American LPGA player Dale Eggeling has a personal rule: if she's on a roll, she doesn't go to the toilet during a round. This policy goes back to August 1994, when she was five under par for the first 16 holes of the Chicago Challenge. The call of nature was summoning her to what Americans euphemistically call "the bathroom". She ignored that call at the 17th and bogied the hole. Rather than wait to get back to the clubhouse she ran for a Portaloo between the 17th green and 18th tee. She then proceeded to double-bogey the 18th after her worst drive of the day and finished with a modest 2-under-par 70.

In July 1993, to celebrate the British Open of that year the Reverend Norman Faulds turned the aisle of his church in Gullane into a putting green and undertook a ceremony which he called "The Blessing of the Putters".

A dog called Chico was made an honorary member, in 1971, of Waihi GC in Hamilton, New Zealand. He was trained to find lost balls which were then sold to provide extra funds for the club. (One wonders did he have all his teeth extracted first.)

In 1987 Jeff Sluman was in a play-off with Sandy Lyle for the Players Championship (the so-called "Fifth Major"). He had an eight-foot birdie putt for victory and was lining it up when a fan jumped into the water adjoining the green. Sluman had to step back and wait for officials to grab the man and pull him ashore before he could resume. When he did, he missed the putt and lost the play-off at the next hole. It later transpired that the man, a student from Florida State University, had pulled the same stunt earlier in the day, had been warned about his subsequent behaviour but had been allowed to remain where he was.

A device has recently been developed, by (naturally) an American company, which lets golfers know how slowly they are playing. You attach it to the steering post of a golf cart and start it when you tee off. The face of the clock features the eighteen holes of a golf course and the hand tells you where you should be at any given time in the course of your round.

Beware of electric caddy car batteries. In 1993, one Sandy Duncan was driving home when the battery of his trolley went on fire in the boot of his car. The metal shafts of his clubs touched the battery terminals and the resulting sparks started the blaze. Duncan got away with his life, but six of his clubs and his car stereo were destroyed.

In the 19th Century the now famous Old Course at St Andrew's was (and still is) a municipal course. It might have hosted a number of prestigious events but locals didn't take kindly to being told the course might have to be "rested" before staging a championship. One year, the British Amateur and Open were being staged within a month of each other and professionals like Old Tom Morris wanted the course at its best for both events but, more particularly, for the latter. Morris came up with an ingenious solution for keeping people off the course who were fully entitled to play it during that month. He simply filled in all the cups!

John McDermott won the US Open championship in consecutive years (1911 and 1912), but he had a problem with dates. In 1914, he arrived from the USA for the British Open pre-qualifying tournament, in the wrong week! By the time he got there, pre-qualifying was over.

A gang of burglars who were attempting to rob a house adjacent to Warley Park Golf Club in Essex in England discovered they'd picked the wrong house when they were nicked by 24 off-duty policemen who were playing in a society day at Warley Park, and who spotted the raid taking place.

Harry Vardon and Ted Ray, on a tour of the USA, were playing a challenge match against Vardon's brother Tom and Jack Burke. On one hole during the morning session Tom, always anxious to best his older brother, holed a long putt. The great man stepped up to his putt, a tricky one but considerably shorter than the one his brother had just seen disappear. Vardon, despite his infamous putting frailties, looked to have sunk the putt as it approached the hole but, just before it dropped, to the chagrin of Vardon and the amusement of the onlookers, a frog leaped out of the hole and stopped the ball in its tracks.

The Nome Ice Classic in Alaska is a bit of a "here today – gone tomorrow" type of event. The six-hole, par-3 course is "built" on the frozen Bering sea and melts into the ocean every spring. While the sea is frozen, "greenkeepers" import sand and construct sand traps. They even drill holes in the ice and put in trees. As no tee known to man can penetrate the ice, the players usually tee up on spent shotgun cartridges.

The late Tony Lema, known as "Champagne Tony", lived his short life to the full. It cost him a lot of money and, according to a story told by

Ken Venturi, may have cost him his life. At the USPGA in Firestone in 1966, Lema was to be honoured, at a dinner, for his 1964 Open Championship victory at St Andrew's. He was being paid $500 to attend the function but pulled out shortly before it was due to begin. Venturi, a good friend and former teacher of Lema, was asked to try and persuade him to honour his commitment. Venturi sought out Lema in the locker room and asked why he had changed his mind about attending the function. Lema told him that he had been booked to play an exhibition game in Lansing, Michigan; that he was being paid $2,000, and that he and his wife Betty were to be flown to the exhibition and flown on to the next tournament. The news angered Venturi.

"I didn't teach you to bow out because of money. I tried to teach you to be honourable," protested the 1964 US Open Champion.

"I don't care. I am going for the money," Lema responded. More prophetically than he could have known, Venturi replied, "You will live to regret those words." Lema shrugged his shoulders and walked out of the locker room. Venturi never saw him again. To calm down after the encounter, he went to a movie. When he checked into his hotel that night he was greeted by a receptionist saying, "Hey, it's too bad about that golfer that got killed." The plane taking Lema to Lansing had crashed.

Playing at a course in Adelaide in Australia, Peter Hobbs, with a wayward shot, hit a woman and knocked her unconscious. She had to be admitted to hospital with concussion. When she came round, Hobbs did the decent thing and paid her a visit to apologise. Did she gracefully accept his apology? Not quite! When she realised that she was in the presence of the man who had hospitalised her, she grabbed her bedpan and dealt him a crushing blow with it.

The BBC took the unusual step of recording a programme in their long-running *Songs of Praise* series from the bleachers at the back of the 17th green at St Andrew's after the final practice round for the 1995 Open Championship. Nobody pointed out that it might not be appropriate for a religious worship programme to be recorded at a course which houses the infamous "Hell Bunker".

Newly-wed Christin Curley had only one doubt about the new man in her life: would responsibilty be shared equally in their married relationship? As a test the 31-handicapper challenged her new spouse, Bill Velez, to a one-hole shoot-out on the 515-yard par-5 18th hole at Sterling Farms GC in Stamford, Connecticut.

Dressed in her wedding finery, she clipped her drive (using a Big Bertha) 175 yards down the fairway. Inspired by the sense of occasion she putted out for a bogey, having seen her ball hit the flagstick and almost drop in for a par. Then she watched as new hubby Bill lined up a thirty-foot putt for par. He lagged it nicely but still left it a foot short, tapping in for his own bogey. Honours even, and the tone of their future relationship now set, the couple headed off to their wedding reception.

A few years ago, an American company came up with a cheap solution to the dilemma of what to do with a club which has just let you down badly. Do you, sensibly, blame yourself rather than the club and, breathing more deeply, replace it in the bag? Do you toss it in an adjacent lake, ensuring that it is recoverable when your anger with it abates? Or do you break it in two across your knee, thus ending its natural life and putting you to the expense of buying a replacement? The Temper Tamer, developed by Schering Enterprises, introduced a fourth option, a club made of lightweight aluminium with a rubber clubhead, which can be bent, twisted, tied in a knot, bashed against the side of a caddy-car (or a caddy), and then simply straightened and replaced in the bag after abuse. An excellent idea, but beware! Ask yourself does it constitute a "club" under the Rules of Golf and would it therefore be included in the complement of fourteen clubs which you are allowed carry in your bag?

The notion of golf courses appearing on TV is hardly unusual, but TVs on a golf course??? Muswell Hill Golf Club in North London has been the target of a colourful environmental protest action which became known as the Transvestite Golf War. A group of London-based transvestites decided that golf courses were a misuse of urban green space, available only to the well-heeled. Donning their own heels (and their fish-net stockings, make-up, etc.), they made their way to Muswell Hill and picnicked on the fairways, offering incensed golfers cucumber sandwiches as they passed. One refused the offer of a cake, observing that "There's enough tarts around here already."

An afternoon watching the procession of hackers who populate most golf courses caused one of the "trannies", "Daisy", to opine that transvestites and golfers have more in common than might be immediately apparent. "They dress up to go out and do their thing in the same way we do. It's just they haven't got as good a dress sense as us."

As the picnic things were cleared away, and the environmental protest came to an end, one of the prime movers, "Trudi", remarked on the reactions of the golfers. "I think they like it, really. We're probably the nearest thing to women they have seen on this course for a long time." Ouch!

There have been any number of sad stories of golfers failing to turn up for their tee times and being disqualified or otherwise penalised, but what do you say to a player who turns up when he's not supposed to be there? In February 1995, Mark O'Meara arrived in California from Florida for the Nissan Open to discover that he hadn't entered it. So he went home.

A grocery store in the USA decided to garner some publicity for itself by offering $25,000 dollars to the winner of a sweepstake if he could hole a 10 foot putt. The problem was that the winner, 66-year-old William James, had never played golf in his life. In preparation for the putt, he practised for weeks but when it came to the big day he missed it, by about three inches on the left side.

Henry Longhurst records the unlikely coincidence of a friend of his, Major Gerald Moxon, playing in the Army Championship at Sandy Lodge as a young man, being knocked unconscious on the fifth tee by another player's ball in flight. The following year, playing in the same championship at the same venue, when he got to the fifth tee he regaled his playing partners with the details of the accident twelve months before. Whereupon another ball emerged from the ether, hit him on the head and knocked him unconscious.

USPGA Senior Tour players Dave Hill and JC Snead were hitting balls from opposite ends of a range, while practising for a tournament at the Silverado Country Club in Napa Valley. Snead was using a 3-wood and his balls were falling perilously close to Hill and his wife who was sitting in a golf cart. To warn Snead off Hill took out a towel and raised it above his head. Snead, seeing Hill's gesture, put away his 3-wood . . . and took out his driver instead. His first ball bounced off Mrs Hill's golf cart. Incensed, Hill grabbed a five-iron from his bag and walked around the range until he got to Snead. He then raised the club above his head, intending to bring it down on top of Snead. Snead parried the blow with his driver, which shattered in his hands. Throwing away the ruined clubs, both men set to punching the living daylights out of each other until they could be pulled apart. Bear in mind . . . these men were SENIORS!